TIME FOR REVOLUTION

TIME FOR REVOLUTION

Antonio Negri

Translated by Matteo Mandarini

continuum
LONDON • NEW YORK

Continuum

The Tower Building   15 East 26th Street
11 York Road   New York
London SE1 7NX   NY 10010

www.continuumbooks.com

British Library Cataloguing in Publication Data
A catalogue record for this book is available
from the British Library.

Library of Congress Cataloging in Publication Data
A catalog record for this book is available from the Library of Congress

ISBN 0–8264–7931–6

Typeset by RefineCatch Limited, Bungay, Suffolk
Printed and bound in Great Britain by Antony Rowe, Chippenham, Wiltshire

Contents

Kairòs, Alma Venus, Multitudo

Acknowledgements

I would like to start by thanking Tristan Palmer and Rowan Wilson at Continuum for their patience and assistance throughout this project. I have also been fortunate to have had the encouragement of Michael Hardt, whose skills as a reader have been invaluable. I am indebted to Stephen Houlgate for tracing a reference to Hegel from a single (mistranslated) word. Susan and Francesco Mandarini provided indispensable support and advice from the beginning to the end of this project – it could not have happened without them. Thanks to Juliet Rufford for showing extraordinary patience and perseverance with my syntax and me. The introduction is a good deal less opaque thanks to her hard work. And I would also like to thank Eliot Albert, Tariq Goddard and Alberto Toscano for many hours of debate that, in one way or another, found their way into this book. Alberto Toscano provided typically incisive comments on several drafts of this introduction and suggestions for the notes to the translations themselves.

Finally, I am most grateful to Antonio Negri for suggesting that I bring together these two texts in the first place. I have gained a great deal from reading, translating and writing about his work but even more from his intellectual generosity and commitment.

Matteo Mandarini

Translator's Introduction

> Labour is the living, form-giving fire; it is the transitoriness of things, their temporality, as their formation by living time.
>
> (Karl Marx, *Grundrisse*)

The two texts by Antonio Negri, translated into English and brought together here for the first time, display a formidable capacity for compression. *The Constitution of Time* (1981) – originally published as the final chapter of the collection of essays *Macchina tempo* (Negri 1982a), covering the period 1976–81 – arguably represents the high point of the theoretical and practical work carried out over the course of a decade or more by Antonio Negri and his comrades and collaborators, while it also exhibits the productive aporias,[1] the resolution of which would occupy Negri over the next decade. *Kairòs, Alma Venus, Multitudo* (2000a), Negri's latest book, matches the earlier work in terms of its force of concentration, drawing together in a single, dense text the results of the work that followed *The Constitution of Time* in the 1980s and 1990s. *Kairòs, Alma Venus, Multitudo* was written after Negri's work on *Empire* was finished, yet it represents a deepening of the conceptual assemblage provided in the latter collaborative work.

Antonio Negri's writings are notoriously difficult in the Italian, and they become doubly so for a reader who is largely unacquainted with the debates of *Operaismo*.[2] The situation has not been helped by the almost complete self-censorship of the Italian publishing world following the suppression of *il Movimento* and the 'counter-revolution' of the 1980s, which saw many of the writings of some of the major theorists of the 1970s (including those of Negri) disappear from circulation.[3] Raniero Panzieri's *Lotte Operaie Nello Sviluppo Capitalistico* (1976b) and extracts from Mario Tronti's seminal *Operai e Capitale* (1966) were translated into English, if only in relatively obscure journals and collections, in the late 1970s and early 1980s,[4] but their isolation from *il Movimento* (many of whose members were either in prison or exile) meant that they were never able to become components of a broader international debate and social movement. In recent years, a number of thinkers have begun to remedy this situation.[5] But the works they have produced, and even *Empire* itself, would have failed to make the impact that they have made outside the academy had their publication not intersected with the emerging, global subjectivities of what, in Italy, has become known as *Il popolo di Seattle* and the new cycle of struggles that has – so far – led from the American city to Genoa, Barcelona and Florence.

For *The Constitution of Time*, I have provided some further information for the reader (mainly drawn from Negri's own writings) in the translator's notes. In the case of *Kairòs, Alma Venus, Multitudo*, I have let what is a remarkably self-sufficient text speak largely for itself. Its development is driven by an autonomous logic, a cumulative composition, and exhibits constant feedback-effects that perpetually unground and refound it. From first, second, third . . . to nth foundation. Too many notes would only dislocate the consistency of the composition, as would too many external references. Conversely, *The Constitution of Time* is heavily interspersed with citations and references. While in prison Antonio Negri used notebooks to jot these down from the limited number of books he was allowed to have at any one time. As he recalled in his 1997 Introduction (reprinted here as an Afterword), many of these notebooks were 'destroyed in the piss and fire of the repressors, for no other reason than that dictated by the revenge of a rabble of cowardly and ignorant prison guards'. Despite his and my best efforts, it has been impossible to track some of these references down. The Bibliography is thus reconstructed almost entirely from memory and guesswork.

In 1981 Antonio Negri had been in prison for almost two years pending trial. He would remain there for another two before his election as Radical Party member to parliament and, following the subsequent Chamber of Deputies' vote to rescind his parliamentary immunity, his flight into exile in Paris. Perhaps these particular circumstances, in which 're-education to virtue is reached through idleness' (*Kairòs*) as Negri would say with some irony when he once again found himself two years into an Italian prison sentence (1999),[6] were those most conducive to taking stock of the theoretical and practical work accomplished over the preceding years. Two different prisons; two different books.

But it is not just the circumstances of composition that link these texts together. Nor is it simply the recapitulative force, the extraordinary compression and the desire to make sense of the intense years that preceded, common to both these texts, that make the present volume more than an arbitrary collection. It provides indispensable material for understanding the development of Negri's thought – not only that carried out in his years of exile, but also the collaborative work with Michael Hardt – and for grasping the new possibilities for collective action in the face of the new *Imperial* forms of capitalist accumulation, which represent the abiding concern of Negri's theoretical labour. Taken together, then, the texts elucidate the course of Negri's thinking from *Marx Beyond Marx* (1979) to *Empire* (2000), from proletarian self-valorization to the constellations of co-operating multitudes. The red thread that links the two, as the title for this collection suggests, is that of temporality.

I

In order to situate the two texts translated here a brief account of *Empire* is in order. The widely debated theoretical synthesis that *Empire* represents has been able to 'tap into' and give rational expression to the optimism expressed in the new age of militancy that emerged in the mid-1990s – thus bringing to a welcome conclusion the short-lived triumphalism of the champions of the 'end of history'. Taking up again some of the founding principles of *Operaismo*, Hardt and Negri argue that during the last quarter of the twentieth century, capital has been forced to restructure in order to break the workers' and anti-colonial struggles that had shattered its previous regime of accumulation. Restructuring followed upon struggle. As Hardt and Negri put it in their account of the power of the multitude – the antagonistic subject of 'Empire' – when the 'action of Empire is effective, this is due not to its own force but to the fact that it is driven by the rebound from the resistance of the multitude against imperial power' (Hardt and Negri 2000, p. 360). Thus, the much vaunted triumph of capital that globalization is supposed to embody is not a sign of the health and creativity of capital but rather the effect of struggles that could no longer be regulated within the nation state. Capital's response to such struggles

3

was to decentralize production, raise the mobility of capital and the (relative) mobility of workers, but the corollary of this was that the nation state could no longer regulate the flows that now exceeded it. However, with the relative decline of the sovereign power of nation states, sovereignty as such has not disappeared – political controls, state functions and regulation persist – but simply changed its form. Empire is the name that Hardt and Negri give to the political form of globalization. Crucially, what is at stake here is not the emergence of a new (perhaps US-based) imperialism. As Hardt argues in an interview with the Italian daily *Il Manifesto*, imperialism 'constitutes a veritable extension of the sovereignty of European nations beyond their very borders'[7] and is characterized by a complex dialectic of inside and outside.[8] On the other hand, with the notion of Empire, Hardt and Negri are outlining a radical paradigm shift. As they argue in a pivotal chapter of the book ('Imperial Sovereignty', 2000, pp. 183–204), '[w]hat has changed in the passage to the imperial world [. . .] is that this border place no longer exists' (ibid., p. 183). In other words Empire has no centre and no limits. Rather, it is a decentred and deterritorialized apparatus of rule that progressively incorporates the whole globe (ibid., p. xii).

The constitution of Empire is understood on the model of the mixed constitution that Polybius provides us with in his discussion of the Roman Empire (1979), where the three principal forms of government – monarchy, aristocracy and democracy – are brought together. Their modern-day successors are represented by the International Monetary Fund (IMF), World Bank, the World Trade Organization (WTO), NATO (monarchy); transnational capital (aristocracy); and nation states and non-governmental organizations (NGOs) (democracy). This model is not meant to be understood as metaphorical – it is formally the same. Such an understanding of the global constitution allows for a modulated and non-univocal understanding of the lines and operations of Power.[9] This global juridical constitution points to changes in the material constitution. In other words, it presupposes that capitalist relations had been expanding 'to subsume all aspects of social production and reproduction, the entire realm of life' (Hardt and Negri 2000, p. 275).[10] This total subsumption expresses the material conditions grounding the claim that in Empire there is no longer an outside. Capital subsumes the whole of social life and the emerging juridical constitution watches over the process, supervising and regulating the relations at a global level.

The 'general apparatus of imperial command' consists of three distinct moments or what Hardt and Negri term 'the triple imperative of Empire' (ibid., pp. 198–9). The first element is the 'magnanimous, liberal face of Empire' (ibid., p. 198), where everyone is welcomed and included 'within its boundaries, regardless of race, creed, color, gender, sexual orientation, and so forth'. By formally setting aside differences, Empire seeks to neutralize much of the terrain of possible conflict. The second is the differential moment where differences – considered cultural and contingent rather than natural or biological and thus non-exclusionary – are championed as a 'force of peaceful regional identification' (ibid., p. 199). Finally, there comes the 'management and hierarchization of these differences within the general economy of command'. No longer divide and conquer then, '[m]ore often than not, the Empire does not create division but rather recognizes existing or potential differences, celebrates them, and manages them within a general economy of command' (ibid., p. 201).

Yet Negri and Hardt insist that the totalizing nature of the process leading towards the consolidation of Empire should not be a cause for despair. In a paper given at the university *La Sapienza* in Rome, Negri went so far as to claim that this is 'damnably positive, it is a sign of freedom, a sign of the force of the historical processes that break open the infernal cage that is the nation state'.[11] For on the one hand, workers' struggles bring to an end the previous – nation state-based – regime of accumulation[12] and thereby reveal their ontological and creative power; while on the other, it is precisely the paradigm shift in the form of sovereignty that signals the emergence of the multitude as the other subject of *Empire*, one that

> acts as an absolutely positive force that pushes the dominating power towards an abstract and empty unification, to which it appears as a distinct alternative [. . .] whereas Empire is a mere apparatus of capture that lives off the vitality of the multitude – as Marx would say, a vampire regime of accumulated dead labour that survives only by sucking the blood of living labour.
>
> (Hardt and Negri 2000, pp. 61, 62).[13]

'Multitude' is both the pivotal notion of *Empire*, while at the same time being unsettlingly under-theorized. In a paper entitled 'The Politics of the Multitude' given in London in 2001,[14] Hardt spoke of the concept of the multitude being left at a 'poetic level' in the former collaborative work. It would be hard to argue against such a characterization of it at least as far as *Empire* is concerned. An important and perhaps not immediately apparent feature of the concept of the multitude, one that is a useful corrective to the merely 'poetic' understanding of the multitude, is its class content. Class distinctions are not, however, there ready-made; they are always an effect of struggle. That is to say, class is a political concept. Hardt takes the example of race as another concept that is determined politically, so that, for example, for Jean-Paul Sartre it is anti-Semitism that produces the Jew (and not any sort of essence or nature). But this is insufficient, for it seems to provide Power with constitutive force, leaving the subject as a passive recipient of determination. Rather 'race arises through collective acts of resistance' (Hardt 2001). Hardt goes on to say that '[c]lass is similarly formed through collective acts of resistance' and should be investigated not through 'a mere catalogue of empirical differences but rather with the lines of collective resistance to power'. Such resistance is not reactive, 'it is entirely positive' (Hardt and Negri 2000, pp. 361–2), which is to say, constitutive. One should understand the multitude as a substantive multiplicity. Deleuze and Guattari, perhaps the major theorists of multiplicity, claim that the concept

> was created in order to escape the abstract opposition between the multiple and the one, to escape dialectics, to succeed in conceiving the multiple in the pure state, to cease treating it as an organic element of a Unity or Totality yet to come.
>
> (Deleuze and Guattari, 1988 p. 32)

The multitude – understood as a multiplicity – serves then, among other things, to separate the former from the notion of 'the people', in which the many are subsumed under the unity of the State.[15]

All the same the notion of the multitude remains relatively undetermined in social or sociological terms. I would contend that it is only through an exploration of the transformation of the class composition of the working class that one can arrive at an adequate notion of the multitude. To do this it is necessary to pass through the articulations of the *social* or *socialized worker* that Negri explores in the 1970s and 1980s.[16] Indeed, at the risk of conflating the two, my claim is that the determination of the composition of the social worker is the condition for determining the composition of the multitude.[17] To see this we will need to turn to Negri's *The Constitution of Time* before returning to this question at the end of Part II.

II

The Constitution of Time was written after the long wave of struggles that began in 1968–69 had been thoroughly crushed by the State apparatus. Elsewhere, student and workers' struggles were shorter but brought important new forces into the cultural and political arena of many Western democracies (whatever the deformities produced by the entrism of some of these in the party system). In Italy, the State's response was one of brute repression. *Il Movimento* was defeated by the military power of the State,[18] although it was the very intensity of the State's response that confirmed the arguments of Negri and those other theorists and militants who had been engaged in mapping the changing forms of class composition of the working class in those years. A new social subject was in the process of becoming hegemonic, one that had displaced the role of the traditional factory-based, de-skilled *mass worker* of the Fordist-Taylorist factory and that refused the discipline of the factory and the mediation of its union representatives. This new subject came to be known as the social or socialized worker.

Raniero Panzieri and Mario Tronti's analyses of the class composition of the mass worker in the late 1950s and 1960s in the founding texts of *Operaismo* had, in accordance with Marx's account of 'real subsumption' and of the *'General Intellect'*,[19] argued that the whole of society was becoming integrated and entirely (re-)produced by capital itself. The class composition of the mass worker was still largely determined by the technical conditions within the immediate process of production. However, Fordism's reliance on Keynesian regulatory mechanisms meant that the mass worker could not be understood independently of this politically determined mechanism that extended well beyond the factory walls. Keynesianism made consumption an integral part of (re-)production through its regulation of the wage, in such a way that the State took on a directly economic function, increasingly rendering consumption productive.[20] The reorganization of production that broke the hegemony of the Fordist factory, and hence of the mass worker, meant that the 'terrain of confrontation began to shift from the factory to the overall mechanisms of the labor market, public spending, the reproduction of the proletariat and young people, and the distribution of income independent of remuneration for work' ('Do You Remember Revolution?', in Virno and Hardt 1996, p. 230). With the emergence of the socialized worker, class composition could no longer be determined by the workers' role in the immediate process of factory production. As Marx had argued a century before, capital's response to workers' struggles – in this case, those of the emerging mass worker – would be to restructure its operations in order to bring an ever-increasing number of types of labour under the 'immediate concept of *productive labour*, [such that] those who perform it are classed as productive labourers, workers directly exploited by capital and *subordinated* to its process of production and expansion' (Marx 1990, p. 1040). These were the conditions that allowed for the extension of the realm of exploitation across the social sphere. In the Italy of the 1970s, the political context and privileged object of the analyses of the later *Operaismo*, it became increasingly evident that the labour performed by the social or socialized worker was ever more social and co-operative, defined specifically by its mobility and its abstract, immaterial and intellectual nature:[21] 'The new social subjects reflected or anticipated in their struggles the growing identity between new productive processes and forms of communication, represented, for example, in the new reality of the computerized factory and the advanced tertiary sector' ('Do You Remember Revolution?', in Virno and Hardt 1996, p. 234). It was thus plain that labour was no longer determined in and through the discipline instituted by the factory regime.[22] But this signalled that working-class subjectivity was no longer determined immediately by capital, and that co-operation was no longer something brought to labour from the outside by capital but was inherent in labour itself: *'co-operation is completely immanent to the labouring activity itself'* (Hardt and Negri 2000, p. 294). Capital's operation of restructuring aimed at bringing increasing numbers of this new, complex form of socialized, co-operative labour under its rule, extending exploitation across the social totality. It is at this point that exploitation becomes the 'expropriation of the form and the product of social co-operation' (Negri 1996a, p. 153).[23]

So the operation of restructuring, stepped up under Reagan and Thatcher, aimed to neutralize this new social subject, finding in its regulatory regime ever more effective forms of exploitation, while replacing the Fordist-Keynesian model destroyed by the struggles of the previous decades. Against the mass workers' fight to de-link the wage from the strategy of Keynesian accumulation, capital had mobilized its new strategy, one that saw mounting mobility of capital, the decentralization of production and an ever-increasing segmentation and disciplining of the new forms of mobile and flexible social labour. Now the 'models of regulation are extended along multinational lines, and the regulation passes through monetary dimensions which cover the world market to a continually greater extent' (Negri 1996a, p. 156). But by restructuring production in order to bring growing numbers of subjects under its rule, capital displaced antagonism to a higher, more socialized level.

This restructuring was a response to the transformation in the quality of labour – immaterial, mass intellectuality – to which capital had to make itself and its strategies of exploitation adequate. If the actions of the mass worker unmasked the State's direct involvement in the process of production and exploitation, it was only with the social worker that it became clear one had to raise the conflict to the social terrain. In order to combat more and more socialized forms of exploitation, one would have to attack the social relations of capitalist command themselves. The subsequent 'military' and political defeat of the social worker merely confirmed the analysis of the new subject. *The Constitution of Time* is a bold reassertion of the theoretical and conceptual achievements of those years. As Negri puts it in the 1997 Introduction to the book:

> The richness of the 'Prolegomena on Time' consists simply in its being the summary of the thinking, within the revolutionary movement of the final years of the 1970s, on the transformation of the time of exploitation (no longer reducible to a measure based upon the time of use-value, but) brought into relation with the new forms of social exploitation of labour-power and with the new organization of social temporality.

Having said this, it may be disconcerting to find *The Constitution of Time* open with a difficult but vital first chapter on Part One of Marx's *Capital Vol. 1*. But Negri quickly abandons the classical, doctrinal figure of a Marx who had sustained the myriad theoretical debates of orthodox Marxism. The Marx of *The Constitution of Time* is familiar to us from Negri's seminal *Marx Beyond Marx* (1979). In the latter book, his close reading of the *Grundrisse* and the *1857 Introduction* led Negri to formulate a number of methodological tools for understanding the transformations of contemporary capitalism. He also went to work on the notion of real subsumption and the general intellect. If we are to make sense of the importance of Negri's contribution here we will need to take a brief detour through Marx's theory of value. In Part One of the first volume of *Capital* Marx argues that if, in commodity exchange, equivalents are always exchanged for equivalents, it is impossible to understand how an increase in value is possible. Bar trickery and swindle, it is only by finding a commodity that produces more value than it costs that one can make sense of *surplus*-value. Marx discovers such a commodity by turning away from the realm of exchange towards the 'hidden abode of production' (Marx 1990, p. 279). This shift enables him to indicate labour-power as just such a commodity. Labour-power produces more than it costs because the capitalist, who pays – in the form of the wage – the cost of reproduction of the worker, gets into the bargain the worker's *capacity* for labour – labour-power – for a full working day (which is fixed by a number of different factors, including the intensity of the class struggle of the time).[24] The level of surplus-value produced is determined by the length of time that the worker is forced to work beyond that necessary for the production of the value the worker receives in the form of the wage. But, and this is where the problems begin, in order to calculate this quantitatively, it was necessary to have a common temporal unit by which labour-power could be measured as well as a means of reducing the various concrete forms of labour to a simple unit of *abstract* labour.[25] Concrete or complex labour would thus be a multiplication of simple abstract social labour. 'The various proportions in which different kinds of labour are reduced to simple labour as their unit of measurement are established by a social process that goes on behind the backs of the producers' (ibid., p. 135) – that is, these determinations are immediately social.

This is where we find ourselves after the first few pages of *The Constitution of Time* and it is here that Negri intervenes in order to highlight the aporias in Marx's theory of value stemming from his notion of capitalist time-as-measure: time 'measures [quantities of] labour in so far as it reduces it to homogenous substance, but [. . .] also determines its productive power in the same form', i.e. through multiplication. The central aporia is born of the failure of Marx's attempt to reduce the complex, material, qualitative elements – of struggle, of antagonism, of new social subjectivities, of productive innovation – to the analytic, synchronic elements. But by highlighting this aporia, Negri was able to show how Marx held the key to moving beyond the Marx of classical economic theory. The aporia is resolved by displacing the terrain upon which it operates. The labour theory of value demanded that labour-power existed, in some sense, outside capital (outside its disciplinary regime) and needed to be drawn in. One could only think of measuring value by understanding the unit of measure through which it would be calculated as formed outside the capitalist process of production and reproduction of society (as a use-value relatively independent of exchange-value). But historically capital had increasingly brought (subsumed) labour-power under its rule and redefined the use-value of labour-power in terms of its exchange-value. This is what Marx terms the 'specifically capitalist mode of production' or *'real subsumption'*. Increasingly the real subsumption of society by capital reaches a stage in which it is no longer possible for use-value even to be conceived of as independent of exchange-value.[26]

Given these circumstances, where is one to find that space of independence, that 'outside', which would be required to form the basis for any unit of measure? This is what Negri means when he says that the law of value is in crisis. But its crisis does not mean that its effects are over. What has changed is its form. With the subsumption of the relative independence of use-value, one is immediately within the dense temporal *Umwelt*[27] of capitalist exchange, in which all is quantity, all is time and the hegemony of time-as-measure is over. As Negri wrote, 'once within real subsumption, we pass *from the aporia* on to a pure and simple tautology'. While Marx's synchronic and linear discourse aimed to render the elements reversible, the diachronic, irreversible and materialist elements produce blockages and aporias that prevent the recuperation of increasingly socialized, collective labour within the analytic categories. It is only by eliminating these irreversible elements that the central aporia is overcome, but this is done at the cost of rendering measure, i.e. time-as-measure, tautological.

Negri's summary reads:

1. in real subsumption all use-value is drawn into exchange-value;
2. but with that the external origin of the measure of time (based on the externality of use-value) recedes and measure is flattened onto the process itself;
3. if measure measures itself, it follows that the process of value concludes in that of command, in tautology and indifference;
4. the trend of productive forces (increase, decrease, transformation) bears no relation to the magnitude of value;
5. complex, productive, scientific labour is definitively irreducible to elementary temporal units;
6. productive force is inexplicable. *In short*, a non-dialectical tautology comes in at the end of the process in place of the initial dialectic.

> And *so* it is only possible to explain the movement of the class struggle by rejecting the notion of temporal measure as equivalence. The *form of equivalence* is simply an *effect of coercion.*

What we are left with is a time that measures itself; it is both 'measure and substance'. The tautology takes an intensive form, exemplified by the inability to distinguish measure from substance, and an extensive form: the inability to '[distinguish] the totality of life [. . .] from the totality from which this life is woven'. All we are left with are quantities of time, and quality is displaced by quantity. We are left in a world of *indifferentiation*, of *indifference*. But more importantly, time no longer appears as a form of measure, calculation – it is the very substance of life, of production and reproduction. Time is constitutive: *'time of constitution, time of composition*. So the *paradigm is ontological.'*

The significance of this ontological move is critical, as we shall see when we turn to the second of the books translated here. But first it is important to note the other critical node that marks his thinking, that of the antagonistic subject. Real subsumption marks both the realization of the law of value and the end of its dialectic of recuperation. If capital subsumes the time of existence, it also returns time to us as *collective substance.* Furthermore, 'abstract, social and mobile labour-power [. . .] subjectivizes itself around its own concept of time, and a temporal constitution of its own' (see Negri 1982b, p. 220). This subjective, antagonistic element serves to introduce differentiation into the apparent indifference of the dense tautological structure of real subsumption.

> The homologies can only by given because the context on which they operate is that of indifference. But if I deny, resist, denounce this fact and its indifference I am not – for this very reason – within indifference, on the contrary I am difference, real determination and practical determination.
>
> (Negri 1982a, p. 72 – my translation)

As we have argued above, real subsumption is capital's answer to the increasing socialization of labour, where the whole of social life, production and reproduction and co-operation is subsumed by capital. Where time ceases to find a relative independence from the process of exchange and becomes the substance of social life, the 'necessity for capitalism is that of integrating this collective within an *equilibrium* that reduces dialectical possibilities to zero: this is the *new quality of antagonism in real subsumption'*.

In other words, capital rises up again – beyond the apparent indifference of real subsumption – as an antagonistic pole, whose aim is to reduce the time of collective (proletarian) time to zero, to the analytic of capitalist time, to indifference. The production of real subsumption exhibits the global inherence of both the subjects of time – capitalist and proletarian. In other words, it is this ontology of immanence that enables the emergence of the antagonistic collective subjects: '*the mechanism of logical production of the dualism is the same as that which produces the qualitative existence of the separate subjects.*' The law of value ceases to be a theory of measure and becomes an operation of command. Antagonism no longer comes from outside – as Hardt and Negri declare in *Empire*, 'There is no more outside' (2000, p. 186) – it must be sought within. And it is to this that *The Constitution of Time* addresses itself, charting the operations of this closed, capitalist analytic time of re-equilibrium with a tendency to zero and the modulated, constitutive time of proletarian composition.

To conclude this section let us return briefly to the discussion of the multitude that formed the conclusion of Part I of this Introduction. It should now be apparent that the technical composition of the social worker is in line with that of the multitude. Hardt and Negri's exposition of the composition of the multitude in *Empire* runs as follows:

> [T]he object of exploitation and domination tend not to be specific productive activities but the universal capacity to produce, that is, abstract social activity and its comprehensive power. This abstract labour is an activity without place, and yet it is very powerful. It is the co-operating set of brains and hands, minds and bodies; it is both the non-belonging and the creative social diffusion of living labour; it is the desire and striving of the multitude of mobile and flexible workers; and at the same time it is intellectual energy and linguistic communicative construction of the multitude of intellectual and affective labour.
>
> (ibid., p. 209)

But if that is the case, what are the shortcomings of the notion of the social worker that are overcome through that of the multitude? Or more precisely, what transformations in the material (economic, political, social) conditions lead to the emergence of the multitude? The core transformation is that of globalization and the concurrent shift in sovereignty from nation states to Empire as discussed in Part I above. Arguably, the social worker is still overly tied to the nation state. Although production is ever more decentralized and capital ever more mobile and transnational, the regimentation of labour is still largely contained within the nation state. That is to say, with the hegemony of the social worker the globalization of production had not yet reached the stage that it called forth a globalization of sovereignty. At this point, shifting register from that of political economy to that of political philosophy, Hardt and Negri insist upon the need for a 'postmodern republicanism', that is Machiavelli and Spinoza *contra* Hobbes: 'The people coincide with sovereignty [of the nation state, this] is now meaningless at the level of globalization', the multitude is the subject of Empire.[28] What this requires in practice is a further change in political composition. The concluding section of the book seeks to formulate these demands: the demand for the right to global citizenship, to a social wage and to reappropriation. It is perhaps precisely in this shift in the political composition, a response to the exacerbation of the material conditions (mobility of capital, labour and decentralization of production) that one could discern already – but at lesser levels – in the technical composition of the social worker, that we can discover the point at which a new subject is called for. This subject is the multitude.[29]

III

Kairòs, Alma Venus, Multitudo sets out to explore the immanent plane of the dense 'phenomenological fabric' of real subsumption discussed in the earlier text.[30] The terminological innovations of the later text give the impression of a radical shift of terrain but the continuities are at least as strong as the differences. In another essay, composed around the same time as *The Constitution of Time*, Negri had argued that:

> All the categories that have operated – as keys to antagonism – towards the production of real subsumption, now, within the realm of real subsumption, reveal themselves to be no longer able to describe the general framework of subsumed society, nor are they able any more to organize antagonism.
>
> (Negri 1982a, p. 224 – my translation)

His awareness of this would lead him to explore other tools, other concepts to unlock the world of real subsumption (that he would go on simply to call *postmodernity*) and to discover within it immanent and antagonistic subjectivities. *Kairòs, Alma Venus, Multitudo* can be situated at the far end of his investigations into postmodern society, modes of regulation and subjectivity that began with *The Constitution of Time*. My account will inevitably be somewhat impressionistic for the logic of the text is autonomous and cumulative – building layer upon layer as the ontological consistency is articulated – and it is not possible here to trace the force of the logical derivation of the emerging material composition, I can only attempt to give a sense of its constitutive force.

In this text, rich with internal allusions and cross-references (and that clearly draws some of its inspiration from Spinoza's *Ethics*), Negri sets out from *practice*, a practice of language and knowledge constructed in concert with an ontology. That is to say, the one constructs the other. The emerging ontology determines in its turn the conditions for an adequate epistemology and both the one and the other are determined in terms of the instant (*kairòs*) in which naming and the thing named attain existence, i.e. in terms of time. 'It is in a temporal context that we establish the relationship between knowledge and being, and their adequation.' Therefore the *phenomenological fabric* of *The Constitution of Time* becomes explicitly an *ontological fabric*.[31] Central to this production of an immanent field of production and reproduction is the recognition that 'the capitalist process has subsumed the world, turning it into a dead creature, and that on the contrary living labour is *kairòs*, the restless creator of the *to-come*'. To take up again the comparison with Spinoza, or rather with Negri's reading of Spinoza, we are provided with an ontology that sets out from the 'modes', from practice in order to construct 'substance',[32] so that:

> when Spinoza defines the concept as a common notion, he affirms it as a construction of a means for knowing reality, in nominalist terms, but he also recognizes in this logical structure the path that leads to a growth of being as an assemblage, a project.
>
> (Hardt and Negri 1994, p. 287)

Negri had argued in the 1997 Introduction to *The Constitution of Time* that one of the theoretical shortcomings of the text was the impossibility of providing an adequate account of the nature of proletarian constitution, of proletarian creativity, of proletarian time after having described it 'in a sort of symmetry with the analytic temporality of capital'. This is overcome in *Kairòs, Alma Venus, Multitudo* by, on the one hand, construing being as a plenitude conceived in temporal terms as the eternal, i.e. the limitless, or rather Negri reconceives the limit of the eternal as the opening on the edge of being, the edge of the eternal that always opens onto a time *to-come* and, on the other hand, by understanding proletarian practice, proletarian constitution in terms of a creation of *new* being, a construction *in common*: *praxis*, the productive co-operation of the multitudes.[33] What is generated is new being, which perpetually augments the eternal:

> This eternal is prior to us, because it is at its edge that we create and that we augment being, that is to say, eternity. [. . .] And so we are at once responsible for eternity and for producing it.

In this way, capital's attempt to render irreversible material processes reversible through a reduction to zero – synchrony, dead labour – is broken by the irreducibility, the *immeasurability* of the common, which constitutes the very fabric of the making and unmaking of being by the productive multitudes. Commonality, which comes to be articulated in the forms of 'linguistic-being', 'being as production of subjectivity' and 'biopolitical being', forms both the ontological fabric and the (temporal) practice of the productive multitudes (ontological practice): the ungrounded ground of being augmented and prolonged in and through the practice of the multitudes.

> Everything flows and everything hybridizes on the edge of time. On all sides, in the face of the void, the singularities mount assaults on the limit so as to construct in common another plenitude for life. That is what the biopolitical production of the multitude consists in: stretching itself out from fullness to emptiness so as to fill the void.

It is no coincidence that Negri should take up his study of Spinoza (1981) at exactly the time that his attention was fixed on the escalating level of the real subsumption of society by capital, its totalizing and totalitarian character. For, in Spinoza, we find ourselves on a fully immanent ontological terrain where resistance must be discovered on the same plane as that of Power, because *there is no exteriority* in Spinoza either. The same concern forms a refrain throughout *The Constitution of Time* and *Kairòs, Alma Venus, Multitudo*: 'There is no exteriority on which to fall back on, on any occasion'; 'That which I think it is necessary to theoretically combat is the exogenous character of the possible alternative' (*The Constitution of Time*); 'How, within an experience that has no exteriority, is one able to sketch a line of flight out from the crisis of the common?' (*Kairòs,*

Alma Venus, Multitudo). Such a flight, such a resistance should be understood as a productive practice in common: ontological practice, biopolitics.[34]

The loss of the outside reappears as a central notion in the definition of Empire. There is no outside; there is no centre. Indeed, '[e]mpire constitutes the ontological fabric in which all relations of power are woven together' (Hardt and Negri 2000, p. 354). However, the ontological fabric of the Imperial order is not constitutive but *constituted*, which is to say, 'resistance is actually prior to power' (ibid., p. 360). *Kairòs, Alma Venus, Multitudo* gives us the tools to think through this ontological priority of the multitude. Empire operates by folding back over and appropriating the productivity of the multitude, 'stripping from the social process of productive cooperation the command over its own functioning [. . .] closing social productive power within the griddings of the system of Power' (Negri 1996a, p. 154).[35]

As Negri and Hardt argue in *Empire*, this radically innovates the meaning and practice of politics: 'When we say that political theory must deal with ontology, we mean first of all that politics cannot be constructed from the outside. Politics is given immediately; it is a field of pure immanence' (2000, p. 354). This could be described as the elaboration of a political ontology of time. Thus, for Hardt and Negri, 'Ontology is not a theory of foundation. It is a theory about our immersion in being and being's continuous construction' (Hardt and Negri 1994, p. 287). In place of politics, is *biopolitics*: the constitutive movement and productive force of the multitudes. It is likely that the projected second volume of *Empire*, which will extend and intensify the ontological, the biopolitical and empirical determination of the multitude, will take its cue from the account provided in *Kairòs, Alma Venus, Multitudo*.

THE CONSTITUTION OF TIME

**The timepieces of capital and
communist liberation**

Preamble

... *voici le temps*
ou l'on connnaîtra l'avenir
sans mourir de connaissance ...
(Apollinaire)

These notes constitute some pure and simple prolegomena to the construction of the communist idea of time, to a new proletarian practice of time. The level of discussion is abstract, but the analysis is directed towards and supported by the interpretation of concrete behaviours. I say concrete and not simply real for the good reason that all that is concrete is real while not all that is real is concrete. By insisting on the concrete, I insist on the surface and the opening of life and of the struggle against metaphysical and mystificatory hypostasis. Time is the concrete reality of my life in so far as it is the substance of my collective, productive and constitutive-of-the-new being. Outside of a materialist, dynamic and collective conception of time it is impossible to think the revolution. Time is not only a horizon, however, it is also a measure. It has been conceived of as the quantitative measure of exploitation; now it can be thought of as the qualitative measure of the alternative and of change. Reactionary mysticism (and there exist no other forms) has always constituted itself around the unreality of time, and thus of its exploitation – revolution is born from the pathways of a constitutive phenomenology of temporality. The needs, the desires, their organization in the working day of exploitation and of repression are all in play here; in the face of this organization, they have constituted temporal aporias that dictate the practical innovation of the paradigm of the working day – that is to say, of its creative destruction. The enormous power of scientific labour, of the intellectual organization of associated human labour, enables us to repropose the project of the imagination to Power, or better, against Power. As the classics teach us, the imagination is the most concrete of temporal powers.

I ask my readers to forgive me for presenting only some notes/prolegomena, but the destructive fury of State repression has destroyed the materials gathered over a long year of work. Here only broken fragments are offered for discussion in a collage *that I nevertheless consider useful. I dedicate these prolegomena to two dear teachers: Giulio Preti and Enzo Paci.*

1

First Displacement: the time of subsumed being

1.1 Time-as-measure and productive time

A use-value, or useful article, therefore, has *value* only because abstract human *labour* is *objectified* or *materialized* in it. How, then, is the *magnitude* of this value to be measured? By means of the *quantity* of the 'value-forming substance', the labour, contained in the article. This quantity is measured by its *duration*, and the *labour-time* is itself measured in *determinate portions of time* such as hours, days, etc.

(Marx 1990, p. 129 – translation modified)

All the problems begin here. In fact, if time is quantity, it is not only quantity. Time does not only *measure* labour, but *reduces* it to homogenous substance.

[T]he labour that forms the substance of value is equal human labour, the expenditure of equal human labour-power . . . Socially necessary labour-time is the labour-time required to produce any use-value under the conditions of production normal for a given society and with the average degree of skill and intensity of labour.

(Ibid.)

This reduction is dialectical. Marx refers explicitly to Hegel's *Philosophy of Right* (ibid., p. 135, n. 14). That is to say, the homogenous temporal substance is at once the medium [*medietà*] of labour and the overcoming of that medium [*medietà*];[1] it is at once the form of equivalence (and of reversibility) and the form of productive power.

> The value of a commodity is related to the value of any other commodity as the labour-time necessary for the production of the one is related to the labour-time necessary for the production of the other ... [it] changes with every variation in the *productive force of labour*.
>
> (ibid., p. 130 – translation modified)

Therefore, time measures labour in so far as it reduces it to homogenous substance, but it also determines its productive power in the same form: through the multiplication of average temporal units. Therefore, in relation to labour, time is at once *measure* and *matter*, *form* and *substance*.

With these first propositions in mind we are able to note some *possible* aporias. The first aporia concerns the definition of the temporal unit of measure itself. This unit of measure is an abstract element, a quantity of simple necessary labour that is established 'by a social process that goes on behind the backs of the producers' (ibid., p. 135). A social process *behind the backs of*, that is, *external* – but to what? External to production. So 'external' can only be understood with a reference to use-value. The measure of exchange-value is determined from outside, that is by temporal quantities founded on use-value, determined immediately. The *immediacy* of the determination, considered in relation to the function of *mediation* that the quantitative unit determines, is a real enigma. It is an enigma that is at the very least exhibited by these aporias, or rather, by these insurmountable theoretical difficulties that emerge in the process of exposition: (1) the definition of qualified or complex labour, (2) of productive as opposed to unproductive labour, (3) of productive labour-power, and (4) of the productive function of intellectual or scientific labour. At least in these cases, but also in others, *qualified labour* is not reducible to simple labour, to the accumulation of units of measure. A substantive element – an increased productivity of this labour-power, an intensification of its use-value – lies at the basis of the definition and shows this element to be an irreversible component. The same is true of the definition of *productive labour*. In this case also the definition is given in an equivocal way: on the one hand productive labour, in so far as it produces surplus-value, is reduced to the simple temporal unit of measure. But this is not true absolutely. Another element intervenes in the distinction of productive from unproductive labour, and that is the formal participation of productive labour in the whole machine of capitalist production – so that in this case also the use-value of productive labour is multiplied, not primarily as a quantitative increment, so much as substantively, on the basis of a functional relationship, and is in this way contrasted with the use-value of unproductive labour. Thirdly, the *productive force of* human *labour* is irreducible to pure temporal measurement: to this is added the use-value of co-operation (as such) that raises and modifies qualitatively the value of labour-power as productive force. Also insoluble is the problem of the *productive* value of *intellectual* and scientific *forces*. In each case the insurmountable theoretical difficulty consists in the impossibility of loading or making homologous a reversible, equivalent temporal unit with substantive qualitative multiplicators. Marx resorts to use-value – however qualified – that is to an *external* element, in order to explain what is most *internal*: productive power. This is a veritable enigma.

The aporia dissolves, at least in this first form with its resort to an extraneous element, only when we enter the phase of labour's real subsumption by the regime of capital. As I have already demonstrated in my *Marx Beyond Marx* [1991b], one can say without doubt that the whole systematic development of Marx's thinking is dominated by the necessity of resolving the aforementioned aporias. Or, one could go as far as to say that Marx's systematic thinking *presupposes* the theoretical model of subsumption, and only then adapts it to the empirical analytic. Or even, once within real subsumption, we pass *from the aporia* on to a pure and simple tautology. In fact, at the stage of the real subsumption of labour by capital, capitalist production (therefore the production of exchange-values) is not only the effect, but also the *condition* of production.

> This immanent tendency of capitalist relations is realized adequately – and becomes a *necessary condition* even from the technological point of view – only when the specifically capitalist mode of production is developed and, with it, the real subsumption of labour by capital.
>
> (Marx 1990, p. 1037 – translation modified)

Here use-value cannot appear except under the guise of exchange-value. There is no longer an external vantage point upon which use-value can depend. The overcoming of capitalism occurs on the basis of needs constructed by capitalism. But in that case, time-as-measure of value is identical to the value of labour, to time of labour as substance. To say that time measures labour is here but a pure and simple tautology.

Let us deepen our analysis. Two *threads* run through all of Marx's thinking, one *analytic*, another *materialistic*.[2] The first thread, particularly evident in some of Marx's writings (especially in the *Grundrisse* [1973], in the first chapters of *Capital Vol. 1* [1990], and also in the 'Results of the Immediate Process of Production'),[3] focuses on the abstract linear elements of the capitalist relations of production – here the analytic is fundamentally synchronic. The second thread is materialistic and fundamentally diachronic. It is particularly evident in the *Theories of Surplus Value* and in the unfinished volumes of *Capital*. Historical, material, weighty, irreversible elements serve here to qualify the relations of production. In Marx it is indubitably the case that the *dialectical apparel of the exposition* serves to mollify these opposed approaches. But dialectical manipulation does not remove the *logical struggle* that traverses the system. On the contrary, dialectics often plays the coquette, it does not cleave to substance: the system is returned to us in its aporetic form. An absolutely clear example of the aporia's return, even within the most polished parts of Marx's theory, is provided in the celebrated pages on the working day (Marx 1990, Chapter 10). In these pages, whether the working day is considered in terms of its length, its form, or of the dynamics of its transformation, the relationship between the capitalist drive towards the limitlessness of the working day and the worker's exertion towards its limitation remains always unresolved. While the analytic and linear discourse continuously renders the constitutive elements of the working day reversible, the materialistic moment places the irreversibility of the struggle, of the 'civil war', at the forefront: 'our worker leaves the productive process differently from how he entered it' (ibid., pp. 412, 415). But this *difference* destroys the analytic premises that had founded the equivalence of the temporal measure on natural and physical concepts. The aporia is a potent one in this case also. How are we to overcome it? The only possibility for a logical solution Marx provides is through the destruction of all the irreversible and static premises of the analysis. Only when the working day becomes a global flow (and therefore conceivable at the level of real subsumption), only then is the aporia removed and time-as-measure has no need to fix its foundations outside the productive circuit. The measure is in the *flow* between labour and time. A continuous time. A tautological time.

Let us continue. Wherever the passage towards real subsumption occurs (one can always bear in mind the 'Results of the Immediate Process of Production' as an example), time-as-measure, as equivalent, as reversible, etc., manifests its aporias in definitively tautological form. The relationship between the analytic and materialistic threads of the exposition was in fact based on the possibility of recourse to an external element.

(Some, such as Agnes Heller, have considered this external element so fundamental as to link its supposed natural and humanist qualities to the worth of Marx's thought.) When the dialectic is resolved (and we know that under real subsumption that indeed occurs), tautology reigns. Real subsumption means the complete realization of the law of value. At first glance *indifference* rules in real subsumption. Labour is quality, time is quantity; in real subsumption quality falls away, so all labour is reduced to mere quantity, to time. Before us we have only quantities of time. Use-value, which in *Capital* was still given as separation from, and irreducible to, value *tout court*, is here absorbed by capital. The aporia consists in the fact that since time has become entirely hegemonic over the process, in so far as it is its only measure, it also reveals itself as its only substance. But this complete superimposition of measure and substance denies any dialectical significance to the relationship, reducing it therefore to pure and simple tautology.

To summarize: (1) in real subsumption all use-value is drawn into exchange-value; (2) but with that the external origin of the measure of time (based on the externality of use-value) recedes and measure is flattened onto the process itself; (3) if measure measures itself, it follows that the process of value concludes in that of command, in tautology and indifference; (4) the trend of productive forces (increase, decrease, transformation) bears no relation to the magnitude of value; (5) complex, productive, scientific labour is definitively irreducible to elementary temporal units; (6) productive force is inexplicable. *In short*, a non-dialectical tautology comes in at the end of the process in place of the initial dialectic. And *so* it is only possible to explain the movement of the class struggle by rejecting the notion of temporal measure as equivalence. The *form of equivalence* is simply an *effect of coercion*. For example, every mutation in the composition of labour-power (equivalent to different forms of the composition of the temporal units of measure of the productivity of labour) is in the dialectical Marx submitted to a mechanism of reversibility, of equivalence and of command. This reversibility needs to be broken. Here we see the exceptional importance of the *Grundrisse* [Marx 1973], where the equivalent is all in the hands of capital, given in the form of surplus-value – consequently the antagonism comes at the beginning and *irreversibility is the key to the process.*

But the argumentation that reveals, in the course of Marx's thought, the reduction of the aporia of time-as-measure and time-as-substance to tautology is, when we enter the stage of real subsumption (which summarizes in intensive form the argument so far), confirmed by another series of observations that we can call *extensive*, that is to say, that concern the extension of the realization of the tautology. Real subsumption once again:

> First, with the development of the *real subsumption of labour under capital*, or the *specifically capitalist mode of production*, the *real functionary* of the overall labour process is increasingly not the individual worker. Instead, *labour-power socially combined* and the various competing labour-powers which together form the entire productive machine participate in very different ways in the immediate process of making commodities, or, more accurately in this context, creating the product. Some work better with their hands, others with their brains, one as a manager, engineer, technologist, etc., the other as overseer, the third as manual labourer or even drudge. An ever increasing number of *types of labour-power* are included in the immediate concept of *productive labour*, and those who perform it are classed as *productive workers*, workers directly exploited by capital and *subordinated* to its process of production and valorization. If we consider that *collective worker* that is the factory, then we see that its *combined activity* results materially in an *aggregate product*, which is at the same time a *total mass of goods*. And here it is quite immaterial whether the function of a particular worker, who is merely a member of the *collective worker*, is at a greater or smaller distance from the actual manual labour. But then: the activity of this collective labour-power is its *immediate productive consumption by capital*, i.e. it is the self-valorization process of capital, the immediate production of surplus-value, the *immediate transformation of this latter into capital*.
>
> (Marx 1990, pp. 1039–40 – translation modified)

We have seen elsewhere (and it is widely accepted throughout Marxist interpretation) that the concept of the socially combined worker represents the subsumption of the *social whole* by capital and therefore renders the social relations of production, reproduction and exploitation, one-dimensional.

That said, let us ask: *in what form can time be the measure of social labour?* If social labour covers all the time of life, and invests all of its regions, how can time measure the substantive totality in which it is implicit? In this way we are brought back to the earlier conclusions. We find ourselves before a tautology that after presenting itself *intensively* as the impossibility of distinguishing the measure of the differentiation of the substance of value, reproposes itself *extensively* as the impossibility of distinguishing the totality of life (of the social relations of production and reproduction) from the totality of time from which this life is woven. When the entire time of life has become the time of production, who measures whom?

Does this mean that Marx's theory of value and time should be put out to pasture? The answer is probably yes for a sizeable part of it, and certainly its aporetic form should, as we shall see – although it is precisely the theoretical dissatisfaction produced by the aporia that drives forward Marx's analysis. But, on the other hand, this final tautology seems to us to be extraordinarily productive from the theoretical and revolutionary standpoint. For now we know that time cannot be presented as measure, but must rather be presented as the global phenomenological fabric, as base, substance and flow of production in its entirety.

1.2 Tautology and composition

The impasse in which the orthodox Marx – the Marx who does not step *beyond* Marx – finds himself, the web of aporias in which his thinking on time is caught, represents, however, the highest point of development of the materialist idea of time. In order to understand the specificity of the Marxian 'limit' we must understand that his idea of time is nevertheless the most consummate conceptualization of the *pre-Einsteinian materialist perspective* – for Marx moves beyond the terms of the theoretical debate on time of his day, beyond the potentialities which materialist thought concerning time had set for itself over the preceding few centuries.

To test these assertions a few historical remarks will prove sufficient. Putting aside some contemporary subtleties on the idea of time, the philosophical tradition offers us – aside from subterranean threads, such as the Democritean and Epicurean to which we shall return given their exceptional importance (but it should be underlined, they are subterranean threads!) – two consolidated positions. One is the *theological*. Time is the mystery of divinity. 'What then is time? I know well enough what it is, provided that nobody asks me; but if I am asked what it is and try to explain, I am baffled' (Saint Augustine 1986, Book XI, Part 14, p. 264). When the practice of theory is directed simply towards the constitution of the transcendent, time is non-existence. Time is multiplicity. Time is a theological scandal. Time is rebellious. Time is only resolved by transcendence and constraint. '[The demiurge] mingled them all into one form, compressing by force the reluctant and unsociable nature of the different into the same' (Plato 1961, line 35a). Demiurge and constraint are inseparably united against time. Therefore reality is a constrained unity, *that is, dominable space*. When studying the history of the idea of time, it is absolutely necessary to bear in mind this fundamental *reduction of time to space* – which is as much present in materialist theory as it is *foundational* to spiritualism. The *hard core* of the idea of time in the Western tradition is its eternal *Parmenideanism*: the spatialization of time. The negated time is reconstructed in an illusory manner in accordance with the model of space. Time is pure and simple taboo in the spiritualist philosophical tradition; and yet this is the tradition of Power, of the knowledge of the temple and the palace. It is difficult to think of another concept around which Western thought has, with the same efficacy, cast its spells. How different are things in the Eastern tradition, and particularly in the Chinese! (Those unforgettable passages by Marcel Granet, or Needham, on the density of Eastern time, on its capacity to portray the collective, to represent the social!) The contemporary subtleties of the theory of time, the theorists who, faithful to disciplinary specificities, move between Nietzsche and Hesse with a dash of Theodore Roszak, take up the magical – and reactionary – effects that inevitably spring from the insolubility of the problem of time. While still leaving aside the beguiling and fascistic illuminations: 'I have a vague intuition of the substance of which time is made; for it is that which changes the past into the future' (Borges).

The power of the spiritualist tradition that reduces the problem of time to that of death, the problem of the temporal being to that of non-being, empirical time to space, is so powerful that even the *materialist tradition's* thinking on time – and this is a unique phenomenon in the history of Western thought – is induced into continuous theoretical conjuring tricks. 'In a word, science in its effort to become 'rational' tends more and more to suppress variation in time' (E. Meyerson).[4] For centuries, time has been thought of – materialistically – from within the categories of space. Modern, bourgeois, revolutionary thought – even in the finest moments of its development – has not in truth been able to think time autonomously. Even the turning point of the Renaissance (Telesio, Bruno, Gassendi), which succeeded in making time absolute as against space, was not able to define it outside of the spatial cipher. Every pompous *Geschichte des Materialismus* omits to mention this shameful fact. This reaches the point of paradox: in the whole history of modern (pre-Einsteinian) scientific thought the most accomplished formulation of the definition of time is given by the perpetually renewed Gnostic hotchpotch of neo-Platonism, in other words, in the transcendental figure of space (Koyré). And when finally a breach occurs, a fundamental breach of the tradition, the same *relativistic conceptions* of the spatio-temporal relationship have long had to fight to unfasten themselves from the postulation of an *isotopic homology*, with exclusion of any *asymmetry*, so as to liberate themselves from a continual attempt at a *geometrical rigidifying of the idea of time* (Meyerson, Čapek, etc.). And this is where we stand long after Marx and his epoch! But of all this later, as these notes develop. Materialism is thus mutilated here. Or more correctly, castrated: since the thematic of time is the only one that could have taken it towards a positive resolution of the problem of the *productivity of matter*, that is, that could have toppled theology into revolution and pushed the anxiety for revolution towards the perspective of the abolition of death. (Ernst Bloch, when he glimpses the problem, prudently withdraws.)

However, we cannot deny that modern materialism has achieved some results in its elaboration of the idea of time, although the junk of the theological and spiritualist imagination – surreptitiously, but not any less effectively infiltrated – is ever present. Hypocrisy becomes a characteristic of the materialist tradition's conception of time. However, there are two high points to the (hypocritical) materialist and modern conception of time: the Newtonian and the Kantian. (Obviously here I take Newton and Kant to be the main exponents of the scientific thinking of the seventeenth century, the Enlightenment, and the materialist currents of which they are the bearers, but which are clearly not exhausted in their thinking.) In both cases, and in accordance with G. H. von Wright's formulation, time is in the end considered as the *envelope* of the order of temporal events and hence as the 'nature of the temporal medium'; the attainment of this *independence* of the concept is doubtless a huge step forward. Except that in the case of Newton, the nature of the temporal medium is objectified in a theological sense: time as the 'sensorium Dei'; while in the case of Kant, the nature of the temporal medium recovers its objectivity by way of the transcendent position of the subject. (We will return later to further important aspects of the Kantian idea of time.) In both cases theological and spiritualist echoes render the innovative approach timid and diminished.

Is this the definitive demonstration of the idiosyncrasy, the obtuseness of materialism when confronted with the problem of time? In fact it is precisely on the back of this presumption that new theoretical experiences emerge: hybrid experiences that are nonetheless effective. Beginning with the insistence with which the (Newtonian but especially the) Kantian analysis had demonstrated the flowing interchangeability of the idea of time, Hegel attempts to reach a stronger identity of the mediation, providing it with a real interiority and necessity. With the violence which characterises his thought (and that renders it effective), for Hegel the problem of the order of temporal events becomes dialectical, and thus is linked with the force of necessity to the subjective and transcendental medium by rendering the 'whole' absolute. In the words of von Wright: some distinct references are given for the concept *time* – namely, *(a)* time as *order of temporal events*, *(b)* time as *envelope and measure of this order*. The proposition 'envelope of the order of temporal events', or *(b)* of *(a)*, is not, however, the equivalent of *(c)*, time as *nature of the temporal medium*. Now, while Newton founds a natural philosophy of *(b)* of *(a)*, Kant proposes problem *(c)*, or rather, proposes the transformation of *(b)* into *(c)* – finally Hegel proposes an *independent* problematic of *(c)*. Hegel makes time take on the role of general mediator, which the spatial principle of divinity was on the way to surrendering. Hegelian time enables thought to escape Zeno's paradoxes of space for the first time, shifting the ground of the antinomies. That is to say, with Hegel a specific definition for the *temporal* measure, of measure as temporal specificity, is secured – where before that, even in the Newtonian school, time was brought back to the cipher of the *spatial measure*, 'between before and after' (Piperno). The effect of the Hegelian operation is unquestionably the definitive erasure of the rigidity of the spatial definition of time that the history of ideas had handed down.

One cannot exaggerate the importance of this move. Some authors maintain that 'the Hegelian theory of *becoming* brought time onto the philosophical scene' (Fernando Gil).[5] Maybe so: however, Colli's irony in this regard is apposite to this reasoning ('becoming: a dark word'). Others (von Wright, Prior, etc.), continue to maintain that it was, rather, Kant who established the image of time as the way out from contradictions. I think it is not worth either underestimating or exaggerating the importance of the transition signalled by transcendental idealism. As we have already seen, Marx himself refers to it as an essential precedent. However, despite the innovation, the temporal mediation of contradictions is in effect still prey to theological remainders and, consequently, the contradictions are brought back within the spatial horizon. For example, the Hegelian 'vanishing' of spiritual time (Hegel 1977, 'Spirit', par. 508) is still spatial – a conjurer's trick, *temporal fuzziness*. Time is not yet conceived fully in the independence and autonomy of its concept. The problem is posed, the matter of the enquiry is defined, but the solution is anything but attained.

Nor does the contemporary logic of time and of temporal modalities alter this picture in any significant way. Whatever the initial approach, and it is often extremely well developed, it ends up fixing the foundation of time spatially in accordance with the criteria of a physical ontology. It could be a structural referral, in terms of its operations, or a physicalist postulation of time atomism.[6] In each case the newly represented contradictions of a materialism that is unable to free the conception of time from subordination to the idea of space, although it is so intentionally, is unable to conceive of time as its own essence, as immanent, as human. Time is unable to become materialist power, and so to operate on the terrain of epistemology. The logic of time and of the temporal modalities, however much it pushes on in its approximation to and desire for being, is unable to escape from a sort of uncertain spatial compromise. It is probably only when, though caught in numerous ambiguities, Einstein insists on the *physical construction of the asymmetry* of time and of space such that the conception does not contradict the development of *thermodynamics*; probably only then, can one overcome the perpetual reflux towards an irreducible geometricism and the logical strictures that oppose themselves to an epistemology of time. But of this more later, as we proceed in our work.

Let us return to Marx. In his writings, the limits of the history of materialism and the difficulty of liberating the idea of time from a geometric foundation and the presuppositions of a metaphysics of space are both traversed and overcome. In Marx, time is not only the route out from the contradiction of change, not only the instrument that constructs the effective possibility of change (von Wright) – time is also the tautology of life. To begin with, in Marx, time is given to us as the matter of equivalence and the measure of the equivalent. Bit by bit, however, alongside the abstract development of social mediatization[7] and of the subjectification of abstract labour, time itself becomes substance, to the point that time becomes the fabric of the whole of being, because all of being is implicated in the web of the relations of production: *being* is equal to *product of labour*: *temporal being*. We need to pause at this point. Indeed, in Marx this necessary and tendential superimposition of time and life liberates and fixes the hegemony of the epistemological significance of time over and against the purely logical one. What does this mean? It means that time is *a before* and not *an after*. It means that time is existence, and not the product of reflection or of the mediation of existence:

determination and not abstraction, the irreversible not the reversible. At the level at which the institutional development of the capitalist system invests the whole of life, time is not the measure of life, but is life itself. Marx grasps the passage from time reduced to a convention derived from space, to medium [*medietà*], to measure of exploitation, up to its pure and simple general abstraction, and therefore, to its total, mystified realization in the world of life in the phase of real subsumption.

Therefore, Marx's tautology of time, life and production at the level of real subsumption is both the consummation of the materialist tradition (and the overcoming of its substantial deficiencies) as well as the eruption of a new horizon of reflection on time. In Marx, in the theory of capitalist development up to real subsumption, the *traditional relationship of time to space is definitively overturned*. Space is temporalized, it becomes dynamic: it is a condition of the constitutive realization of time. With Marx, time becomes the exclusive material of the construction of life.

It is well known that each scientific culture has a temporal paradigm, that is to say, a particular conception of time as its systematic referent, one that is even present in contemporary – even if contradictory – tendencies.[8] The originality of the *Marxian paradigm* consists in the fact that here time is constitutive; it is *time of constitution, time of composition*. So the *paradigm is ontological*. In Marx, time begins to come into view as the measure of labour (a Hegelian step forward with respect to the deficiencies of modern science), but, step by step, as the course of the class struggle and the abstraction of labour asserts itself, time increasingly becomes *interior to class composition*, to the point of being the motor of its very existence and of its specific configuration. The process develops so that the maximal temporalization of the labour process (and of the production process) leads to the maximal reappropriation of all the spatial conditions of existence. When work has become mobility, pure and simple mobility – when, that is, it is time pure and simple – then it is the possibility and actuality of the constitution of the world. O'Connor and Hossfeld, Paul Virilio, Jean-Paul de Gaudemar have all recently come to this awareness in writings of varying degrees of importance – an awareness which is alone adequate to the development of mature capitalism: *mobility comes to be the very definition of the proletarian class* today.[9] It should be pointed out that, as we shall see below, *to the different scientific paradigms of time* there correspond *different forms of class composition*. And this is said so as to underline, in the first place, how time is inextricable from the foundation of *composition*; in second place, how the constitutive reality of temporality has a *sense* and *direction*, that is to say how it develops materially, in a tendential and necessary sense, towards the *tautology of time and life*. The concept of time is immediately epistemological, that is it cleaves to reality. When time is taken as productive force, in the infinite multiplicity of the effects and actions it delineates, in no circumstance will it be representable as mediation. Here mediation has become *a before* with respect to events, with respect to actions, *not an after*; it is not thought but it is lived as such. Thought approximates reality, thought describes real composition – time is the real composition.

1.3 An *Umwelt* of antagonism

The Marxian tautology of being and time in real subsumption is only a base from which to take up our journey again. Time constitutes the immediate ground of reference, an average social time that has invested all the sections of society – production, reproduction and circulation – and within which all the articulations of being are given. Productive space is in the first place restructured in accordance with productive social management strategies – on the basis of this fluidification, every component element taken together reaches an aleatory presence and a global inherence to this ontological framework.[10] The *presence* of each element is mobile and fast; *the inherence* to being is global and absolute. Being is materially given in the form of time. Every productive activity, every human action is within this *Umwelt*: a dense and strong *temporal envelopment of existence* is the first feature by which contemporary being reveals itself. There is a contemporaneity in the description of which one can discern, in a suggestive manner, the reappearance of the characteristics of pre-Socratic being. Genesis is repeated at the conclusion of the millennium? 'We have returned to the beginning, except for those that are departing rather than arriving' (Burroughs): no, we too depart; not eternal return, but innovation. (And no decadent banalities). Eternal return? The thing is excluded on principle, from the very concept of the temporal ontology of subsumed being. The Stoic paradox of the eternal return effects the – Aristotelian – spatial conception of time and renders it cosmologically absurd. If time has a spatial cipher, if the line represents it geometrically, what prevents the line from being circular? If anything, if it is true that fire perpetually burns being, the circular paradox is more realistic than the linear conception of time. This is not, however, the –

mythical – situation from which we set out. The analytic of this firm being-in-the-world has no need of circularity. The *phenomenological Heidegger* correctly sees the task of the enquiry as follows:

> these are both ways in which Dasein's Being takes on a definite character, and they must be seen and understood *a priori* as grounded upon that state of Being which we have called '*Being-in-the-world*'. An interpretation of this constitutive state is needed if we are to set up our analytic of Dasein correctly.
>
> (Heidegger 1962, p. 78)

At first glance this reality presents itself as restlessness and as open surface. Phenomenology, psychology, and the analytic logic of time have, as is well known (I am thinking of the works by Michotte, Piaget and Vicario), tried to identify a paradigm that, with the assumption of the totality of the temporal involvement and the impossibility of fixing external reference points, arrives at an immanent *relative definition* of time, as a *relationship of times*, as a tension between velocity and local times, as co-ordination of different velocities. The structural foundation of the temporal dimension attested to by this paradigm is linked to a dynamic of times that are equally structural and constitutive of the temporal medium; so that it is only *genetically* that the compact material of the order of events and the composing mesh of the medium are themselves articulated and defined. The totality of temporal being is disarticulated and recomposed from within. At the same time in which every pre-constituted form is disarticulated, we find ourselves within the real, global process of the formation of events. The contradiction then, as the logician himself (von Wright) finally admits, is the real: time opens itself, in its interior, to a real contradiction while the real contradiction itself constitutes it in structural totality.

These observations are important, but they remain superficial and uncertain. For at the moment in which they yield to the necessity of a structural understanding of time, they relativize the materiality and weight of the experience of time. Frankly, it seems to me that what is given with one hand is taken back with the other. The dissymmetries, the *hysteresies*,[11] the real differences around which the conception of time-as-measure goes into crisis, and the logical difficulties; all this is pacified through a general modification of the framework which does not alter the nature of the composing elements. Time is acknowledged as real contradiction but it continues to be hypostasized as the envelope of real contradiction. Rather than following the real contradictions within the interior of the envelope, the envelope itself comes to be assumed as the nature that provides the foundation for their solution. *So time as contradiction is not contradiction but solution.* So that the equilibrium vainly sought by the old paradigms, which is its problem, is *not resolved but given as resolved* in the new paradigm. A typical paralogism of pure reason.

We will return to the methodological implications of these procedures repeatedly so as to criticize their foundations and their redundancies (but also to learn from the richness of their insights). But now I wish to critique the delight that philosophy seems to express in proposing such paralogisms. The word 'paralogism' takes us back to Kant. Not only the word itself, for the Kantian critique of the paralogisms of pure reason is where contemporary critique is founded. Indeed it is here, in this renewed initiative on paradigms, that one witnesses the fulfilment and the mystification of a Kantian enterprise – that is to say one witnesses the opportunistic development and paradoxical realization of the *transcendental schematism*. It is well known with how much realism Kant posed the problem of the 'thing in itself', that is of the impossibility of objectively, materially guaranteeing the operation of reason outside of reason itself. On the terrain of knowledge, the only instrument to allow a real 'approximation' is the transcendental schema (a sort of Epicurean experience of 'anticipation'). But the schema of reason is regulated by dialectics; it does not construct reality to resolve problems but it resolves problems and thereby works itself out in reality. *What is accomplished here, on the other hand, is the upsetting of the schema understood as a formal system of substitution of a fictional reality for an unknowable reality.* The schematism reproduces paralogisms. Already in Kant's lifetime *formalism* – the science of paralogisms, conjugated with a naive and acritical conception of the transcendental schematism – began to develop, especially in the juridical and social sciences, with constant and disparate references back to a supposed Kantian orthodoxy.[12] The demands of bourgeois ideology have continuously nourished and renewed this mystificatory thread: command; the more it demands 'rationalization', the more it loses as a project.[13]

It is worth remembering that the only justification for the hypothetical, hypostatic falsity of the paralogism is that it follows on from a real and irrepressible need. Nor can one deny that the need to define time becomes ever more real and profound as the temporal rootedness of existence becomes more disquieting and pervasive. In effect it is precisely this leap forward of all the parameters of existence, this discovery of this enormous and dense temporal *Umwelt* that throws thought into confusion! From here stems the urgent need for a solution; but also of the philistine happiness of make-believe, subterfuge and paralogism. The schematism of reason appears to offer the possibility of traversing this dense universe flattened on time and to control it. Applied to the multiplicity of local times and real differences, the schematism appears able to found a new dialectic that recomposes unity, extolling the functional aspects of the process: schema as function. The utilitarian aspects of the paradigm can at this point reveal themselves as elements of truth. How can we not be reminded here that Heidegger's *Being and Time*, in its *metaphysical* aspect, ambiguously poses itself the task of realizing the Kantian programme of the transcendental schematism as the commencement of the problematic of temporality?[14] But Heideggerian panic and tragedy in the face of the dramatic and compact multiplicity of temporal being become, in the contemporary theories of multiple time, functional games, doltish happiness: 'There is no other itinerary between *Dasein* and *Dasein* than that which passes through a world of Forms'! (Cassirer). What's more, in the social sciences, they become elements of legitimation: communicative interaction discovers its symbolic form in productive relations! (Habermas).

Let us return to the real contradiction. The true question is not how it can be *resolved across* the whole of the temporal *Umwelt*. The true question is how can it be lived, how it can embed itself and develop, how it can be *described within* the temporal *Umwelt*. *The tautology of being and of time must be opened up, but within and only within the* Umwelt. Let us reconsider once again the situation defined by Marx. Contradiction, antagonistic development and struggle impose real subsumption; at this point all the parameters that have defined the unfolding of the contradiction are thrown into crisis. Above all, we have emphasized the modification that occurs to the fundamental temporal dimension. Time becomes substantial, given in the form of real constitution – as totality. Here then, within this historical, logical and ontological displacement, the problem of time is proposed anew. What is to be seen is *if and how* – within this temporal *Umwelt*, within its totality – *far from triumphing over indifference, contradiction re-emerges and antagonism is reborn.*

What we must confront here is the problem of the *if*. In effect we find ourselves before a determinate negation, a specific criticism: those same concepts which capture the passage from time-as-measure to time-as-substance and on to multiple times, deny that within subsumption time presents itself again as antagonistic materiality. In truth, when the problem is that of the *mediation of multiple times*, the result cannot but be the *re-invention of time as envelope*. The problem of time is laid out in schematic terms and resolved within the perspective of the re-legitimation of a unitary form of time – thus providing totality with a new foundation. The dialectical content may increase, but the schema remains functional, formal and unifying (sublimating). The so-called *postmodern ideologies* – despite the confusion of their concepts – operate on this level. Recently, Prigogine and other scientists that have intervened in the debate seem to maintain that the temporal irreversibility of events is reducible and controllable within the categories of the reversible totality. *But* time, when it becomes substantial, is not less but rather more contradictory. The general, global displacement of the level of analysis modifies the structure of the antagonism, meaning that it dislocates it, but it does so concomitantly with the contents of the antagonism. Nevertheless the contents remain antagonistic. The archipelago of real times presented to us by the temporal *Umwelt* does not tend towards the zero of neutralization, of reciprocal dampening, but rather towards explosion and diffusion. This *positive entropy* is richly described in that beautiful tract of the phenomenology of time and times that is Deleuze and Guattari's *A Thousand Plateaus* [1988]. Real subsumption, notwithstanding the many elements of the old relations of production that are reduced to insignificance, does not amount to indifference. Rather, it produces and displays a *complete transcription of the real relations* (individual, of class, of force), and introduces a maximization of plurality and dynamism. Antagonistic *dipositifs* open up and consolidate themselves starting precisely from a new irreducibility of action to average value, or to unified time. Therefore, the form of the theoretical exposition of this displacement will in essence have to capture the points of view given within this unified compass. Not as indifference, but as rooted difference, and so as more ontologically radical.

But there's more. This general displacement of the terms of the antagonism, inserted within the temporal matrix, returns the *collective* to us as a multiplicity of subjects. The more the processes of subsumption are realized, the more they create the collective. Time gives itself as collective already from the point of view of capitalism: collective capital, collective worker, etc. But it is not a simple operation. *In destroying time-as-measure, capital constructs time as collective substance*. This collective substance is a *multiplicity of antagonistic subjects*.[15] The necessity for capitalism is that of integrating this collective within an *equilibrium* that reduces dialectical possibilities to zero: this is the *new quality of antagonism in real subsumption*. Keynes and Polanyi – two of the most acute theoreticians of the *great transformation*, that is to say of the passage into real subsumption – insist maniacally on the necessity for equilibrium (neoclassical in the case of Keynes, institutional in the case of Polanyi) as the soul of the collective, of the planned, of the State. Keynes and Polanyi, as bourgeois champions of the transformation and of the great crisis, present the project of *re-equilibrating the modified components* within this passage. The construction of the collective is for them the construction of scientific and political conditions of reversibility, of a re-equilibrating calculus.[16] And it is precisely this that we are *unable* to concede logically. The substantial radicality of time collectively founds subjects and places antagonism on a new temporal and collective foundation, with new dimensions. The transition to real subsumption, in so far as it affirms the collective as sole temporal and real substrate of action, not only does not reduce it to the formal indifference of equilibrium, but reproduces, reproposes, refounds the antagonism of subjects. So collective time, the temporal *Umwelt*, tend to present themselves to us immediately within *two horizons*: that of the closed time of legitimation and of equilibrium, the zero tendency of the absolute circularity of the social; and that of multiple, antagonistic, productive, constitutive, open time. 'In short, the difference is not at all between the ephemeral and the durable, nor even between the regular and the irregular, but between two modes of individuation, two modes of temporality' (Deleuze and Guattari 1988, p. 262).

Therefore it is not a question as to *whether* the antagonism is born again in the *Umwelt* of real subsumption. The phenomenology is sumptuous. Decisive as well is the fact that early traces of *how* the antagonism unfolds in the *Umwelt* reveal themselves within that same analysis that asserts the displaced rebirth of the antagonism.

1.4 Displacement, hysteresis, asymmetry, innovation

In my *Marx Beyond Marx* [1991] I demonstrated in depth how the mechanism of *displacement* dominates Marx's logic – in other words, that of the scientific standpoint of class. When real subsumption is reached through the development of productive forces and of the relations of production, the displacement of all the constitutive parameters is thereby determined.

The synchronic rules are modified within the framework of the diachronic transition.

As we have seen in the displacement produced by the realization of subsumption, the unitary paradigm of time-as-measure of value is smashed. Subsumption generates a completely enveloping temporal *Umwelt* that dissolves the possibility of measure. With the dissolution of measure, two tendencies present themselves to us on the terrain of theory itself: the first reproposes a *formal* schema of manifold time, a scientific centralization of the combination of multiple times, a concept of the *envelope* of the multiple – in other words a new *space* of organization of time, therefore an analytic of the combination of these modalities; the other tendency displays the situation in materialist terms, and so respects multiplicity for what it is, as irreducibility of the many to the one, *time* conceived in its founding dynamic – and therefore, molecular *reality* as against any molar projection. From the methodological standpoint, it seems important to me to mention that once the analysis of time has been displaced onto the terrain of real subsumption, the first problem becomes that of the hysteresis of the concepts of time. The antagonism of the paradigms (or if one prefers, of the *style of thought*, or even better, of the *principle of individuation* connected to each paradigm) appears immediately on stage. On one side, the formal and analytic tendency, the idea of equilibrium. On the other, the materialist tendency and the insistence on multiplicity. The impossibility of considering time as the measure of value, and therefore of taking it as the solution to a real contradiction, pushes contradiction onto two opposing fronts, therefore freeing up its antagonistic potentialities.

It is well established that once the law of value is no longer current or functional, it determines on the terrain of the relations of production the hegemonic accentuation of the political precept, of the rules of command. When we analyse the idea of time and its transformation, we understand the thread of that real displacement: the idea of time will be articulated along with that of command, tending to become the fabric of the analytic of command; as against this, in the hysteresis of the dissociation of multiple times we find opposed tendencies, material tendencies constituting themselves as the negation of command, and therefore as logics of liberation.[17] But all this occurs at the *level of displacement*, and so *within the great unitary base, the new social nature of existence of the collective* Umwelt. The displacement of the law of value in real subsumption is both its negation and its realization: the realization of a general and collective substratum that opens towards a new transition, dominated by a new antagonism. The hysteresis of the concept of time, the catastrophe of its experience, the fact that it presents itself to us according to antagonistic tendencies, all this represents the chief qualities of the displacement. Therefore, we must methodically underline the problem of the *hysteresis within the displacement* as the first step in determining our enquiry qualitatively.[18]

But still from the standpoint of methodology, and keeping to the terrain that cleaves only to the ghost of reality, one can immediately add some further important remarks. If the destruction of time-as-measure of value places us before a compact, socialized, standardized, subsumed world; if this world can be seen from two points of view, and these two points of view are real because the displacement is given as a hysteresis of the tendencies – the logic of time, in order to enable the emergence of the *dual* and antagonistic character that the experience of displacement (of the crisis of the law of value) produces, must initially demonstrate the irreducibility, the impossibility of superimposing dialectically the two faces of the hysteresis, of the separation. For, as soon as we see the phenomena that interest us, we note the profound, the radical *asymmetry* between the polarities of the crisis.

I will give just one example. The displacement is given through the process of real subsumption. Now, from the formal point of view the tendency of subsumption presents itself in terms of a linear logic: the reality of capitalist dominion is realized as systemic and totalitarian. The whole of society becomes productive. The time of production is the time of life. At this point, however, the formal and linear tendency must recall its own reality: it is the tendency of capitalist development. But *capital is a relation*, a relation of exploitation. The displacement of development onto the level of real subsumption is – therefore – an *antagonistic displacement*. The fact that all has become productive does not negate the asymmetry of the productive relation: in other words, it does not negate the fact that it is exploitation that constitutes the relation of production. The social realization of the relation of capitalist production, over-determines and accentuates the relation of exploitation, it does not negate it. But we have already seen how at this level the unitary idea of time-as-measure goes into crisis, and there arise within the fabric of the multiplicity of real times, at least two opposing tendencies. These displaced times are in a material opposition adequate to the original asymmetric relation. In the *Umwelt* of real subsumption (of enveloping time) there emerges not only the hysteresis of the analytic of time and of multiple real times, but also and above all *the asymmetry of the time of command and of the times of liberation from exploitation*. Asymmetry is the initial and powerful, radical and insoluble form of antagonism within the displacement.

Perhaps we should here recall a minor tradition in the history of the idea of time, but one that is not any less important or suggestive. It is the hypothesis of classical materialism, that of Democritus, Epicurus and Lucretius. It is an entirely ontological hypothesis that, on the basis of a relation between mutation and time, on the basis of a tendential unity of movement and time, proposes the definition of time as innovation and/or corruption; that is to say, time as direction, as significant ontological vector, as asymmetry, as displacement. 'Epicurus and Lucretius, before Spinoza, released Sisiphus from Hell' (Serres 2000, p. 38). It worth recalling this tradition because it symbolizes – with the value of a symbol and nothing else (it is in fact very dangerous to posit, as some contemporary authors do, this 'relationist' conception of time – one that is linked to fixed and determined spatial parameters – as a way of overcoming the Ancient spatial concept of time and as anticipation of the 'relativistic' contemporary theories. The atomistic theory has merely the force of a symbol, that is all!) – the radical alterity of a libertarian, materialistic and collective conception of time: we like – we very much want – to reconnect ourselves to these origins. Against time as 'number of motion in respect of "before" and "after"' (Aristotle),[19] against the conception of time as the universal reverberation of the 'harmony of the celestial spheres', against Aristotle and Plato – and therefore against every conception of time-as-measure (even more so if it happens to be the absolute measure of the astral movements) – here time shows itself as fullness and as difference. We insist on the *co-presence of the plenitude* of the capitalist subsumption of labour, which is a veritable *coining* of collective being, *of difference*, of asymmetry, of the corruption and the innovation of being, and of its mutation. This paradox represents the situation we find ourselves in well.

> Nature does not codify the universe, there is no code to the equilibrium [. . .]. The *clinamen* appears as freedom because it is that turbulence which refuses the forced movement. It cannot be understood by the scientific theory of the constructors of wells and aqueducts, it cannot be understood by the master of the waters.
>
> (Serres)

In fact the master of the waters, of this liquid universe of the temporal *Umwelt* of subsumption cannot but understand time as 'appearance', as 'not being in-itself', as 'accident of accidents'! Against this Democritus, Epicurus and Lucretius take a stand in favour of the ontological reality of time.

At this point it seems possible to provide a few remarks on how to advance the enquiry into the definition of the communist idea of time or, the time of communism. We will start from the analysis of *collective time* as determined by the displacement marked by real subsumption, identifying on the one hand the *capitalist analytic* of the subsumption of labour by capital, and on the other, its specific antagonism – that is – social work, the *social worker* as the crisis of the social analytic of capital (Chapters 2 and 3). Secondly, we will define *productive time* in the specificity of its antagonism: on the one side, time as productive of surplus-value, time as *money and circulation;* but on the other, time as productive *co-operation*, from complex labour to self-valorization (Chapters 4 and 5). Thirdly, *time* will be seen in its *constitutive* form: the constitution of capitalist Power in the *State*, in the global and articulated organization of command, when the analytic of capitalist time becomes Power. And on the other hand, the worker time of a *global working day* that erupts from self-valorization to self-organization, to the *new* proletarian *institutionality* (Chapters 6 and 7). Finally, we will find ourselves before the definitive irreducibility of the different temporal series: the capitalist series annuls itself in the formality of the time of *destruction*, of disintegration, of waste; the series of multiple times of the antagonistic standpoint is resolved in the long and consistent *revolutionary time* of the communist constitution (Chapters 8 and 9). In reality, with these last two points, we find ourselves before a *second* fundamental *displacement*, so that the path travelled in these prolegomena is that which goes from the subsumption of labour in capital and of society in the State (first displacement) to the explosion of this relation.

We are travelling the path which orthodox theory called the problem of *transition*, which it flattened onto that of socialism. Here – in truth we have had to consider many things – we start from the concept of *subsumption as crisis*, of *socialism as antagonistic displacement*. If there is a transition it happens in the form of antagonism and certainly not in the form of a linear utopia. The idea of time is central not only because it places itself at the heart of the critical genesis of the theory of value – the appearance of real subsumption and the opening of the problem of transition (which happens to be a real problem) – but above all because it presents itself as the matrix of the dystopia of communism, of the reality of its immensely powerful collective advance. Time will increasingly appear to us as the real material from which communism is constituted. *The scientific innovation is that of the second displacement.* We must work at this; we must anticipate the course of that path. Probably some truths will emerge, but we must bear in mind that, although we work at innovation, we are still within the terrain of subsumption, and hence of the hysteresis of forces and the asymmetry of relations: we live in the forms of contradiction and of antagonism. Here the truth and the concept of communist time will appear to us as fireworks and flares rather than as a secure trajectory of physical time. And yet it is necessary to begin.

2

First Construction: collective time A

2.1 Ascesis and ecstasy: analytic of circulation

In real subsumption, the *collective appears in the form of the analytic whole: capitalist socialization appears indifferent, equivalent and circular*. Society is a superstructure, but an all too real one: from the superstructure it takes the possibility of being logical; from the real it takes the possibility of being put into practice. The society reconstructed within the capitalist analytic, as the product of capitalist power, is a structural horizon. A philosophical ideal has been achieved: synthesis, synchrony of organization and of command, of the one and the many. Only one thing is missing from this analytic society, from this compact socialization, from this monetarization of collective being: time. Or rather, *time* is given in the form of *measure* and accountability, of command and function. The aporias, the crises and the conflicts have an indifferent content and determination. Nevertheless they can and must be resolved within the circularity of the social flow. The motor and measure of this circulation is the *functional equivalent*, i.e. the money of command. Time, in so far as it is an ontological determination, is the attribute of servants; hated if recalled, it is nothing but necessity. From another perspective, time can be entrusted to aesthetics, to genius and recklessness, to music. In order to guarantee its own formal perfection, circulation must avoid time: *faux frais*[20] are to be annulled – a *non-temporal* act of production should creatively (or at least functionally) comprehend all of circulation, all of time and all of value. To accumulate and to govern capitalist circulation is equivalent to Genesis. This transcendental of the society of real subsumption is the transformation of Prometheus into

Narcissus, the ideal of the complete self-sufficiency of the schema of production and of automatic functioning. *Ecstasy.* A regulative logic, a generalized jurisprudence, a self-grounded independent semantics, circuits of simulation. There is no time: jurisprudence is the fixating of time; the automatic regulative logic is the de-potentialization of time; time becomes uncrossable. Every relation becomes relative: merely the comparison between two monetary quantities. Every 'natural rate' fails: *surplus-value* is annulled in the indifference of interest. The realm within which one moves is that of *the reified equivalent,* which is thus indifferent to determination, and hence is entirely circular. There is bourgeois ecstasy in the face of this construction.

Forgive me for this impressionistic and pretentious approach. Ecstasy cannot be described other than by those who feel it, and I must go begging to these lucky ones. Nor does ecstasy have an internal order: the accumulation of sensations is therefore the only description. Drugs are not inappropriate at this node of bourgeois understanding.

But this folklore of capitalism in the phase of real subsumption should be disassembled. The *ecstasy* should be reduced to the ascesis that produces it. The uncertainty of the framework should be broken down into the analytic that composes it. We know what the framework of the problematic is: the ensemble of the effects determined by the complete socialization of capital, hence of its relation, of its antagonism. The displacement has modified the nature of the process: the relation between command and organization cannot but be given within the productive social block. The old techniques do not work. There is no exteriority on which to fall back, on any occasion. But there's more: this collective and structural time that envelops and constructs life seems to lack all distinction. Never have destinies been so interwoven. Work is time of life, time of all collective life. It is the condition of its existence. The restoration of time-as-measure in this structural reality is a material operation – whether enforced and consensual little does it matter now. It is, however, functional, analytic. *Complexity is reduced to articulation, ontological time to discrete and manoeuvrable time.* The analytic is an authentic transcendental operation – a display of transcendental schematism. That administrative procedures and acts organize this process changes little as regards its metaphysical nature. For example, the terrain to which Luhmann is constrained remains that of Heidegger's ontology. The operation is intelligent, is judicious: restructure continuously the compactness of collective temporality on the basis of a functional schema – time is to be reconstructed as the measure of the reproduction of the system, it is to be reconstructed as an ensemble of functions forming a temporal matrix.[21] Restructuring is not a rule pertaining to a phase, but an operation that should be developed in all phases, at every moment of the social process. It is *now-time* (*Jetzt-Zeit*)[22] unfolded in succession.

The process has three fundamental characteristics: it must be *endogenous* to the system; it must be continuously *productive* of functions and systemic innovations; and it must reach *equilibrium*. What we are seeking is a veritable *thermodynamics of society*. The more the analysis deepens and produces real redundancies, the more the contradictory content of the process becomes manifest. But the multiple times of the collective and their dissipative effects must be reconceived all the more in a dynamic of reversible trajectories that can be brought back to equilibrium, to the rule of equivalence, to the equilibrium of micro-conflicts within the recapitulative totality.[23]

How this process resembles that *old alliance* of dialectical materialism, which linked the social sciences to the physical sciences! But there is little mileage in insisting on formal assonance here; it is more important to stress that through cultural analogies, *different political and social systems* display a *tendency to unity*. The folklore of capitalism answers that of real socialism. But further, how can one not see in the analytic fanaticism of the 'ought' (*Sollen*) of recomposition and refounding of equilibrium, the capitalist recognition of the end of the real function of measuring and the will to posit it once again despite this? Marx had alluded to the capitalist dream of circulation without *faux frais*, without time. When the productive and revolutionary reality draws near to this utopia, renewing the experience of time, capital must restore time-as-measure as its reason for existence. 'In this way capital becomes a terribly mysterious being' (Marx). *Ecstasy forms the basis of ascetics.*

The problem is indeed a formidable one. The entire history of bourgeois thought saw equilibrium (to which it tended as to its own absolute) in terms of *mediation*. Hence in terms of a linear process of rationalization, of supersession (*Aufhebung*), of criteria of preferential rationality and of natural rate. Here rather the regime of the production of truth anticipates reality, and the paths of functional rationalization are always interrupted, are always problematic and mobile – thought is transformed into a *constitutive strategy*. Bourgeois science must reconstitute itself as abstract measure, over and against a collective irreversible time; and so as a function of equivalence and circulation, in other words, *as money*. In order to make mediation work, Hegel must cross out the sections on 'The Enlighten-ment' and 'Absolute Freedom and Terror' in the *The Phenomenology of the Spirit* – because in these sections it *is not* the struggle against superstition and the regulation of the absolute freedom of capital that generate sci-ence, it is generated *rather* by superstition and terror. The transcendence and the circularity of science do not come together in 'supersession' but rather in 'foundation'. It is here that we see the insufficiency of 'negative thought' and the thinking on the *Krisis*[24] today, in whatever form: in the Hegelian sources that mark it out, negative thought is like an inside out glove, unsure whether it represents the hand or the turning inside out, whether it is clarifying the reality of mediation or is speaking simply of its necessity. Formal *Krisis*. This character of Italian ideology is entirely obsolete.[25]

The capitalist analytic of social labour subsumed in capital is therefore a veritable *coining* of social being. The constitutive thought of capital does not set out from individuals so as to form the criteria of obligation as in Hobbes, it begins with the obligation; it does not begin with the contract between all and the general will as in Rousseau, it starts rather from the general will: mediation precedes being, it pre-forms it, it pre-constitutes it. The economic plan of the State does not resolve the class contradictions but rather it encircles them, it systematizes and dominates them. Time-as-measure, mediation and equilibrium are the will and foundation of an analytic of Power, of a prior and arbitrary monetization of the real, of an aggressive coining of being. Occupying in advance the whole of the social space so as to measure it through the abstraction of time – rather than assuming the plural, multiversal and substantial temporal constitution of the world. This is the problem that capital must resolve.[26]

Here then, after the initial impressionistic account, the transformation of Prometheus into Narcissus becomes clear. How far we are from the crisis, from the disenchantment that bourgeois science experienced when the awareness of the fading away of Prometheus, of the exhaustion of the project, became apparent! At that time science lived its tragedy in ethical form. The mysticism of Wittgenstein – in the passage from the *Tractatus Logico-Philosophicus* [1974] to the *Philosophical Investigations* [1958] – still contained, though ambiguously, the concept and the experience of a real referent. That is, to a new reality, to the compact world of subsumption. When Wittgenstein exclaims that the limits of one's existence are the limits of logic, he certainly destroys physicalist atomism, the 'picture' the-ory of the real simulacrum, and every other empirical schema – *but he captures the sense of the tautology of society, of value and of language.* The tragedy arose from the comparison between the mystical and exhaustive apperception of the tautology, and the individualism, the solipsism of the framework of enquiry; that is to say, of the consciousness of the author as philosophical, hence as universal subject. This was a real tragedy, for throwing away the ladder, truly leaving it in one's wake, came at an enormous price. From individualism to collectivism: there are those who live this passage as tragedy – when instead struggle and reality show it to be a blessing! When in its mature form Husserlian phenomenology unfolds ascetically in the process which constitutes the world, in the universal human analogy of the world, in a theoretical praxis (always unmentioned but) effective – through a timid medley between acts on the part of the transcendental subject and activities constitutive of the collective subject – even in this case the tautology of the world subsumed in capital is touched upon. It is done so *ascetically in Husserl and mystically in Wittgenstein.* But tragedy is also Husserl's context. Because this human analogy of the world, practised ascetically, allusive of the collective, is unable to definitively break with the idealist position of the 'I think' that produces science. The systematic caesura, the *epoché* is the sign of the impossibility of bringing together Prometheus and the world. Whether one throws the ladder away or not, the analytic of subsumed being – understood theoretically for the first time as constituted totality – was anything but satisfied, it was merely accomplished hypostatically. Wittgensteinian mysticism and Husserlian asceticism bring tragedy into the Promethean work of capital as subject and author of the subsumption of society.

Today the ethical tragedy is over. There is only ecstasy. The linear path of time must become circular because the totality is presupposed. Rather than the paradox of the spatial conception of time, the theory of the eternal return presents itself as the justification for the meaninglessness of any temporally directed arrow. The cosmological fire is extinguished: this is the difference that runs from the Ancients to Nietzsche. The analytic of capital operates on a *totality without genesis*, without contradictions, without process. An *analytic of totality where the totality is the presupposition*. Time is removed – the mind is, as Gertrude Stein wants, a space; theory is the geography of this space. Time is a transcendental schematism accomplished because presupposed. Therefore it is ecstasy of effectual Power, of the capitalist analytic of subsumption. And if there remain any contradictory and aporetic elements, it is the ascesis of evanescence that controls and resolves them. Narcissus.[27]

3

First Construction: collective time B

3.1 Crisis: towards a phenomenology of collective praxis

To speak of the real subsumption of labour in social capital is to speak of average social labour (given by abstraction, by limit and measure) becoming substance. As we have seen, for capital it is a case of systematizing and moulding this substance. The analytic of subsumed labour is a process that aims to fix the 'compound totality' (*synolos*): collective capital – social labour-power – that wishes thus to exclude social labour-power as the potentiality for crisis. It is well established that the entire history of the bourgeoisie is nothing other than the permanent attempt to live through crisis, that crisis is linked to the definition of the bourgeoisie itself. Even to say 'the market' is, in a way, to say crisis. But it is also well known that the bourgeoisie makes crisis the key to the progress of capital, and so succeeds in its project to organize productive time and to exert its dominion over crisis. From this standpoint, the seventeenth century is the emblematic century: the century of great crises and, at the same time, the one that is foundational for the capitalist constitution of society. It is emblematic of this relationship. Koselleck was able to call a precious little book on the idea of critical bourgeois culture *Pathogenese der bürgerlichen Welt* [1979]. I have insisted vigorously on this paradox in my own studies of seventeenth- century philosophy.[28]

The situation changes, however, at the level of real subsumption. When social production founds the tautology of time and value, *crisis* is not linear and/or periodic in the relations of production, but rather it is *simultaneous* and *stable*. The global institution of the social does not in general allow for periodizations or diachronic lines, but only for synchronic cross-ings of a homogenous reality. Therefore, the world of real subsumption is the world of crisis because it is entirely traversed by the antagonisms of displacement – nor can they be isolated: at best they are systematically reproducible and, for this reason, controllable. *Crisis is, from this point of view, synonymous with real subsumption.* We can say the same thing in other words. As I have shown elsewhere (*La forma stato* [1977], Chapter X, pp. 306–34), crisis cannot be defined as a crisis *of* circulation, in the sense that at some points in circulation blockages are generated and therefore the cumulative processes break the measure of equilibrium. The crisis is *in* circulation, at *every point*, and does not so much concern the *paths* of needs, of commodities and information (which can be perfectly planned and guaranteed), as the *emergence* of plural, multiversal and mobile times of subjects. The old concept of crisis presupposes the *reversibility* of the circuits: in real subsumption, in global productive circulation, the crisis is rather the emergence of *irreversible times*.[29] In this way, the passage through the tautology of time and value gives us the possibility of appreci-ating a concept of crisis that is *consubstantial with the current phase of capital-ist development*. Real, global and simultaneous crisis founded on the antagonism that the plural substantial times of subjects oppose to the analytic of command.

Therefore crisis is the correct standpoint in the face of real subsumption. A crisis that is founded on the antagonism of plural times, of collective subjects that the displacement of real subsumption places at the centre of social space. But what does this definition of plural, substantive and antagonistic times mean? In Marxist jargon, even the most recent, antagonistic substantiality is brought back to *use-value* as independence and autonomy from *exchange-value*. What then is the relationship between the traditional understanding of use-value and the antagonism of sub-jects, of plural times? To pose the problem in this way is to pose the problem of the *displacement* (of the new quality) of *use-value* within the real subsumption of labour by capital.

In order to confront these problems, and to give them a solution, we propose the following *intermediate theses*:

(a) Use-value – the fundamental form, labour-power – offers itself up for exchange. It becomes exchange-value.
(b) Within exchange, capital – because it is constructive power – *reforms*, restructures use-value in the combination of productive factors.

(c) Within the capitalist constitution of exchange value, the *relative independence* of use-value can be grasped through (a dialectic that shows) successive displacements in the *composition* of labour-power.

(d) But within the totalitarian *real subsumption* of society in capital, this relative independence is no longer conceivable.

If – to accept for the moment this absurdity – this relative independence continued to be possible, it would mean that the process would be undefined (undefined dialectically). But it is not, unless one assumes circularity and the eternal return as true images of the process, as is anticipated in a mystified way by the analytic of capital. The Marxist theory of the 'normal' working day is important – though in many ways ambiguous – because it poses a 'superior' *limit* (the working day itself), which is essential in all equations. It is equally useful to recall here, in terms of fixing a limit, Harrod's temporal paradox, which demonstrates the impossibility of a 'total affluence' on the side of consumption (there is insufficient time to acquire all the commodities on offer).

(e) Use-value could at this point be defined as *subtraction*, antagonistic in so far as it is a negative, against and within real subsumption. This subtraction is formal or material.

(f) By *formal subtraction* we mean generic subtraction from capitalist command. The ghetto. The crisis of the law of value, in its realization, is here understood as the falling away of any paradigm of value, and one rebels against this fall of values. Nevertheless it is an illusory condition. Although it could still count as an ethico-political precondition: a sort of 'radical doubt' with utopian functions (see my *Il comunismo e la guerra* [1980]).

(g) *Subtraction* understood *materially* is break, de-structuring and struggle. Use-value as crisis. It is the only possible form of independence of use-value. (But the break and the crisis *are not* sufficient to render the independence of use-value active).

If – to accept this absurdity – a relative independence of the composition at the level of real subsumption were still possible, this would mean that the capitalist process (apart from being temporally undefined – which is not the case) would have to be *spatially* discrete (in this way the conditions for the functioning of the analytic model would be given). But this is not the case because the composition presents itself as *absolute mobility*. At the level of the antagonism determined in real subsumption, class composition is given in the form of time.

(h) Late capitalism would like to think of itself as *undefined time on a discrete spatial base* (neo-liberalism). This is pure ideology. *In reality* it is *constrained to a limited time on the basis of a continuous space. Use-value is the point of intersection between the undefined mobility of the composition and the determined temporality of the constitution.*

(i) Late capitalism experiences the *cleavage of the spatio-temporal conditions* of the reproduction of capital. These spatio-temporal antagonistic conditions are represented by *use-value* (time of life).

When introducing these theses we have called them *intermediate theses*. In fact, in order to consolidate them from the standpoint of the argument, it is necessary to move forward and define more clearly the *temporal and collective status of use-value*. But already we have objections against these intermediate theses, ones that we would do well to overcome, as overcoming them can advance our enquiry. Now, proceeding by extremes, there are those (such as Agnes Heller and her school of thought) who negate the possibility of giving use-value a social and collective dimension, while insisting on its antagonistic character; there are others (Baudrillard, Formenti and the so-called postmodernists generally) who seize the collective and temporal displacement of use-value with great intensity but deny it its antagonistic valence. To contrast two theories in order that they may critique one another is not the best method that one can follow, partly because the intention behind this approach is to give as proven the intermediate thesis, in this case our own, without in fact doing so. It is nevertheless the case that the linearity (antagonistic and materialistic) of Heller's system of needs (and of all phenomenologies, which we may call 'Jena inspired'), and on the other hand the *New Wave* idea of the pure systemic simulation and the complete indifferent displacement of values, have for us a unifying characteristic, which can be submitted to summary criticism: and that is the localization of the possible antagonism in a space *exogenous* to the system. So it is only *before* – at the time of foundation, of the taking root of needs – or *after* – on the margins of a world systematically achieved – that a point can be discovered from which *resistance* can proceed. As in Rosa Luxemburg the opposition is born on the system's outer limit – it remains *exogenous*. That which I think it is necessary to theoretically combat is the exogenous character of the possible alternative. Indeed, we believe that if the logic of displacement and antagonism operates, use-value as resistance and struggle is identifiable within the *endogenous* dimensions of the process – and that this fundamental characteristic, which is part and parcel of a correct usage of the logic of displacement gives us – once again – *use-value* as an element of crisis within the process, one that is adequate to the dimensions reached in subsumption by the productive process. Therefore, it is to the temporal and collective status of use-value that we must return.[30]

Let us turn back to the heart of the analysis. To me it seems that the capitalist analytic runs into insoluble aporias when in real subsumption time and work tend towards unity. It is clear that if time shows work as a real and present medium [*medietà*], and no longer as simply abstract, indifferent, merely equivalent, but already touched by the principle of subjectivity – *then the concept of use-value we find before us is a new one.* Before real subsumption is given, average social labour *opposes* itself to use-value (which is immediate emergence).[31] Here in real subsumption, on the other hand, *use-value and average social time are given as identical.* Time as sociality and use-value as sociality. *Social use-value.* Not private, individualist immediacy, but rather immediately social value. Here to say social use-value, to say temporality constitutive of value in the collective medium [*medietà*], is to speak of *the immediacy of mediation. Irreversibility.* Socially average labour (time) does not mediate between use-values, but displays their new reality. Use-value opposes itself to the analytic circulation of the system in so far as – *within the same dimensions* – it presents itself as the immediacy of mediation. And if time is the element, the function, the foundation of the process, we find ourselves before the *constitution of time as the collective essence, as the machine constitutive of the subject.* The eminent form of the crisis of the analytic of capital consists in the temporal and collective emergence of the antagonistic subject; it consists in the transformation of use-value and in its social average displacement.

The capitalist analytic constitutes a collective horizon. Temporality marks out this collective horizon. But the analytic goes into crisis on the terrain of temporality, through the aporias of circulation. Antagonism emerges on the terrain of collective displacement. *Antagonism is plural collective subjectivity in the face of the capitalist reduction of complexity.* It is clear that at this point we will have to follow the emergence of antagonism around the following four points: (1) synchronically, as the *impossibility* of reducing the antagonistic subject to the totality of the temporal equivalence: 'The idea of a "total affluence" is a logical fallacy' (R. F. Harrod); (2)

diachronically, as the *impossibility* of reducing the antagonistic subject to the circularity of production (the postulates of rigidity in Bronfenbrenner, for example); (3) then, *on the positive side*, synchronically, as the immediate emergence of the sense of social antagonism, of the asymmetry of treatment: 'Tout le mal provien de l'inégalité' (Starobinski); (4) again positively and diachronically, as the ontological experience of the continuity of the development of the subject within the framework and in relation to the analytic universes. To enter upon this path is to place oneself *on the terrain of a phenomenology of collective praxis*, of the analysis of temporality as ontologically constitutive identity, *Lebenswelt* – in the antagonistic complexity that opposes it to the empty, circular, equivalent unity of the command-time of capital. We shall confront these subjects directly further on in our enquiry.

But for now let us dwell further on the topic of the antagonistic foundation. To me it seems that, in the history of thought, the hypothesis of a collective constitution of time as an operation antagonistic to the spatial and mediatory conception of time, becomes an increasingly observable element – and one that is always characteristic of revolutionary thought. Elsewhere (*The Savage Anomaly* [1991]), I have tried to define the 'damned' current of Western thought – from Machiavelli to Spinoza to Marx – that is part and parcel of this terrain. It is a red thread that should be woven further and more widely.[32] (In particular, and after having so roundly condemned the Kantian transcendental schematism, I think it necessary to do Kant justice, because his thought is 'damnedly' complex and it should be read as such. Let me then make what appears to be a digression. Looking at the *Critique of Pure Reason* [Kant 1990], we have to bear in mind the *two* great motifs with respect to time and the dialectic. *The first* is the essence of a fundamentally bourgeois thematics. It is the conception of time as an internal sense, as an internal transcendental form – from this point of view, it is *superior* to that of space which is external, though still formal, while time is the internal form in as much as it dominates the outside as well [for this see the *Transcendental Aesthetic*, section II, 'Time' in ibid.]. But within this framework the form of time takes on other fundamental functions. Precisely because of its character as strong 'internal' and 'external' element, time is the force that supports the *project* of the intellect towards reality. Reality is unreachable of course, but that does not mean that the intellect's project is any less real. It is the project on which the power of reason is formed: empirically as transcendental imagination, rationally as transcendental apperception [*Analytic of*

Principles, chapter 1, 'The Schematism of the Pure Concepts of the Under-standing']. From this first point of view then, the *Critique of Pure Reason* serves to found the bourgeois conception of time, both in its *superior form* [internal and external, *not* internal and/or external], and in its schematic *project*. We rediscover this conception of time [interior and projective] at every point of Kantian thought: in the aesthetic as the theory of the internal form, in the analytic of the understanding as the schematic the-ory of judgement, in the dialectic of reason as the fabric of transcendental apperception [and to this are linked the developments which lead to the *Critique of Judgement* (Kant 1987)]. The core of Kantian teaching should be considered from this perspective right through to its mature formulations in the contemporary analytic – and in particular, as already hinted at, as it is found in Heidegger. Having said this, let us look at the *second motif* of the Kantian approach: the relation of time to the dialectic. In Kant this rela-tion is absolutely problematic. The dialectic, unlike what will occur later with Hegel [and on the basis of a Kantian framework], is for now a pure and simple 'logic of illusion' [*Transcendental Logic*, 'Introduction' in Kant 1990]. In reality, the relation of time to the dialectic is in any case substan-tive, *but negative*. On the one hand time is internal sense and the founda-tion of the imagination, on the other the dialectic is the pure 'logic' of illusion [*Schein*]. Time, in organizing faculties of knowledge, cleaves to reality although it does not exhaust it; the dialectic, on the other hand, is the prisoner of the *Analytic Amphiboly*, that is, prisoner of reason's errone-ous and vain wandering between empiricism and productive rationalism. In Hegel the analytic amphiboly will be resolved in the dialectical process of reason; in Heidegger it will be dissolved in the ontological advance of meaning. In both cases time becomes the structure that conveys the dia-lectic. In Kant, time is saved by the dialectic, as the dialectic is the pure logic of illusion [*Transcendental Dialectic*, 'Introduction' and *The Dialectical Inferences of Pure Reason*, both in Kant 1990]. It is in this *dual* sense that Kantian thought takes on for us the value of a fundamental shift. *Firstly*, because it gives us a concept of time as the form of subjectivity – a revo-lutionary idea of time as the project of subjectivity; *secondly*, it is precisely because the conception of subjectivity is revolutionary, that the concept of time refuses to become dialectical – that is, to become closure of the pro-ject in a generality that passes itself off as universal. Of course, from the standpoint of a materialist critique one can truly say that the separation 'time/dialectic' in Kant represents enlightenment, individualistic and bourgeois thinking which has yet to arrive at the thought of profit. In other areas of his thinking, however, Kant is well aware of this question. But this does not prevent the logical force of Kant's thinking from arriving in advance at the de-mystification of the capitalist solution to the antinomy, the mystificatory presumption of an analytic operation within the dialectical process – while having entirely understood its significance. Kantian time is able to resolve the contradictions of the project, without falling into dialectics [von Wright]. In Kant the primitive, the originary separation of the concept of time from the development of the dialectic is fundamental. *In Kant the concept of time founds the separation and the project at one and the same moment.* And it does so on the terrain of individualism, of course. But it is important for us, who move on the terrain of collectivity, to evaluate this experiment.)

That these pages on Kant do not constitute an empty digression is clear as soon as we return to our theme. That is to say, to that fabric of the phenomenology of collective praxis which is constituted by the identification of use-value as the active, collective, antagonistic element within real subsumption as crisis. We then find ourselves before the solution to a historic problem that has existed since the dawn of bourgeois civilization and capitalist culture: it is the solution to the *problem of imagination and of antagonism.* Thousands of interpretations have been given of this fundamental experience: spirit develops by investing reality, but it continuously runs into an obstacle. We have two solutions at opposite extremes of the spectrum. The first is the *utopian* one. In the recent studies by B. Baczko, the analysis of the aspects of this experience of the imaginative reduction of reality, of the progressive time that constitutes the heart of utopia, reveals fully the truly constitutive collective dimension of this experience. But the utopia remains utopia: living labour and dead labour, action and heaviness resolved. In *this contrast the concept of time is broken*: the non-contemporaneity of the times of Ernst Bloch is not a *multiversum* image, it is an image of destructive contemporaneity – real time is broken by utopian time and vice versa. *The other extreme* is represented by the desperate and heroic conceptions of the *spatial duplicity of the temporal matrices.* From Bergson to Weil to the Sartre of the *Critique of Dialectical Reason* we find ourselves perpetually standing before a temporal *universe* that displays antagonism as the tension of constructive (and collective) time before the practico-inert, with all its heaviness, density and its insolubility. The idea of time is broken in this case as well – though it fails to tear itself away from an inertial, linear, spatial conception – and it is this that breaks it. The antagonism is romantic, spiritual. Only Marxism and the conception of displacement take up the Kantian provocation of a *time* that is always *internal-external* – hence collective, foundational – and *at once antagonism*. In real subsumption *time divides itself in reality*: on the one side time of living labour, on the other time of dead labour. Both are internal and external, both are rooted to the dimension of the collective, although they are materially and historically different and antagonistic. If the crisis traverses the analytic horizon of real subsumption, then antagonism constitutes the proletarian subject, it constitutes mobile, real, collective living labour. The Kantian intuition of separation as inherent in the idea of time does not fix utopian and improbable contemporaneities, it does not block separation within the irresolvable heaviness, always residual and inertial, of the practico-inert – but instead rediscovers it in the formal and material completeness of 'a priori' independent subjects. Thus the *dream of a constitutive time of antagonism*, developed from Machiavelli to Spinoza to Marx, finds a real foundation.

This seems the right moment to summarize the moments of the transition we have undergone. In destroying time-as-measure *capital constitutes time as collective substance*. But for capital this temporal collectivity cannot show itself as such; it must rather be reduced to an analytic collectivity, to a collectivity without time. It is here that the *antagonism* erupts. The time of co-operation constitutes itself as a subject against capital. It is *use-value*. It is *principle of crisis*, latent or actual – but always principle of crisis. Often in Marxist literature use-value is taken as a naturalistic foundation or merely as the function of exchange-value. It could still, one way or another, be understood as such prior to the transition to real subsumption. In the phase of subsumption, time presents itself as collective substance of value and as antagonistic subject. The more use-value – labour-power – becomes an abstract commodity and pure and simple expropriated time, the more any exogenous reference falls away and instead the antagonistic character of production, of crisis, of use-value, is affirmed. *Use-value* is simply *the determination of the collective liberation of time from exploitation*. But only to the extent that it is – in itself – an element of *crisis, coextensive and synchronic* with the existence of capital. Collective time is constituted in global terms by subsumption, and put in crisis and antagonism by the collective proletarian subject.

4

Second Construction: productive time A

4.1 Money, value, nomenclature: between timepiece and war

Genesis tells of how creation was completed when God gave to each thing its name. The analytic of circulation is a Genesis; it is a *horizon of nomenclature*. *The passage* from the collective imaginary of circulation to the *real world of production*, from the asymmetries and aporias of the system of circulation *to the world of value*, is for capital an ontological deepening of the process of denomination. It is a passage evidently endowed with *power*: from sense to reference; this is the relationship in which circulation and production stand to one another, and power dominates the passage. We have crossed the territory of circulation. The first displacement, beyond the market, shows us simply the collectivization of every social relation as well as its monetarization. It is an imaginary, schematic, superstructural horizon. It is the realm of a general-universal equivalence. The first difficulty to appear in the sphere of circulation consists in the fact that the regime of names – that presents itself as independent of social elements, of the universes of the real, and thus as virginally functional in its reproduction of the collective imaginary – clashes with a *regime of things*, of subjects, of temporal dimensions that is irreducible to the former. The measure of circulation (which has meaning only in terms of the arrow's circulatory direction) is dashed against the measures of the collective subjects – a specific antinomy is born of the irreversibility of the relations set down here. *The critique of political economy* must therefore retain its traditional and dignified function of critique of theology (of ideal and hypostatic circulation). The commodified definition of *money* in terms of pure universal equivalent must be withdrawn, and it must be redefined as the *form of value*. (It is here that one can locate the dissolution of the theories of money as pure nomenclature so characteristic of the post-Keynsian schools, both on this side and the other of the Atlantic – whose concern is merely to pose the 'postmodern' problem of circulation and to define its character.) But that means insisting on the fact that, in real subsumption, monetary circulation must and wants to be directly *productive circulation*.

This move is no small thing. Through it we are drawn by the analytic nomenclature onto a terrain of stronger ontological intensity. The passage installs itself within a universe of value that productive circulation demands as its own fabric. It is not a case of organization of the general-universal equivalent, but rather of operations productive of commodities that form the matter of the world, of nature – the only nature that today capitalist subsumption allows us to know. Here time is nature – nature of capital, average accumulated social time, value.[33]

But in the tautology determined by the social displacement of production, the relation value-time cannot be measured – or rather, it can only be measured on the basis of the relations that stretch between the unity of command (of the form of social organization) and the plurality of the times of subjects. The material, natural, productive relation *can* only therefore be worked out in the *form of command*. The process of *nomenclature* transforms itself into that of *disciplining*: in the labour process discipline is the homologue of hierarchy in the social redistribution of wealth; it represents the hierarchy of functions in the process of social production. The collective essence of the social producers, their rich complexity must, as the condition of capitalist organization, be reduced to labour-power dispersed across the market. Value is surplus-value, is command, is hierarchical and disciplinary absoluteness of command, it is – to use a merely suggestive term – *absolute surplus-value*. If production is only given as social productive circulation, *productivity is systemic*. In that case the internal differentials become irrelevant. And above all, if determined in this way, the canonical *distinction* between mechanisms of extraction of absolute surplus-value (lengthening of the working day) and of relative surplus-value (intensification of the productivity of labour) falls away. There is only abstraction of surplus-value on the basis of the functional co-operation of all of social labour; there is only organization of exploitation as command that expresses itself over the whole of social labour. If we say *absolute surplus-value* it is because we lay claim to the hard core of Marx's theory, the concept of the brutality of capitalist Power as it approaches the accumulation of surplus-value proper to slavery: let us then say absolute productive command of capital over social labour in real subsumption. (A specific exception, which takes the definition of absolute surplus-value back to its origins as an individual measure of exploitation, concerns female labour – housework and the reproduction of the species – with its unlimited extension of the working day.)

Within the disciplinary horizon, command presents itself (1) as *centralized ordering* of production; (2) as *social organization* of production; and finally, (3) as *structure* of social productive command, as foundation and abstract 'natural' synthesis – and this fundamental, tendential and necessary abstraction of capital wants to present itself as more powerful than the concrete. Let us look at each of these three articulations in turn.

1. The first is the one that gives us capital as the *presupposition* of society. The time of accumulation is accumulated time, its ontological freedom taken away; it is blocked and shaped power. One must here be wary of not being dazzled by Bergsonianisms: this accumulated, objectified time is not weakened but is more powerful. Its lack of human qualities does not render it any less efficacious. Accumulated time, in the form of technological structures, of weaponry, of metropolises, of 'nature', is as chaotic as it is Powerful. *This mass of accumulated social time is predisposed for command.* Veritable absolute surplus-value, in the sense that the maximum time, the totality of the time of life, is presupposed as a condition, as matter and functionality of command. (And as we have said, this is the case even if the concept of absolute surplus-value can no longer be logically distinguished from relative surplus-value due to the inexistence of the real relations that the distinction presupposes.) Social time is thus constructed as *mass* of potentiality of command ordered in its entirety and in accordance with the exigencies of accumulation. One could say that here capital reintroduces time-as-measure – as the subjective will of command, as its norm; but it would be wrong to say so because here time is not *measure* but *imperiousness,*and imperiousness is not *timepiece* but *rule of war*. (For these concepts I refer you to my *Il comunismo e la guerra* [1980]. But these concepts can only be fleshed out further on in our discussion.)

2. These remarks are all the more valid when we consider command in terms of the organization of social labour flows. In this case time,

already presented as norm and hence as presupposition, is *executed* in the disciplinary and hierarchical articulations of the social labour processes. The norm, prearranged for the totality, made to count as the indicator of equilibrium and of reproduction of the system, becomes here *administrative procedure* – in a broad sense, naturally, so that the terminology may change.[34] The analytic of equilibrium is pushed by its own aporias into infiltrating reality, operating as function of organization and surveillance. This occurs across the entirety of social relations. The collective time which we came across in the analytic of capital as the result of an operation of transfer, of symbolic transvaluation that functions as a superstructure – is here brought completely back to, and rediscovered within reality, and is all the more unyielding the more it fluctuates across and within the determinations of production. (It would be useful here, and I underline it as an element that serves to bring together the elements of our enquiry, to work on the analysis of the time of productive decentralization and of imperialism so as to verify, precisely, both the extension of dominion and its internal organizational compactness.) The market, the multiple times of capital (free competition) have been absorbed in integral fashion: the illusion of the multifarious aspects of the market is simply the effect of the productive temporalisation that traverses it. Nomenclature of time = forced disciplining of time = reduction (to this measure of command and surplus-value, as essence of exploitation) of all the pores, of the *whole dimension of life*. The crisis that affected the first collective constitution of time in the analytic of circulation thus imposes this strange, forceful – but not any less effective – return to reality. Nomenclature and genetic codes had been displayed to us as wanting in reality, as on the edge of crisis: to revive them it is necessary that the time of circulation adjusts itself, remoulds itself within the time of accumulation and of reproduction.[35]

3. It has been said that time lies between timepiece and war. This thought should be expanded upon. Time-as-timepiece is – as is well known – that of capitalist accumulation in the classical era. We have been presented with numerous very fine essays on the subject from Benjamin Franklin to E. P. Thompson. On the other hand, the time-as-measure that becomes command within the complexity of the productive circulation of capital has something to do with political and administrative time. It is a time that is measured on the basis of the uniformity of the command flow *and* above all on the capacity to

create (to control and destroy) every exception. 'The sovereign is he who decides on the exception' (Carl Schmitt).[36] The nature of the time of command is given therefore by the possibility of its being the time of exception (of its creation and of its destruction); that is of the *State of exception* and of necessity. But the State of exception is generally the *State of war*. The realization of the capitalist analytic in money, in value, in nomenclature, and their ontological rendition occur within the crisis. In turn, the crisis is determined by the collective constitution of praxis through real subsumption. Now, the *self-recognition of the analytic in the crisis is the production of war*. From the capitalist standpoint, commanded time fluctuates between timepiece and war, between normality and exception, between passivity and *terror*. Absolute surplus-value, as the mass of commanded social time at the level of social exploitation, can become terror to the degree that capitalist accumulation ceases to be a relation and is *the organization of a separation. The time of the timepiece here becomes time zero: tendency towards the time zero of terror.*

With this we have gone beyond the topic under discussion. The structure of socially productive command takes us back to the analytic of command as *institutional time* (a subject we will discuss further below). To summarize specific elements of this passage, we have therefore emphasised the characteristics of commanded time in the productive circulation of capital. That which best determines it is the conjunction of absolute surplus-value – as the mass of time commanded in society – and of the extension of diffuse, sinuous, all-encompassing social disciplining. Time between timepiece and war: between the measure of exploitation analysed and developed spatially and its reduction to zero, to exception. A time then that has gone beyond the level of the transcendental schematism, made concrete in a variety of forms, and has attempted to resolve within itself the reality of productive space. This *reduction of space to time* is the fundamental characteristic of productive circulation in real subsumption.[37] Now the characteristics of *evanescence* that previously had been qualities of time have all been acquired by space, while the time of command is the solid foundation of the productive reality of capital.

4.2 Energy: evanescence of space

In this crisis the collective and objectified time of real subsumption tries to link itself to ontology. Indeed the horizons of logic are not enough for it. The time of command tries, it must try to hook itself on to the real beyond the analytic universe, and thus tries to discover an equivalent that gives it a premium of reality. The form of the relation must correspond to the *function*: a reality must be provided for evanescence also, the reality of a measure that clashes with and must annul the antagonist. When the great crisis of the second half of our century arises, many see *energy* as the new real *standard*: energy as value that is independent of the crisis, energy as natural rate, as the matter of value. It looks as though in this way nomenclature and discipline can once again be given meaning; it looks as though austerity and hierarchy can be given a rational motivation. The universal equivalent seems to be linked to the most general functions: that is to energy, which is to say, to that commodity which composes all other commodities – i.e. that is productive of reality. *Natura naturans* and *natura naturata*, where the former is the *standard* of the latter.[38]

So far so much illusion! In effect the proposal, and the materiality of the political and constitutive project that accompanied it, did not hold out the length of an afternoon. At the level of real subsumption, no *standard*, no *meaning* is given outside of collective time; no nature is given because *nature is realized subsumption*. It is comprehended, reproduced by collective capital. Nature is also a problem of subsumption. So that oil, as nature, as natural fixed point of exchange, as new spatial foundation of value, has been immediately reabsorbed at the highest level of the circulation of command: it did not appear as the rate of rates, as value of values – it appeared rather as the confusion of values and evanescence, as inflation and multiplier of aporias of circulation. Not as firm spatial foundation of value but as already infiltrated nature, summed-up finally in the temporal mechanism of production and social command.

Stream and evanescence. It is only in time, within its dense ontological reality that, in an endogenous manner, a relation can be born, and not through another external simulacrum. Everything is reduced to time – space also – and to the evanescence of time – of collective time also – until it clashes with the plurality of local times of liberation. Oil is space summarized in time, and here it loses any potential for measure.

The other fount of energy of our century is in truth more suited to express a capitalist measure of value, already realistically placed in the ambit of the temporal evanescence of space and considered precisely not as generic measure of value of the entire universe of productive circulation, but rather as the expression of the specific valorizing function that is command. The *nuclear* is value, is measure in so far as it is function of command. *It does not circulate but it overdetermines*. In real subsumption the only value that command allows is overdetermination: a *surplus* of command, a *surplus* of value. *Terror*. The possibility and the presence of terror. The earth is at this point pregnant with nuclear deposits, with nonbiodegradable shit – a vertigo that implicates nature in its entirety. The nuclear industry and its deposits of excrements are the continual evocation of – accidental – destructive demons. The nuclear is an entirely negative space; space and time linked in the zero of explosion.

There is no realistic opportunity therefore of reaching a *space* that is foundational for a norm of valorization adequate to productive circulation. Productive circulation is only time, temporal evanescence – or rather, in a non-mystified way, a clash of diverse and antagonistic temporalities. The energetic terrain, far from representing the terrain of the regrounding of the functions of value, presents itself as perhaps one of the most significant territories for the explosion of the crisis and of the manifestation of its conceptual narration. In social production, value is not given other than as a function of antagonistic subjects, as the expression of logical and effectual clash.

5

Second Construction: productive time B

5.1 Refusal of work and productive co-operation

Let us begin once again from surplus-value, this time from *relative surplus-value*. The theory of relative surplus-value is fundamental in Marx for it introduces diachrony, development, the differentiation of evolving forms, the dynamism of the system. Relative surplus-value is the intensification of labour, its productive force: reduction in the utilization of labour-power and increase of productivity; an increase in the quantity of abstract average time, *simultaneous* with the reduction in the utilization of concrete labour-power. It is difficult to maintain this conceptual assemblage in the regime of the real subsumption of society by capital. In real subsumption, capital presents itself as capitalist society, and hence as tautology of life and value, of time and labour. The relations of magnitude between the constitutive parts of the working day are imperceptible. The immensity of fixed capital stands before the totality (omniversality) of variable capital. Capital is given as the social medium and it reflects the qualitative medium of labour-power, which itself carries out a revolution in the objective conditions of the labour process in as much as it is immediately social co-operation. There is no longer any relation between the intensity of the organic composition of capital and the levels of production: Sraffa, the Marxist economist, lucidly and decisively demonstrated this. Of course *productive differentials* exist, but they are not marked by the difference in the quality of labour but rather by the lines of command that traverse society: they are productive differentials in as much as they are expressions of (hierarchical) *disciplinary asymmetries*. The enigmas already indicated, which emerge in the Marxist theory of qualified, complex, technico-scientific labour, do not dissolve here: they are simply presented anew at the level of the real displacement.

But that said, the fact remains that Marx's conception of relative surplus-value is of great value for us. (After all it is the dynamic of relative surplus-value that leads to real subsumption, and we can point to no other analysis than Marx's to describe this development. Marx prepares and suggests the *scientific displacement as the effect of the real displacement* whose dynamic he describes perfectly.) Marx's conception of relative surplus-value should be seen as indicating a path of enquiry, while its original definition and its positioning in relation to absolute surplus-value should be purely and simply *overturned*. In Marx there is *first* absolute surplus value, then the dialectic of relative surplus-value. The problem should now be seen as *reversed*. Because what interests us – after relative surplus-value as a category of time-as-measure ceases to be useful – is the diachronic element that Marx's conception introduces: *relative surplus-value* provides an explanation of the productivity of labour that, given the impossibility of breaking the tautology through measuring mechanisms, *breaks the totality of subsumed society*, and displays the productivity of labour as a (non-dialectical but rather) *separate* function of the relations of production and command. *Separation of the capitalist* Umwelt *of subsumption; qualitative and composed time as the basis of separation*. We must start from complex, co-operative, technico-scientific labour: it is the originary basis of the productivity of labour. Marx himself recognizes the irreducibility (irreversibility) of the *time of co-operation* to abstract time:

> the special *productive power* of the combined working day is [. . .] the *social productive power of labour*, or the *productive power of social labour*. This power arises from co-operation itself. When the worker co-operates in a planned way with others, he strips off the fetters of his individuality, and develops the capabilities of his species.
>
> (Marx 1990, p. 447 – italics added)

Productive labour is therefore *not* founded on the relation with capital but on its own co-operative essence. (Marx's definition is based on: (a) the productive force of the *social* worker as productive *autonomy*; (b) on the capitalist determination of the conditions of co-operation; and so, (c) the one-dimensional capitalist nature of the process corresponds only to a first phase of capitalist development, and *only* to that.) *Complex labour* and *technico-scientific labour* are not therefore numerical summations of abstract quantities of labour time – of 'tempuscles' (as such they would be scientific enigmas, as Roman Rosdolsky, the best interpreter of Marx, must in the end acknowledge), they are rather the exemplification of co-operation, the highest expression of the collective dimension of time. Productive time.[39] Relative surplus-value, which already in its genesis is constrained by capitalist command, signals a subtraction of time from capital. Behind the category of relative surplus-value hide the movements of productive co-operation that – *originally* (it should be forcefully underlined) – presents itself as the *refusal* of capitalist command over production and as the attempt, always frustrated but not for that less real, of constructing an autonomous time. When the displacement of co-operation is determined on the terrain of real subsumption, then that *refusal* which was previously hidden and lived in cahoots with capitalist development (within the *refusal-information-innovation dialectic*), becomes entirely explicit as the basis itself of co-operation (*Operai e capitale* by Mario Tronti [1966] is the unsurpassed demonstration of this proposition). The refusal of work counts as the basis of complex labour and technico-scientific labour. The basis of the complexification of labour, the increase in its creative power, the practical universality of its project – all this is related back to the character of refusal that qualifies the collective body of labour. In the development of capital, relative surplus-value is an interweaving of sabotage and dominion (a dialectical interweaving only when seen *ex post*); in real subsumption relative surplus-value marks the proletarian break and independence from dominion. In capitalist development the superior productivity evidenced by the production of relative surplus-value indicates a violent relationship between the subtraction of time from capital and capitalist innovation; in real subsumption relative surplus-value dissolves as a category and leaves and displays the productivity of labour-power. In this way the *relation* located *between absolute surplus-value and relative surplus-value* dissolves in its classical theoretical formulation. And we have seen how absolute surplus-value was pushed back to the horizon of war, and it is clear that within such a horizon it consumes the active forces specific to relative surplus-value. Absolute surplus-value comes *after* relative surplus-value in as much as it is the absolute category of command over the *mass* of social exploitation – that is after the dynamic of relative surplus-value has pushed capital towards real subsumption. What needs now to be underlined is just how much the concept of relative surplus-value *leaves behind*: it *leaves behind* an articulation between the struggle against the time of capital and the independence, quality, creativity, in short, the *productivity of co-operation. Collective time comes to be realized through the productive time of the proletariat.* Relative surplus-value should then be dissected: *surplus-value* should be left to the absoluteness of the command of capital; while on the other hand historical and dynamic *relativity* should be brought back to the definition of the proletariat itself – thus to productivity as the struggle against capitalist time and to co-operation as the quality of work that knows and is able to fight against that time. And thus, to the construction of a *temporal dimension proper to the proletariat.*[40]

Having reached this point in our theoretical proposal, the time of co-operation presents itself to us as laden with responsibility: it is (1) above all *time of struggle* and sabotage, and therefore factor of crisis, of subtraction of time from capital; (2) higher quality of work and therefore origin of all forms of *productivity*; (3) 'aversive' element (Doereinger and Piore use this term for the industrial working class, but I feel it can be generalized), in the sense that this qualified temporal constitution is, for the constitution of the worker, an element of irreversibility – of rigidity, or on the other hand of mobility, irreversible nonetheless, stage by stage – that is constitutive of the real identity of the *proletarian subject.*

With this we enter upon new ground, further deepening our understanding of the material characteristics of the concept of time. Relative surplus-value alludes to the themes that form the basis of the category of the *proletariat*, and thus to the themes that enable the founding of the antagonistic characteristics of co-operation in a subjective figure; and further, enables one to determine the latter – diachronically – in the concept of *proletarian composition*. Thus subjective determination, antagonistic characteristics, and historicity of the composition (inflexibly determined in the relation between rigidity and mutation), now become diverse and concomitant aspects of *temporal constitution.*

Time conceived of as *appropriation* that, at the same time as it passes the threshold of mere subtraction from capital, presents – historically and materially – its radically *alternative* vocation. An alternative time because its matter – its use-value, is alternative, and now more than ever it is impossible for it to be drawn into the ambiguity of the relation of capital, because (a) time is the totality of the existence of use-value; and (b) the time of its existence antagonistically opposes that of capital. Pierre Naville and De Gaudemar have insisted extensively on this fluidification of working-class time in the real subsumption of capital – arriving at conclusions that posit the tendency to the exclusivity of time as the criterion of determination. Here the results of these studies can be confirmed.

But one should insist even further on the other element, that is, on the radical difference of the two *practices* of time: *analytic* on the capitalist side, *productive* on the proletarian. Since capitalist time is analytic, its onto-logical practice makes itself manifest in the necessity of breaking and dis-solving every value, so as to reconstruct it only as circular function of command – with a tendency to zero – destroying any productivity of the system that is not reproduction of command and of the possibility of ter-ror. But all this only happens because productivity is now found entirely within the time of co-operation. Alternative time, productive time. (The general premises, within the totality of subsumption, should be taken up again in the same way as in Chapter 3.)

The composition of the proletariat now presents itself as an autono-mous force proper to it (as aversive element). Drawing back from any dialectical relation with capital, the composition presents itself in the combination of subsumption and antagonism, of displacement and asymmetry, as a structure of *self-valorization*.[41] The underscored elements – co-operation and productivity – rise to the surface of the current defin-ition of the paradigm of co-operation, and thus in the paradigm's specific activity of self-valorization. I have already spoken of this in depth in *Il comunismo e la guerra* [1980] and I refer the reader to it, as I do to the work of E. P. Thompson and Karl Heinz Roth.[42] But one should add that the solidity of the notion of composition *is not* in any way subjected to a *historicist influence* – of whatever origin – whatever the nature of this his-toricism, be it idealist or materialist, which in Ranke as in Engels, in Croce as in Gramsci, is still subject to a dialectic of continuity. Not at all. Dis-placement, irreversibility, the rules of subsumption and antagonism are in force here. So that even with respect to the paradigms of class composition and the temporal practice that support them, we find ourselves here before *difference*. Let us set out the series of the paradigms of composition.

(a) *Undifferentiated worker* (1848–70). Time as natural envelope, the time of the proletarian-slave.
(b) *Professional worker* (1870–1917). Time as timepiece. Time as dialect-ical mediation. The time of the product.
(c) *Mass worker* (1917–68). Time flux. The time of production.
(d) *Social-multinational worker* (1968 onwards). Time as structure, social time. The time of reappropriation and self-valorization.

This succession is merely apparent, because between *a*, *b*, *c* and in contrast *d* – there is a total *displacement*. Today's paradigm of class composition is qualitatively different: it is no longer in a dialectical relationship with the structure of capital. It maintains a relation that is non-dialectical but is rather one of *separation*. Separation means self-valorization. The relationship is transvaluated. The terms that characterize *a*, *b* and *c* are not homologous with *d*.[43]

Let us take a look at the problem from another point of view, one that is not historical but structural. The concept of *class composition* comes to be defined by Marx on the basis of a conceptual assemblage that goes something like this: (1) definition with reference to the *form of the labour process* and that is with respect to the form of co-operation; (2) definition with reference to the contents of the labour process and therefore to the *parts of the working day*, to the division between quantity of necessary labour and surplus-value; (3) definition with reference to the objective level of the needs expanding historically and determined by the *historical structure of the wage*; (4) definition with reference to the *level of struggle* and organization. Now the definitions given above (*a*, *b*, *c*) effectively look as though they can be determined upon this basis. That is not the case for *d*.[44] In fact, even when in purely descriptive terms the concept of time-as-measure – as relation, whether formal or dialectical – founders, and *temporality* becomes the *constitutive matrix* of the social composition of the proletariat, then all the terms, all the points of view, all the differences are recomposed within the separate reality of the subject. Time is not relation, nor residue, nor subtraction: it is the ontology of the proletariat and its possibility of self-valorization. And self-valorization is liberation.

5.2 Internal time and external time

Once we have reached the point where we can grasp the autonomy and independence of class composition, and concurrently, once we have defined the relations between different and successive forms of the composition and of the temporal paradigms, our discourse then shapes the *anthropological identity* of the proletariat. It then becomes possible to grasp the relation between *external time* (as the time of composition) and *internal time* (as the human time of the subjects that compose it).

Before taking our analysis further on this terrain, let us return for a moment to a consideration of the *generic relation* between theoretical

paradigms of time and proletarian composition (proletarian composi-
tions). Leaving aside the theological perspectives (whose conception of
time accomplishes nothing more than, as Alfred Sohn-Rethel has shown,
the definition of the empty abstraction of exchange in the form of the
commodity, i.e. as the simple monetary presupposition of the productive
exchange of the commodity form of labour), I believe that one can say
(in relation to, and perfecting the classification presented in Chapter 1,
Section 1.2) that: (1) the *Newtonian hypothesis* of time as absolute envelope
of the order of events, corresponds to the whole of the first phase of
capitalist accumulation and therefore to the epoch of the *undifferentiated*
worker, to the phase of the creation of the wage labourer. In his study of
the watch market in England in the phase of primitive accumulation, E. P.
Thompson engages in a micro-history of this development and demonstrates how theological time makes way for the natural time of production. (2) *The Kantian paradigm* is a variant of the Newtonian: that is to say
that with Kant we witness the *transition* from the undifferentiated worker
to the qualified worker. Time becomes internal to the individual productive capacity. Kant does not arrive at the totalitarian dialectical conception
that with Hegel corresponds to the composition of the qualified worker, to
the circulation of his actions and his productive knowledge within the
fabric of capital in its entirety, and in relation to the new specificity of
valorization of complex labour. But perhaps it is for this reason that the
Kantian paradigm is so important, because it gives us a *formal* signal of a
moment of *crisis* and of transition, that is to say, it clarifies in critical form
the link between internal and external. (3) However, it is not until Hegel
that the dialectical conception of time, and hence of the specificity of
the paradigm *of the qualified worker is reached*. (4) In Marx we observe, on
the one hand, the reprise and perfecting of the dialectical paradigm, of the
materialization of time as medium [*medietà*] between measure and substance of labour. But on the other hand, the *instability* of the paradigm is
introduced by Marx's tendency to pass beyond, moving on towards real
subsumption. *In the first place*, from this standpoint, Marx's paradigm of
time is a function of the *transition* between qualified worker and mass
worker. (5) But *in the second place*, in Marx we also find the entire *temporal
paradigm of the mass worker*. Here the temporal medium[45] tries to articulate
itself genetically in relation to the flow of social labour processes. The
contemporary structural and genetic theories of time complete the temporal paradigm of the composition of the mass worker, anticipating
already that conception of the complete fluidification of the temporal

structural medium. (6) But nonetheless, the maturity of a paradigm adequate to the overcoming of the mass worker and to the achievement of the *social* worker has yet to be attained by the social sciences. In fact, we have before us only some useful initial propositions that originate with the critique of thermodynamics (Boltzman, Prigogine), and that affirm the irreversibility of the temporal trajectories. But as we have seen, this conception of irreversible time points towards a definition of structural equilibriums rather than to the conjugation of the irreversibility of a plurality of times and antagonism. Perhaps only a renewed analysis of the *Einsteinian* conception of time as the co-ordination of different velocities, as the assertion of both the *irreversibility* of trajectories and of irreducible *asymmetry* of dimensions, could lead us to an adequate definition of the temporal paradigm in the composition of the social worker. But of this more later (Chapter 7, Section 7.2).

Here, after having established this brief framework in which to orientate ourselves, we return to our discussion of the time of composition and to the question of its internal effects *on the human*. Now, it is particularly in the moments of transition, as represented by Kant and Marx, that the internal, the anthropological intensity of temporality is revealed. In Kant this is expressed in the contradiction between the internal time of morality and the external time of science, as a first fundamental example of the process of alienation that the capitalist mode of production brings about. *Separation* had first to be undergone and endured in the form of alienation, before it could be lived and overturned in the form of antagonism. It was not until Marx that the antagonism between time-as-measure proper to capital and time as proletarian productivity attained maturity. But what is of interest to us here is to underline how contradiction impresses itself on the human nature of the temporal effects. That time is contradiction is well known; that contradiction constitutes individuality in as much as it is evanescence of the temporal aspect, emerging between life and death, is even common knowledge. But here the anthropological identity of the temporal contradiction in the human is of interest to us in order to grasp the specific dynamics that it mobilizes. It seems to me that the problem should be set out as follows (and in these prolegomena we will not get much further than setting out the problem). In the history of capitalism, the modification of the composition has, in the internal consciousness of individuals and of the community, the fundamental effect of *opposing* in a different way at each moment (but always specifically connected to the figure of composition) the synchronic moments of life and the diachronic moments of history, human nature (this specific *cultural consolidation* which we call nature) and the development of exploitation. On the anthropological plane it is therefore possible to establish for *each* form of class composition *synchronic series* of temporal behaviours relative to love, violence, community, struggle, organization, utopia, science and revolution. But this conglomeration of interior times, in different forms, is always subjected to the *diachronic series* of exploitation. The anthropological identity of the composition, its transformation into a subject, is *not* achieved. The web of temporal behaviours is traversed by the dialectic of capital. Through diachrony the history of capital imposes itself: the flow of commodities enters the rhythm of composition and insists on the *transformation from working class to labour-power* – this reduction is always necessary for the analytic of capital.

It is only at the moment of *displacement*, initiated by the process of subsumption, that the antinomy between synchronic structures of *consciousness* (of the individual and of the community) and diachronic processes of liberation *escape the dialectic of capital* and thus dissolve capital's specific and traditional antinomic form. Consciousness frees itself from commodification, frees itself from subordination only when, within subsumption, synchronic structures and diachronic movement are *unified*. Therefore, it is a unity which is founded on the overcoming of the capitalist capacity to impose the *asymmetry of Power* along *vertical axes* that traverse life; it is a unity that imposes itself at the level of the horizontality of the collective: so, not division of the class in itself, but *separation of the time of social composition* from the time of the totality of exploitation. Separation that crosses the temporal *Umwelt* of real subsumption and further displaces meaning (from the first to the second displacement). A separation that does not divide the working day by internal lines, but that *coextensively* counter-poses capital and labour. Transformation of the tautology of the first displacement into the unfolded antagonism of the second. *Consciousness* rises up – not as a utopian element, but as a real one – as consciousness of collective antagonism, or rather, of *antagonistic collectivity*. As we have seen, time is collective and productive essence. Collective essence means that *without* collectivity, the only time known by the class and the plurality of individuals that compose it, both internally and externally, is that of capital. Time with tendency to zero. Antagonistic essence means that time is here defined as transformation of refusal into co-operation, of co-operation into production, of production into liberation. In setting out the problem of internal time we come round once again to the basic definition of the phenomenology of collective practice as antagonistic and tendential excavation within the tautology of time and of life. What's more, the analysis carried out so far guarantees us the *effective possibility* of its being carried further. Because real subsumption, in its conjugation of time and of life, and in its antagonistic dissociation of the polarities of the process, assures us of the *tendential unity* of the synchronic series of consciousness and of the diachronic series of history – or rather, they assure us of the conditions of the end of *prehistory*. At this point proletarian consciousness can be placed at the heart of an enquiry into the *anthropological identity* of the composition of the social worker, not only as object, but also as *subject*. The front line of subjectivity. Consciousness and community.[46]

One last brief note. Bearing in mind what has been said up to now, I have the impression that we have done more than merely begin to confront the fundamental problem of internal time according to a logic that follows on from, and is co-ordinated with, the phenomenological process of collective praxis – although this commencement will be developed further elsewhere. Above all we have here demonstrated the heuristic efficacy of the logical mechanism of displacement and antagonism. It not only enables us to destroy some elements of methodological determinism traditional to Marxism, but enables us to problematically and productively constitute objects that Marxism had relegated to a horizon based on an exogenous foundation (and thus, when not an enigmatic one, an acritical one). From use-value to consciousness, from complex labour to technico-scientific labour, we are now able to proceed with rigorous presuppositions and heuristic efficacy. In effect real subsumption constructs, through displacement, a material linguistic universe that antagonism renders distinguishable, and that the achievement of collective and productive consciousness of time allows us – from the proletarian standpoint – to liberate.

6

Third Construction: constitutive time A

6.1 The hard time of the State: information and legitimation

The figures of collective time and of productive time end with this third temporal construction, the point of consolidated command: *the State*. From the analytic operations of the description of the society of real subsumption, to the productive operations of value-command, now the series we have marked 'A' must be given its definitive foundation. In the preceding pages the temporal matter of capitalist organization has been consolidated; we could now say that its specificity, its definitive constitution, should be determined. We call on the State to form this determination. This is certainly not because of any dialectical attitude, be that descriptive or otherwise; we are seeking to identify in the State not the synthesis but rather the 'last instance', not the Hegelian conclusion, but the *Hobbesian condition* of organization and of command over the time of life. And it is the State that presents itself as the only power adequate to the constitution of the extension and intensity, the articulation and centralization of *social capital*. We know, however, that the law of value is in complete crisis, and that therefore the web of homologies that were on other occasions given between capitalist norms and the norms of the State, cannot be constructed peacefully. Out of the crisis of value comes solely the power of command. Command, especially at the level of capitalist socialization, means control and *hegemony over legitimation*, diffusion of the relations of obligation and their coercive strengthening at every level, through every pore and interstitial fissure of society.[47] But in saying this we are doing nothing more than repeating Hobbesian postulates typical of the doctrine of the State, reproposing the generic problem of the nature and the form of obligation. It is not enough. *The problem must be redefined within the specificity of the displacement.* What do juridical obligation and loyalty to the State mean in conditions of real subsumption? What specific dimension do they occupy? What is the hard time of the State, and what does it become in real subsumption? How is it received and positioned within the displacement, within the collective and collective production?

The first and most simple answer to these questions is the one that comes from those who affirm that *this* State has rediscovered and rehabilitated an essentially *authoritarian, fascist foundation.* There are many who maintain this, and the demonstration is also simple. It is indeed unquestionable, and the description of everyday life is sufficient to exemplify it, that the intensification and extension of State command represents an unstoppable tendency, with all the consequences that stem from it: the arrogance of the State, the disintegration of the rights to liberty, the preventative extension and hardening of repression. In other words, that the authoritarian *dispositifs* are tendential and effective is not in question.[48] But evidently, a structural analysis at the level of real subsumption must remember that, in every case, *authoritarianism, fascism, are constitutional*: in the relations of social capital, in conditions of real subsumption, it is impossible to conceive of them as scandal, as deviation from the norm, as exception. The state of exception is normal. Authoritarianism is structural. Fascism is constitutional. The paradox is merely apparent, while on the other hand the actual agreement is fully realized. Yet having said this, when – ingenuously – many subjective wills believe they have found in this reasons for struggle and motives for ethical action, nothing of much significance has been said. An aspect of reality has been emphasized but in such a *unilateral* manner that it almost ends up being a mystification. What I mean is that the authoritarian tendency demonstrated by the contemporary State, that the endemic fascism of its actions, though real, or rather extremely real, do not determine the specificity of the situation or of the concept of the contemporary State.

Let us take a look then: authoritarian State, constitutional State. These two expressions, which appear to constitute a contradiction, do not represent one in reality. In effect, the old constitutional State already contains the possibility of an authoritarian *overdetermination* in terms that are both congruous and tendentially necessary. As I have shown in my *La forma stato* [1977], the contradiction of the constitutional process is shown in its need to transfigure the real subjects *politically*.[49] Nothing new here: the

Marx of the 'Contribution to the Critique of Hegel's Philosophy of Right. Introduction' [1992], and in other early writings, had already clearly said as much. What renders social subjects citizens is a theological operation, and is therefore a functional mystification of Power. To continually renew this *basic truth* is a technico-scientific operation. Because we operate in the realm of real subsumption, we can here take a *little leap forward*. In real subsumption the matter of command is social time. Now the *constitution*, any constitution, is a *slice of time*, a segment, it is a block of temporality.[50] This happens all the more in real subsumption. What definitively *undergoes crisis* is the fundamental concept of *representation*: it is in fact not reactionary here because – according to the classical critiques – it annuls the particular in the general, but fundamentally because it *annuls the being of time*, the reality of movement. Representation is the destruction of collective and productive time. From collective and productive time the constitution takes on only the analytic projection and the systemic function. The time of the bourgeois constitution is an originary time – a *Jacobean time* of nullification, a plenitude of abstraction. (Furet's enquiries into Jacobean constitutions are crucial in this regard.) Note: We are not speaking here solely of constitutional time in a general (material) sense, but of that functional envelope that, starting from the constitution, gives a context to the times of jurisdiction, of administration and of repression. In short, we are speaking of the time of the State.

With regards to *juridical time*: the law affirms 'its continuing validity and therefore its universality by superimposing the fixity of an eternal present over the fluidity of time and therefore, explicating its axiological validity through formal validity' (Opocher).[51] With regard to *administrative time*: it consists simply of operations of transferability, of execution, rendering its validity effective – circularity is its only substance. The *time of penal law* and repression is able to demonstrate in the most incredibly harsh way this nullification of time. Between nothingness and terror, an absolute and mystical temporal nothingness emerges. The more the State of real subsumption, of social capital, develops its command over time, the more it develops in terms of a nullifying identity. In the nothing of the time of the State, the idea of the organization of juridical time tends to reveal itself as the *organization of spatiality*: it is an operation of mystification, an attempt to recover an image that is nevertheless material, so as to give credibility to an imperious formalism. Equilibrium and the spatial balance of forces and of Powers, absolutist ritualism of figures and functions (as in a seraglio – says Grossrichard, with a Montesquieuan analogy), of corporations and parties that repeat within themselves, as in a game of Chinese boxes, the same functions of nullification: it is always a spatial image of evanescent materiality that presides over the immobile essence of constitution. A zero sum game, a Chinese exercise in which a field and rules are given for nothing. What is the difference between the motto of Louis XIV's constitution: 'L'État c'est moi', and the democratic motto: 'L'État c'est nous'? The further real subsumption advances, the more obligation, law, juridical organization, etc. must – cannot but – be constitutional, global, structural – and so the more the idea of time is removed (and only poorly compensated for by that of space).

Now we are perhaps able to grasp the specificity of this passage. As the State becomes the centre of attribution of all of society, that is, it becomes the intimate constitutional structure of the collective and of production, so the State becomes authoritarian, ever more authoritarian and fascist. As we have seen, displacement is not simply socialization. *Displacement is antagonism*. The antagonism of ideas and practices of time, that is of movement. The dissolution of time by the State is the answer to another will of time. The hard time of the State is one aspect of the antagonism within socialization, of socialization. *Just one aspect* of the antagonism. The relation is antagonistic with the character of insolubility. Therefore, the problem of antagonism becomes one of organizing antagonism in some manner. But how is this to be done in the face of these insoluble facts? We have already seen that there is no contradiction between Fascist State and Constitutional State. The phenomenology of antagonism and the revelation of its irreducibility provide us with an explanatory rationale. The State operates under the necessity of removing the collective dimension and the productive autonomy of time, of temporal being, because their emergence means antagonism. But it must do this in the collective, in the productive, assumed as irreversible condition: the removal is fascism; the removal – *within these structural conditions* – is constitutionalism. *The coincidence is not contradictory*. But how can it be organized, how can it be structured?

We have two answers to these questions: the first is the *institutional* one; the second is the *analytic and systemic* one. Both seek some form of *mediation* with the ontology of real time. Let us first consider the institutional attempted solution: it is the attempt to break with the continuity of the temporal flow, and therefore of the density of the antagonism, by stabilizing particular units of time around appropriate forms of *relative equilibrium*. From this standpoint, sociological institutionalism takes up again methodologies and approaches of so-called *juridical realism* as a doctrine of self-sufficient regulations. Here the relation Power-regulation manifests itself as that which *'cannot not be'*. On the other hand, the systemic attempted solution: it is the attempt to create a multifunctional unity whose cohesion is not given by the simplification of material elements and temporal flows (as in the institutional solution) – nor is it given by the presupposition of their organic linkage – but rather, it is given by the *centripetal force* of the functional norm. (In the theories of right, functionalism is called *positivism*, and positivism has the advantage of leading functionalism to the highest level of logical coherence. Here the relation Power-regulation is that which *'must be'*.) In this case the antagonism is *not* removed *from the foundation* through a previous construction of co-ordinates, *but* is resolved *in the course* of the operations that are applied to the multiversal, multifunctional co-ordinates. Complexity is reduced. The neofunctionalist, analytic, systemic framework removed the fixity of the norms that even provided old Parsons with 'enlightenment' solutions: here, in Luhmann for example, but also in some Offe, the mobility of the system and its terminals is always granted. The final solution is no less harsh: thermodynamic, chemically stable. In reality, in both cases it is a certain eclecticism that makes it the boss. An eclecticism that is horribly transparent in the analysis of the current crisis between *Welfare* and *Warfare* for example, between legitimating foundation and repressive foundation; so that as in all eclecticism, even these formulations simply *repeat the very same problem* that was to be resolved *in the solution*. In short, both institutionalism and neo-functionalism apply themselves to the explanation of the contemporaneity of the absolutism of Power (authoritarianism, fascism, etc.) and of the expansion of constitutionalism, but fail to arrive at a solution. In the attempt to approximate the problem of the temporal, real, antagonism that surround this paradox, both attempts fail to tackle the problem and serve simply to re-present it.

The problem of the constitutive time of the State thus remains. The one thing we know for sure is that, at the level of real subsumption, it repeats in extreme terms the old *paradox of the contemporaneity of the negative totality* (the last instance, total asymmetry, foundation of obligation, God on earth) of the centrality of Power *and of the constitutional totality* of the social to be organized. This paradox is tirelessly repeated in eclectic ways.

I believe that it is worth considering the most fully developed of the attempts provided by the modern science of right and of the State to influence and to resolve this theoretical situation. I speak of the work elaborated – in terms that I still consider unsurpassed – by Hans Kelsen and the scholars influenced by him. To what extent the pure doctrine of right dirties its hands and becomes impure with reality, to what extent so-called juridical formalism is realistic, quickly becomes evident. The fact is that Kelsen's reasoning – and this is evident when in a provocative manner and for primarily heuristic ends he confronts the problematic of historical materialism (see, for example, his *Allgemeine Rechtslehre im Lichte materialistischer geschichtsauffasung* [1931], which represents an early anticipation of the *Introduction to the Problems of Legal Theory: A translation of the First Edition of* Reine Rechtslehre *or* Pure Theory of Law [1992]) – arrives at a description of the *ought* (*Sollen*) that forms State's foundation of obligation, as the posing and overcoming of the paradox. Juridical formalism is an anticipation of real subsumption (in critical bourgeois thought). The *ought* (*Sollen*) is in fact presented at the same time as the *transcendental foundation* of regulation and as the *function of* living *labour* that traverses the regulation. In all probability it is here that the time of State, the time of constitution is effectively described. It is explained in State and capitalist terms as the completely unfolded *expression of the collective and productive reality of real subsumption* and as *negation*, equally unfolded and rigorous, *of the real displacement of the antagonism*. Where Kelsen gives the transendentality of the *ought* (*Sollen*) contents, or at least materialist redundancy, where he draws living social labour back into the dynamic of regulation, there all the categories of privacy, of the market, of the old capitalist juridical order are destroyed: what remains is a terrain, integrated between structure and superstructure, that the *ought* (*Sollen*) overdetermines. *Living labour is internal*, for Kelsen, *to the rational constitution of dead labour*. The construction of this transcendental horizon and the analytic completion of the analytic that unfolds it, are a formidable anticipation of real subsumption.[52]

But here the limit of capital's standpoint is also demonstrated, because the internal burden of understanding the entirety of the series marked 'A' reaches the point of in effect positing its *aporia*. The aporetic, critical, perhaps catastrophic fact is that this *ought* (*Sollen*), this totality of obligation, is unable to express living labour as the potentiality of antagonism. It only summarizes it in so far as it contains it in the spatial circularity of the regulations. The irreducibility, the irreversibility of the times of antagonism, cannot but be rejected. The time of co-operation is reduced to that of circulation. The totality of the transcendental time of the *ought* (*Sollen*) will be unable to develop other than through an increasingly exasperated antinomy. The passage from the transcendental totality to the automatic totality seems then to be the only possible route. So from Prometheus to Narcissus once again. But was not the problem that of grasping the effectiveness of living labour within the *ought* (*Sollen*)? But could we not legitimately redefine the problem as that of urgently grasping the antagonism in the displacement? In Kelsen, in the pure science of right, the displacement is grasped, the constitutive temporality of the subsumed world is alluded to, but the antagonism continues to be denied in favour of a continued selection of the functions of the hypostatic unity.

This return to Kelsen has not, however, been in vain. We find ourselves before the timid eclecticism of the schools of institutionalism and neo-functionalism. In contrast, in Kelsen the negation of the antagonism and the search for unity implies specific characteristics. That is to say, if antagonism here goes unrecognized (on principle), if the image that the State has of it is always that of circulation, *the State is in any case forced to present itself as the subject of this antagonism*. The paradox of the relation between diverse and asymmetrical times presents itself here as controlled in so far as it is lived. The transcendence of the *ought* (*Sollen*) is without question not reduced to nothing, *because* this *nothing* of the *ought* (*Sollen*) must be *carried out*, that is imposed. Its logical strength is a physical strength. Carl Schmitt represents the repressed of Hans Kelsen. Vyschinski, on the other hand, represents his realization (is not the antagonism removed by the revolution?). The difference that exists between what we are concerned with in the first displacement and what we find in the second displacement (which we shall see in Chapter 8) consists in this: that here the *nothing of command is still lived as reality*, while in the subsequent displacement the nothing will be lived as such. The State denies the real antagonism in its own constitution and regulations, while it is still constrained to admit it in its *management*, in its administrative existence. The annulment of its temporal being is not yet catastrophe.

If we turn to another example, this time in relation to the theory and practice of the economy of the State of real subsumption, we find ourselves before the same effects. The planned structure of the State, and interventionism, become ever more dominant after the crisis of the 1930s and especially in the crisis of the 1960s; they become veritable transcendentals from the standpoint of the organization of production and of collectivity as well. In this case also, and in the same way, the antagonism must be negated as must the real time of social organization, of the time and the sphere of life as well. 'The element of "time" is the heart of the fundamental difficulty of nearly all economic problems' (Keynes).[53]

Every interventionist theory, all planning, every approximation to the real time of the antagonism must end in *equilibrium* – in the negation of time. In this case also the residual reality of the relation emerges not from the ends of the intervention, which are to nullify the real temporal subjects, but from the recognition by the State of itself as a temporal subject. In this way *the zero of equilibrium is actively attained*. The antagonism is not acknowledged, but one works so that its reduction to unity is realized. The analytic traverses the real times of class composition so as to negate them: in this operation between being and non-being the time of the State is revealed.

No theory expresses this time of the State of real subsumption better than the Heideggerian thinking on the ontology of time, on the nullification of being. The State is *care*, the world of anxiety actively lived. From this standpoint Heidegger produces a metaphysics appropriate to Kelsen's *ought* (*Sollen*), as Bobbio – when at his best, in the post-war year – has frequently underlined.

So we come to our last point. The hard time of the State of real subsumption must attain control of the globe; it must present itself as entirely constitutional. But that 'attaining the world' must exacerbate the pole of the State as activity, while it must deny the antagonistic pole, the proletariat, in so far as it too is activity, antagonism in action. Here we find the same underestimation of the problem of legitimation in the contemporary State: legitimation relies on a counterpart, a relation of activities: the activity of subjects. But here there is only one subject. *In place of legitimation comes information*: that is, lack of activity by the subject, passivity, it is transcription, it is the simulacrum of participation. The hegemony of information over legitimation is the specific form of the activity of the nullification of real time exercised, within subsumption, by the contemporary State.

The construction of constitutive time in the contemporary State (of command in real subsumption) is thus given as the *activity of negation of an irrepressible antagonism*. No analysis of the contemporary State is possible that fails to recognize it as completely invested by the social totality, by the collectivism of life, by the socialization of life – to the point of the transformation of constitutionalism into totalitarianism – but also as traversed by a global antagonism. One that the State must negate. Its identity consists in this necessary activity of negation. But the antagonism is as indestructible as subsumption and the collective dimensions of this life of ours.

7
Third Construction: constitutive time B

7.1 The time of class struggle: the new institutionality

The hard time of the State is an activity of negation. In the series marked 'A' time presents itself as analytic collective dimension, that is, as the dimension of expropriation (of productivity) and of command: time is analytic, time is command. Time is presented to us as non-being but as *active non-being*. In contrast to this, in the development of the series marked 'B', we have – from the beginning – seen time move within a tendency, which in unifying it through collective labour, increasingly materializes time productively. The process that we have witnessed is constitutive; it is a process that leads us to conceive the series marked 'B' as concluding in a *plenitude of being*, one that is *active* and *subjective*. Thus we must underline a first antinomy: *the antinomy of subjectivity*. That is the fact that both being and non-being present themselves to us as figures of attribution and activity, so that – *from within the transitions of the first displacement* – we must conclude by saying that being and non-being cannot be entirely separated, that ambiguities remain, that therefore a further displacement is necessary (only if really and materially possible of course). In this chapter, Section 7.2, I will pause to consider the ambiguity and the determination of the antinomy; for the solution of the antinomy, which rests on a second displacement, we will have to wait until Chapters 8 and 9. But here I want to observe the process of the definition of constitutive time through to its conclusion on level B.

I call *constitutive time* the time of the *class struggles*, or rather, of the *negative labour of self-valorization*.[54] I will consider the analysis of negative labour from five points of view: *(a)* the constitutive time of negative labour in terms of mobility; *(b)* in terms of displaced totality; *(c)* in terms of antagonism; *(d)* in terms of composition; *(e)* in terms of institutionality.

Against the hard time of the State stands the pliant time of negative labour; this is the first observation. The form that its struggles and activities take, on the basis of the collective and productive temporal displacement of class, is first of all that of *mobility*. By mobility I mean *the constant formation and re-formation of the material strata and of the collective subjects of social labour*. At the level of real subsumption the first and fundamental characteristic of the class consists in the omniversality of its dimensions of movement. 'The essence of the unity – and of the concept – of class is that all workers present themselves as migrants, as mobility' (Hossfeld and O'Connor, *Capital Accumulation, Class Struggle and Labour Migration*). Omniversality is pliant. But *not* for that reason is it *reversible*: the articulations of mobility are all composed by irreversible time – as in general is the case with racial, sexual, national distinctions, and in particular, with the relations of force and of composition in the *labour market*. We have already seen in this regard how the labour market is in no way distinguishable from other forms of social organization that influence the distribution of goods and revenues. Therefore, picking up the thread again, the society of real subsumption is at once one of social exchange and antagonism. Mobility is therefore a subjective power both of the labour market and of all society, so what form of distinction is possible then? On the one hand, it becomes ever more difficult to maintain conceptual categories of exclusion and separation of constitutive parts of the labour-power of the (so-called) labour market as a whole – which is no longer *strictly* conceivable as such (hence the complete obsolescence of the concept of the 'reserve army' of labour-power); while on the other hand, the activity of the contemporary State is forced towards the globality of the relation, it reinvents the 'labour market' and tries to separate it, to segment it, to reduce it to analytic functions (see the exemplary essays collected in *Readings in Labour Economics* [1980] by J. E. King) – and beats its fists against the pliant and global time, against the versatility of the movement of the proletariat. In short, here we are able to grasp the *free dimension* of the movement, as the movement of the *social* worker. The fact is that, even in real subsumption – no rather, *a fortiori* in it – work presents itself as *class*, one whose temporal nature was from the beginning irreversible and therefore, where *every attempt to reduce class to labour-power*[55] is, from the beginning, rendered inoperative by the unattainable dimensions of the (omniversal) relation. Negative labour, that is the capacity to produce on the basis of co-operation and freed from command, begins to come about: *mobility is constitutive*; it is the constitutive condition of the free use of time.[56]

The labour market, however omniversal and however weakened it is by the hegemony – over it – of the time of mobility, is still a spatial dimension. The constitutive nature of negative labour appears with greater force as soon as we consider it as a *displaced totality*. Here the field of analysis is the *working day*, which we already know is equivalent to the day of life. And we know how in it production and reproduction are interpenetrated so as to define a single cycle of productive circulation. Finally we know how the alternative is given and struggle develops, *not* relative to parts of the working day and the quantities of time that these parts represent, *but* around the *opposite temporal codes*: of command or of liberation. Because liberation is not the subtraction of value from command (a species of Humboldtism, a theory of the limits of exploitation in the critique of political economy), but is the *investment of the temporal antagonism across the productive totality*. Marx's polemic around 'Senior's last hour' (Marx 1990, Part Three, pp. 333–9), where exploitation is shown to be coexistent with work and not empirically reducible to a fraction of the working day, must here be taken up again and transposed to the entire dimension of the time of life. Negative labour is thus constituted across the global time of life.

And it is constituted as *antagonism*. The demonstration need not linger on the global inherence of the antagonism in the *Umwelt* of subsumption, of which we have spoken at length already. It is enough to insist on the necessary identification of subsumption and crisis that is the real productive machine of the realization of the tendency and of its successive displacements. Here then, rather than *labour*, we emphasize the *negative* – while carefully underlining in the independence of the negative, in the *antagonistic* autonomy *of co-operation*, that specifically economic moment, that is to say, of return to the human search for material wealth and intellectual perfectibility that renders negative labour a labour of *self-valorization*. The time of self-valorization is not the time subtracted from capital (not simply that) – it is the *activity* of subtraction, it is the irreducible basis of every foundation of value. Capital lives by expropriating this activity and reducing its potentiality to the time zero of its regulatory analytic. On the contrary, self-valorization is the time that is constituted through value, and retains this value in the antagonistic composition of the social class of productive labour. To the analytic centrifugation of value that capital imposes, is opposed a centripetal direction, the *reappropriation* that the class effects. This is self-valorization: constitutive time.

Now let us turn to *the constitutive time of composition*. Time, as little by little our abstractions delineate its ontological character concretely, becomes increasingly full. We have also frequently lingered over the notion of composition. But the obvious fact that composition reveals a particularly dense temporal dimension does not yet reveal the determination of a *subject*. For composition to be given as subject, and therefore as determined and finalized negative labour, it is necessary that the collective and productive elements of composition should have accumulated such intensity, such thresholds of transformation, that make it adequate to the dimensions of the social processes of subsumption. The collective time, the productive time of composition, become fully constitutive time only at the level of real subsumption. Therefore the composition becomes what we could call mature. All of its metabolisms are complete. And so it is a case of a figure that has a temporal matter, a finality of self-valorization, and a subjective form that is now socially fully dilated. The mobility of behaviours, the globality of inherences, the antagonism of needs is crowned in the time of constitution. To say *proletarian constitution* is to grasp an already activated ontological thread, a composition already made subject. With this, constitutive time is fully revealed as the dynamic of the movement, filled with a materiality with reference to the satisfaction of needs and the emancipation from exploitation. In the following section we will return to the dynamics of the individual, in the relations unfolded within the composition, underlining the richness of these relations as they become apparent within this approach. For now let us bear in mind that, in accordance with the rhythm of constitutive time, the composition reveals its subjectivity as a *mobile system* in transformation that it is possible to analyse according to synchronic, precise, structural lines, and according to historical, diachronic series; that the analysis stretches between individualities and collectivity; and that time is the substance of this process, in which the multiversal force of the being of the proletariat reveals itself. The construction of value and productive force emerge from this elaborate thread. Always seeking a subjective determination.

Finally time transforms self-valorization into *auto-determination*, into *institutionality*. Negative labour has here taken on a historical and effectual dimension to the point of imposing itself as *rationality*. It is the time of living labour that traverses the whole of society, and that carries and explicates the productive overdetermination that co-operation has determined and determines; so that it, negative labour, constitutive time, presents itself as *sole rationality*. The institutional transition from self-valorization as general and dispersed power to auto-determination as recognized and concentrated power, presents itself as the conclusion of a phase. *Institutionality*: in other words, the present-ness of time organized by worker and proletarian rationality; the *logic of legitimation that derives from this temporal rationality*. To say constitutive time is to say rational time, in the sense that here by *rationality* we intend a *(collective and productive) foundation of time as enjoyed substance* – against the expropriation of time. Rationality as non-work, as negative labour, understood as the liberation of time from the conditions of exploitation – against the reduction of time to measure, to command over life. In the era of real subsumption the institutionality of negative labour represents the only possible form of rationality. In this way the phenomenology of collective practice completes itself, having itself become foundational function of a new horizon of rationality.[57]

Note: When in my *Marx beyond Marx* (1979) and in my *Il comunismo e la guerra* (1980) I described this passage from composition to auto-determination through the mechanisms of self-valorization, the objection was raised that the schism between *subjective quality* of the composition and the *(economico-political) quantity* of wealth and power was not resolvable. But this objection was possible only because the objectors had failed to grasp, or to pay insufficient notice to the density of the constitutive concept of proletarian time. By putting our trust in this autonomous conception of proletarian time, it is in fact possible to define a continuous – if not linear – thread between: (1) individual time, as material and mobile internal sense (of exploitation and of liberation); (1.1) the times of individual auto-recognition (moral, historical, political); (2) the collective time of struggle and liberation; (2.1) the times of the structure of the relation between subjects and events, that is time as composition. We could proceed with a phenomenological enumeration, but we should stop here. Capital intervenes (through social organization, which is the continual reorganization of the mode of production) at various levels and in various forms against this continuity. Between *1* and *1.1* it intervenes in terms of pure economic violence; between *1.1* and *2* in terms of political violence (repression, ghetto); between *2* and *2.1* in terms of juridical-constitutional violence and large-scale economic-State restructuring. Finally, to close the circle, capital can attempt to push each of these powers back to *1* once more. But this passage – which we could call regression of the constitutive paradigm – is possible only on certain occasions and in certain conditions, as we shall soon see. In this case the *restructuring* would be defined as *counter-revolution*. But to what degree and in what form is counter-revolution still possible at the stage of real subsumption? Leaving aside these exceptional cases, in general the law of capitalist development at each moment blocks the workers' passage to a higher structure (capitalist time as the blockage of time, as its inertial and entropic reduction). We could give examples on the subject of the working day, taking up again the classification and the periodizations of the forms of class composition – we would nevertheless see that *every obstacle*, every impediment posited by capital (whether it produced worker and proletarian defeat or not), was nothing but the *premise* to a forward passage in the composition. On this point, and from a subjective perspective – brought back to the dimensions of subsumption of course – I consider Marx's framework as valid. Though recognizing the force of capital and its effects, I insist again that the problem of the unification of *1* and *2*, of internal time and external time, has a solution. To confront this problem from the standpoint of constitutive time means also overturning, in the form that it has been put to us, the thematic of the quality of life, of the personal and of needs. That is to say, in all these theoretical (and reformist) positions, quality is presented as (destructive) alternative to quantity: the quality of life against the quantity of work. To begin with the conception of constitutive time means to travel a reverse path: synthesizing quality and quantity in time, and so grasping the antagonistic nexus in the form of globality. I shall return in later sections to the difficulty of internal synthesis between the aspects of subjectivity and aspects of mobility, between quality and quantity. But on the globality of the process I think there can be few doubts: does the quantitative demand for a diminution of working hours contradict the desire for a better quality of life perhaps? The sophisms that are produced to demonstrate these absurdities evidently cannot be taken seriously. The passage from the multiplicity of processes of co-operation to the unity of the subject in reality occurs as the attainment of the limit between co-operation and rationality, between conditions of production (and reproduction) and their constitutive reappropriation on the basis of a materiality, of a necessity that is that of the time of constitution. Our discourse has revealed that where class-consciousness itself appears as condition, it is first founded materially.

One last note. The time of class struggle is not only the negative time that passes from the mobility inherent in the globality of the working day and to antagonism, on to self-valorization and auto-determination. It is also *prefigurative power*. The time of class struggle in itself contains the future and it continually attempts to shape it. The contemporaneity of the future and of the present at the level of real subsumption does not produce utopian confusion: it is the collective which constructs, the future that is brought back to the dimension of the collective, and it is subordinated to the enormous productive power that class composition, displaced in this way, possesses. Qualified, complex, technico-scientific labour finds the dimension adequate to its power in the future, while the past is memory of the law of value and its abominable effectiveness. But on this relation with the future, other prolegomena need to be written.

7.2 Pluralism and dualism: on the logical matrices

A few problems arise once we are able to grasp this ontological but supple and multiversal figure of time in opposition to the hard but ontological de-potentialized time of the State.

And the fundamental problem is born of the fact that we have in our enquiry so far opposed, in a *dualistic* manner, a series of events (and forms of events) 'A' to a series of events (and forms of events) 'B'. But any correct phenomenology of the events gathered in 'B' shows us that at this level mobility, asymmetry, irreversibility – a multiversal horizon – are already given due to the liberation of ontological time itself. How is it possible to gather all this richness conclusively within a dualistic schema? Will it not be the case that, surreptitiously, a dialectical form is inserted into the reasoning so that, far from being phenomenologically meaningful, the *world of liberation* is nothing other than the *reversed homologue of the world of command*? What assures us that this dualism is not mystificatory?

We must recognize that this is a real difficulty. All the more so since in the history of ideas the concept of *Krisis* has always been given either from the standpoint of a reunifying logical form (hence the operation of the *reversed homologue*), or from the standpoint of nihilism. The first solution denies the possibility of separation (and renders it indifferent); the second renders every possibility of recomposition meaningless. The philosophy of *Krisis* impoverishes the antagonistic significance of the emergence of the different subjects separated in subsumption, while the philosophy of nihilism denies the richness of the articulations of the world of self-valorization, removing the ontological hopes of the project. It is clear that my project is the complete reverse of this: to grasp the two *logical matrices* that, on the one hand, render separation possible, and on the other, give meaning to the pluralism and multiversality of social being.

As we saw above (in Chapter 1), the existence of these two matrices is not difficult to detect. Indeed, within the *Umwelt* of real subsumption, two temporal polarities exist, the one centripetal, tending to spatialize time, giving it a zero value; the other centrifugal, tending to temporalize space, and so providing time with ontological plenitude. The antagonism is given. The dualistic matrix is given. One could quip, space to capital, time to the working class. But what is most important to point out is that the antagonism is not given in forms that can in any way be recuperated within identity. It could be said that the logical essence of dualism, of antagonism, consists in the existence, in the *modal quality* of the two subjects that clash. Equivocal redundancies of the dualistic logic of separation and confusions concerning the pluralistic logic of the proletarian subject are not possible. Considering the problem from within the horizon of the *Umwelt* of subsumption, the dualism is the absolutely fundamental logical matrix.

The opposite objection could be and is made. If the proletarian pole of the process that coexists with the social whole presents itself as essentially plural, multi, no rather omniversal, how can the originary dualism of the subjects be maintained? Will not the dualism of the subjects be drawn into and be confused with the multiversal zone of the proletarian subject? The answer once again relates to the *radical asymmetry of the relation of exploitation*, in as much as it is a relation that opposes one dimension of time to the other dimension, the two paradigms of life in opposition to one another. The dualism of exploitation is in no case reducible to the plurality of social behaviours. It maintains and develops itself around a logical matrix that cannot be resolved within any horizon that is not qualified by the form of antagonism.

The substantial and difficult problem we find before us is not then that of the *compatibility of the two logical matrices*, the one dualistic and antagonistic and the other plural, or rather, omniversal. The real problem is that of defining *the matter and the procedures of the multiversal matrix* in so far as it concerns the proletarian pole, that is, the social dimension of the antagonism.

But even in this regard we cannot but return to the analysis of the existent. That is to say, we cannot but return to the particular quality that the constitution of time assumes from the proletarian standpoint when it becomes collective and productive. *The necessary is given a posteriori.* It is given as the singularity of the multiple. It is given as irreducibility. Important consequences follow from the recognition of this pluralist matrix of liberation, from the discovery and the deepening of this multiplicity of times. It is not a case of examining them more closely here (for this see Chapter 9). Here it is just a case of underlining the perfect logical compatibility of a dualistic, antagonistic, disjunctive matrix that involves the totality of the existent, and *in the same way*, of a pluralist matrix that constitutes and qualifies the social subject of the antagonism.

Note (1): After the publication of *Il comunismo e la guerra* [1980] I set myself the following problem. That is, the problem of the impasse of a discourse that sets the *logical* horizon of command against the *ontological* horizon of self-valorization. In this case two *incommensurable* subjects confronted one another. Nor did the discussions on the continual historical displacements between capitalist restructuring and class recomposition modify the aporetic substance of the reasoning. If anything it introduced complications, giving an evanescent indefiniteness to the process. But on the other hand, to accept a common context that would enable a comparison in terms of commensurability would, it seemed to me, annul the dualism that was so phenomenologically evident. In short, the impasse consisted in the fact that, if there was no context, the dualism became irrational; if a context were given, the dualism fell away. In truth things could not go otherwise while an indifferent, formal context was being presupposed. Thus, overcoming the impasse means identifying a new radically materialist epistemological context along the lines of Marx's teachings. *The epistemology of time* allows this passage and demonstrates the interpenetration of the logical and the ontological horizon. In other words, I feel that I have demonstrated, within the tautology of subsumption, the reality of a global horizon of the collective, and the necessity of its asymmetry – and within the asymmetry, the coexistence of the logic of the one of the capitalist analytic and the logic of the proletarian multiplicity. That is to say, *the mechanism of the logical production of the dualism is the same as the one that produces the qualitative existence of the separate subjects.* In subordinating itself to the ontology of time, logic subordinates itself to existence. Now the destruction of the cynical logicism of the formalism of *Krisis* becomes all the more simple. The logical mechanism does not in fact construct a 'formal a priori' that subordinates or homologates the polarity of the existent, but rather it assimilates the necessity of the a posteriori. The study of Spinoza has been fundamental to me in proceeding down this path. But all the more fundamental has been my taking up the study of the logical positivists, following some of the indications given by Pierre Jacob, *L'empirisme logique* [1980].

Note (2): In the philosophico-scientific theories of time one can apparently find two extremes: (1) that of the absolute theory of time, and (2) that of the relative theory of time. Under the first heading one can put all the definitions, ancient and modern, that take time as the measure of absolute regulation; under the second heading one can put all the definitions that take time as a relational and discontinuous fabric, that is as a possibility and constitution. Some authors – Serres, Prigogine, Piperno – proceed according to the forms of this fable, such that under *(1)* they place Plato and Newton together, under *(2)* the ancient atomists and the contemporary theorists of thermodynamic time. In some ways this is the same procedure as the one I followed in *Il comunismo e la guerra* [1980], so that the distinction between logical matrices, and of the time that sustained them, resulted in total incommensurability. It is evidently an erroneous procedure, as is the historical reconstruction that it foresees and that we have alluded to. In reality, the history of the idea of time (as Milič Čapek has amply demonstrated in *The Concepts of Time and Space* [1976], bearing in mind the fundamental contributions of Duhem and Meyerson) starts from a maximum subordination of time to space to a maximum subordination of space to time; from a maximum *spatialization of time* to a maximum *dynamization of space*. It is not therefore possible to confuse ancients and moderns. The philosophy of the Renaissance constitutes, even in the case of the history of the idea of time, the decisive watershed. Telesio and Bruno pave the way for the modern conception of time, separating it from space – while in the 1600s the capitalist emancipation of time is achieved with Gassendi. It is true, in antiquity we have absolute (Plato), relative (Atomists) and hybrid (Aristotle) theories of time, but they should not be confused with the absolute (Newton), relative (Einstein) or hybrid theories of modernity, because the epistemological framework has been completely modified. (The formidable suggestiveness of the Democritean and Lucretian conceptions of time, so elegantly reconstructed by Serres, should be thought of as simply that, as suggestive.) It is only within this framework, modified through modernization, that the ontology of constitutive time – together: temporal globality of existence and temporal asymmetry of its dimensions – can be conceived. Thus the problem in the epistemology of time is *not* the naive one of opposing a unitary matrix to that of the multiple, or simply measure to constitution, but rather that of putting to work *this opposition* in the area (a) of the modern totalization of constitutive temporality, (b) of the asymmetric relativization of constitutive dimensions. From the standpoint of a strict epistemology of time, *the mechanism of production of the dualism is the same that identifies the totality of the context.* And this conclusion should be placed beside the other conclusion, presented in Note 1, as the epistemological foundation of our procedure: *the mechanism of logical production of the dualism is the same as that which produces the qualitative existence of the separate subjects.*

7.3 The body and the time of constitution

In the fifth chapter (Section 5.2) I stressed the possibility of grasping the anthropological determination of proletarian constitution. Which is to say, one must study the series of phenomenological relations that *from the bodies of individuals* extend to the *materiality of the collective composition*. But here we are able to set out a further problem: the question of the individualization of the social subjectivities of the class composition that arise at the level of subsumption – the problem, in other words, of *collective corporeality*. This relation is characterized by a multiversal logic, by a phenomenology of multiple times that are both individual and collective. The time of the *social worker* presents itself here as a relation between expansive times, as a relation between different but concurrent velocities. The relation of diverse times has two fundamental aspects: the first is that which is taken up by the assemblages of struggle and recomposition under the sign of the conditions of exploitation and of its asymmetrical effects; the second is that of individual liberation, of collective constitution and of the corporeality of the associative and co-operative relations.

Now the specifics of the problem consist in the fact that these two aspects of the multiversal expression of time are not subjected to any law. They express themselves in encounter and collision, in displacement and disjunction, in short, as in an immense firework display. A non-dialectical but collective phenomenology, in the sense that it follows the maturation of the subjective units according to their behaviours, here becomes possible. (That this has nothing to do with the descriptive hybrids and ideal-types of psychological historicism à la Wilhelm Dilthey[58] or with the irrational and formal hybrids of 'Gestalt' is more than evident.) The phenomenology of collective praxis is here a *process* without laws; it is an ensemble of multiple times that only with the fullness of liberation will achieve definite determinations. The asymmetries are here the basis of a relation that develops continuously. We can of course establish genetic paths, thresholds of collective transformation and, if one wants to attempt it, a veritable *theory of morphogenesis*. (L. S. Vygotsky is probably the author who, from the standpoint of revolutionary materialism, has come closest to such a project.) On the other hand, we have nothing against the equilibrium of diverse times, of the different velocities of the geneses and of the developments that must all the same attain, from time to time, moments of compensation and of cumulative rules. One must likewise recall that composition and consciousness present synchronic series and diachronic series of analysis and of development that can finally *coincide* only in the *antagonism of subsumption* – while beforehand they are given as the *crisis* of the individual in his material relations, crises that only the anticipation and the tendency can in some manner heal. The process of collective praxis cuts the *distance* between synchronic series and diachronic series of consciousness, only anticipation can found a human science that does not wrap itself up in dialectical illusions, and that prefigures the bringing together again of consciousness and of its objective conditions. All this should undergo a description and a definition that we cannot provide here in these 'prolegomena'.

One can also add, and this emerges from what has already been said, that the relation between body and bodies, the link between individual and individual, is no different from the dynamic reality of pluralism in so far as it is submitted to the rule of antagonism. Rather, they are a cross-section of this determination of being, a constitutive moment whose internal joyousness we must grasp. And do so as the *dynamic* of a complete temporal constitution. This is the realm of the fullest *freedom*. Where freedom knows how to be *love*. The mechanisms of recomposition are endowed with the highest spontaneity, as spontaneous as the processes and dynamics of differentiation. Here the *difference* is rich and the unity is spontaneous. This is the *temporal territory*, the *body* of the *communist community*.

But all this is a limit as well as an asset. In effect, when we reach the *micro* dynamic of the great process of human liberation and we grasp this spontaneity of collective life, we also perceive, in this relationship between bodies, *elements that are hard*, inertial. (The obscenity of the ghetto, the misery of marginalization, and the drugged illusion of the individual recomposition of bodies: these are caricatures of the difficulty.) Certainly we are completely outside any dialectic that brings back the heaviness of this limit to being, presenting it as though it were intrinsic to the active materiality of the subject: here there is no place for the practico-inert of the various Bergsons, Simon Weils, and of Sartre. But the absence of a negative dialectic cannot hide the existence, the presence, of aporias. *Non-being* insinuates itself in the 'pyrotechnic-like' explosion of the liberated world, of its needs, of its movements. The time of constitution, though lived at the height of the multiversal tensions that traverse it, has nevertheless the reality of the enemy before it. We know that the recomposition moves by its own strength but it is also true that it *corresponds* to the reality of the enemy. The individual life of the *social* worker, his individual search for collectivity, is a tangle of contradictions, of negative conditions, of reified and reifying elements that should be submitted to criticism; and the liberation from which demands the recognition of the collective antagonism, the forming of the antagonism into constitutive instrument, knowing how to reach higher forms of *collective corporeality* (beyond individuality, beyond the family, towards ever more complex and ever more versatile communities). If individual revolt is the condition of liberation, if the continual crisis of individuality and of inter-individual relations, of sexual, racial, national relations, is the condition of anticipation and project – the negative labour that takes root in a manner that emancipates individuality (in Peter Bruckner that is the power of the *Lernprozess*, otherwise mystified in reformist manner by Oskar Negt) – nonetheless it is true that that *beyond* that individualities want here, that *new corporeality* in which negative labour wants to realize itself, is not yet given.

There is to be found in all of the *first displacement*, in all of its series, an aporetic moment. This aporetic moment can be grasped on all levels of the analysis – of collective time and productive time – but above all, at the level of constitution. One could say that here non-being no longer presents itself as obstacle and repression of the ontological reality of negative labour, of the multiversality of being – for it has been defeated in this attempt. Rather, it presents itself as simple activity – active *non-being* – and as such does not prevent the emergence of being, but it does block it from definitively taking flight from its full self-awareness, from its becoming body. The moments of the first displacement display all the *conditions of communism*. But they are not yet it. They are not yet because non-being remains. However, the unity and the recomposition of bodies display the highest level of recomposition and auto-determination of the versatile multiplicity of the singular times of liberation: the bodies and the choruses, the forms of love and of collective recomposition.

(*Reflection or philosophical scherzo*. If we look at the development of communist philosophy in the 1960s and the historical paradigm shift that these years represent, we could summarize them as the condition of the loss of abstract essence in the extinction of the ideological body – and in the proposition of the desire of the real body. Corporeal body: collective, temporal, corporeal communism. In Althusser the height of the desire is defined in a Kantian manner in the schism between theory and workers' movement – a real schism that cannot be overcome because theory is only an industrious tortoise, while the workers' movement is an Achilles gone crazy: the sophism is truer than the reality. But if that is fixed, if we are condemned to live without the subject, the realm of ends is nevertheless given. And a practice could . . .! The whole of 1960s' communist philosophy attempts to embody the realm of ends, to concretize the ideal of reason after the fall of the subject [or it is the arrogant assertion of the objectivism of the Matticks, Altvaters or the terrorists]. The scherzo is real: after Kant come Fichte and Schelling. The naked postulation of desire as the corporeal key, as the pure position wagered on by Marcuse and Krahl; then, the dynamic prefiguring of the class body as abstract composition that is typical of 'Operaismo'. Operaismo: this night in which all cats are grey, and the theology of the political gradually takes the place of the vagueness of the desired body, and the fetishism of the conciliation in the party excludes the joyousness of the body. Nevertheless, after these monstrous Fichte and Schellings, there will be no more of Hegel, not even as a joke: because Althusser's positing of the problem excludes the general solution, the synthesis, the repetition of the arrogance of the universal. This philosophical scherzo lives the explosion, its abstractness, because the presumption of the universal explosion is no longer even imaginable. No delegating, and certainly not to theory. The body is that thing which has taken the place of the realm of ends: collective corporeality as constitution of individuality. Philosophy jokes, the body does not. The last aporetic tensions of this crisis that only the negative labour of the second displacement will be able to resolve, have taken on the intonation of prophetic language. The philosopher Magi. Lullism. The dark ones.

Miserable conjurings. The subject can only be the body, collective corporeality. There are no short cuts and the dream bows to these determinations. In the collective body theory becomes real. Constitutive time. *The end of the scherzo*.)

8

Second Displacement: the time of revolution W

8.1 The project and death: now-time (*Jetzt-Zeit*)

By *second displacement* I understand the realization, no, given that the passage is not dialectical, the uncovering of the separation between the opposition of the tendencies, their conclusive irreversibility, their proper definition and the disjunction of being and of non-being. The two great dimensions of Marx's tautology (revealed in real subsumption), time-as-measure and ontological time, explode into opposed horizons. The series marked 'A' and that marked 'B' lead us to the series marked 'W' and 'Y'. We will see below (in Section 8.2) the formal characteristics of this second displacement. Let us begin with the material ones. The material characteristics of this second displacement are subtle and should be grasped without forgetting the process of development, as well as the density of the *Umwelt* in which they are held from the beginning.

As we have seen, in real subsumption, the idea of time is for capital posed as an idea of command. The time of political economy is nomenclature, auto-declaration of value, command. Therefore, it is negation of the real time which is experienced as antagonistic, or rather, it is a reduction within a *formally dialectical* schema: the cycle and cyclical development, the market and the plan – that is, in the cyclical development, *time* is configured in the form, and follows the criteria of the ordering of economic *space*, as reversibility of all the points, as circulation, as money. *Ideal time* is, from this standpoint, *balanced space*. This reduction is valid for the theories of the State and in general for all of the *human sciences* (as Alain Gras showed so well in *Sociologie des ruptures* [1979a] and in *Diogène*

[1979b]), as well as in political economy. But this is also true of the first displacement. Here, on the other hand, we must grasp the *hard core*, the logical proposal and the practical project that, in conditions of extreme separation, capital brings in to validate, to justify its own existence – justice as the justification of capital's own being.

There are three transitions that should be identified here:

1. Capital not only presents itself as measure and as system, it presents itself as *progress*. This definition is essential to its internal and external legitimation. From this perspective political economy is entirely directed towards drawing the *innovative element* that history – in any case – produces into the time of administration (accumulation like administration, reversible time, eternal return, and cyclical-ness). *Now-time* (*Jetzt-Zeit*), innovative precision, utopia: capital considers them as its own. Progress is the eternal return lit-up by a flash of a *now-time* (*Jetzt-Zeit*). Administration is illuminated by charisma.[59] The city of the devil is illuminated by grace. The elements of innovation are reduced to numerical and quantitative units and only as such are brought back to bear on progress as command and illumination. Progress is the representation of a process that proceeds by leaps forward, in which all factors can be referred back to proportion. Difference is only quantitative. The economic cycle is the clearest example of capitalist progress: all its terms are modified in accordance with effects and trajectories that are substantially quantitative. In short *now-time* (*Jetzt-Zeit*), utopia, present themselves as innovation, as the touch and tact of the real *within the routine* of the temporal being of command. Utopia and routine present themselves as *abstract identity*, as necessity. Economic determinism, the invisible hand which is the natural law that transforms itself into the law of the State by maintaining the numinous and obligatory character of a law of nature – here we are in the hard core, where *necessity* identifies itself with *interest* and with the progressive *self-presentation* of capital.

2. But in bourgeois ideology time can present itself as *alternation* of these two functions, as well as conjugation of economic determinism and utopia. This derives from the experience of the difficulty of retaining the *negative* (and from the opportunity of absorbing it, of sucking its dynamism into the system, as motor of the system). One may well mystify the negative but it is difficult to flatten it. Therefore, let us close it within alternation, as a *conflictual* element (whether logical or

material). The *dialectical* procedure is the form that command takes; the dialectical illusion is the mode in which the hard core of the self-valorization of capital now presents itself. So here utopia is the alternative to determinism. But if we consider the thought of the two most eminent bourgeois theorists of utopia, Karl Mannheim and Ernst Bloch, strange paths appear. In the former, utopia is understood as the possible rational, as project, as the opening of the practico-inert block of ideological and administrative temporality; in the latter, utopia is antagonism that unfolds on an axis synchronic with the temporality of contemporary Power. Now, in both cases *time* is given *in two forms*: as deterministic *immanence* and as utopian *transcendence*. In both cases, however, the *ontological concept of temporal matter does not change*. For it seems to me that alternation is usually fake – merely a functional element on the basis of which the preventative transfiguration of the elements in struggle live and are admitted into the circulation of command, and as such are rendered perfectly ideal and uniform. Kant's thought, more than Hegel's, lies at the basis of the mediation of alternation: a hard *dualism* for *only one axis* of value. Further, the Kantian reference point is also the one that sustains the more mature figures of the bourgeois theorization of dualistic time. Determinism and time are in the *early* Max Weber interpreted as alternation between the immanence of the rational time of organization and the transcendence of charisma; they are, from the *early* writings of Hans Kelsen, interpreted as the immanence of the formal process of regulation and as the transcendence of the *Grundnorm*.[60] The dualism of the neo-Kantian systems is always one between pure reason and practical reason, between formal theory and history-Power, but always within the unitary space of reason. Therefore, it is not a case of different *temporal paradigms*, but rather the alternation is between different spatial functions of the experience of time, between different systemic articulations. System and innovation exist as different modes of the same substance. So the unity of the project comes before its articulation.

3. And yet bourgeois thought barely tolerates even the mere possibility of the dualism of determinism and utopia. Does not this evanescent temporal transcendence hide aporetic and potentially subversive elements? In fact, the dualistic articulation of time is always exposed to radical displacement. (The analysis of revolutionary transformation, which is so common in the thinking of the liberal left, should

be directed towards this limit.) The subversive irony of Spinoza, who denounced any ethical and utopian transcendence as the 'sanctuary of ignorance' (1991, Part I, appendix), is here provocatively placed in the service of the *re-enforcing* [*ricompattamento*] *of the horizon*. Charisma and *Grundnorm*, if we keep to the same example, should *not* be conceived of as dualistic elements, *but* rather as the source of the immanent productivity of the system. Now the critical transition is absolutely clear. The one-dimensional horizon of time is – to all effects – restored within a commutation of the factors that do not alter the result. *We pass from innovation as systemic product, to innovation as systemic motor.* From Prometheus to Narcissus. The *later* Kelsen makes his system realist (in the juridical sense): that is to say the relation between *Grundnorm* and formal system becomes continuous and productive. The *later* Weber (in 'Parliament and Government in Germany under a New Political Order' [see Weber 1994]) also carries out an analogous synthesis: in the constitution charisma presents itself as the foundation of organization. From (the illusion of) dualism we have returned to monism, a productive monism made subject.

But that is not the end of it. The course of the project, from the abstract and progressive character of system and innovation – to the alternation of determinism and utopia and to the conflictual illusion – on to the final systemic synthesis, has been rich in theoretical and practical redundancies. The systemic dimension imposes an extreme coherence on its own foundation. In enquiring into the nature of the temporal foundation of the system, its circular trajectories come to the forefront, thus displaying *temporal nature zero*. (The stoic critique of Aristotelian time-as-measure becomes important again: paradoxically it renders the linear, circular, hence zero value of time, real.) Systemic monism produces that which it can produce: abstraction and reduction of every tension to zero, absolute de-potentialization of the relation to reality. The productive subjectivization of the system develops the bureaucratic routine, *rational legitimacy*, to the point of rendering them absolute. Rational legitimation then becomes *technocratic legitimation*, therefore no longer even legitimation in the strict sense, because in basing everything on itself, on its own necessary function, technocratic legitimacy eliminates the very *relation* of legitimacy. Here, the absolute nature of command, its capacity to absolutely guarantee its systemic rational reproduction, leaps to the fore. Therefore, it should surprise no one that the productive monism of contemporary systemic theories results in the conception and the practice of the *nuclear State*.[61] Here nature and history are filtered by the system and expressly lead to *possibility zero*. The only reality that can be felt here is that of death.

With this I'll bring to an end my account of the path of bourgeois theory, the development of which in reality reveals outcomes that cannot be qualified by simply following infra-systemic routes. I believe that the fundamental point consists in this: the capitalist science and practice of Power operate a veritable displacement of perspective when they become aware of the real unsustainability of the antagonism implicit in subsumption. It is not that they dialectically overcome the aporias, rather, they excavate the system, seeking its hard core in the course of the attempt to make difficulties and checkmates fall away and to control the possible aporias. The *first displacement* is, as we have seen, that of the passage to real subsumption, from which there follows on the capitalist side a series of attempts at regulation specifically directed at the aporias that are revealed in a determinate manner. From here proceeds a permanent and creeping *conjugation* of being and non-being, within the ambit of the first displacement. On the other hand, the *second displacement* recognizes the insolubility of the relation, placing the antagonism at the forefront. Here, the bourgeois standpoint aims to represent *one pole, and only one pole of the relation. If innovation is always aporetic, if it is always nourished by antagonism –* if it is born as an external to the system of Power – then *it must be annulled*. The content of the second displacement, on the side of capital, is the *ontological zero*. The time of capitalist revolution ends with real time being reduced to zero. Absolute hegemony of the war industry. Progress burns up in nothingness.

Here we shall take a long digression. Let us ask ourselves: has it not been the case, and is it not the case, that this idea of the zero time of innovation and of the permanent capitalist revolution has a much more powerful and extensive conceptual development than that which appears from the analysis of its immediate area of application – the world of bourgeois ideology? Is it not the case rather that this myth of innovation as *Krisis*, and as systemic project, is capable of being applied to and of connoting ideological behaviours well beyond even the frontiers of bourgeois thinking? The answer is affirmative: the conception of innovation, understood exclusively as capitalist auto-determination of development, based on the time of command, of measure – the *hysteresis* of development itself, has invested the *thinking of socialist revolution* as well.

> A Historical materialist cannot do without the notion of a present which is not a transition, but in which time stands still and has come to a stop. For this notion defines the present in which he himself is writing history. Historicism gives the eternal image of the past; the historical materialist supplies a unique experience with the past. The historical materialist leaves it to others to be drained by the whore called 'Once upon a time' in historicism's bordello. He remains master of his powers, man enough to blast open the continuum of history.
>
> (Benjamin 1973, Thesis XVI – translation modified)

So says Walter Benjamin in the 'Theses on the Philosophy of History'. He goes on to say, 'History is the object of a construction whose location is not homogenous and empty time, but the full one of now-time (*Jetzt-Zeit*)' (probably from Thesis XVII)[62] . . . 'Now-time [*Jetzt-Zeit*] as the model of messianic time' (Thesis XVIII – translation modified). Well, this conception is ruinous. Far from being the destruction of historicism and of its perverse political results, the conception of the messianic *now-time* (*Jetzt-Zeit*) represents the utmost modernization of reactionary thought: it is the conversion of historical, plural, punctual, multiversal materials into the thaumaturgical illusion of empty innovation. The conception of the messianic *now-time* (*Jetzt-Zeit*) reduces the tautology of real subsumption to *mysticism*, and mysticism always stinks of the boss (no matter what Agamben and Facchinelli say about it). In Benjamin one again experiences the creationist paradox of time-as-measure, which is equivalent and opposed to the stoic one. Saint Augustine of Hippo: 'time was made simultaneously with the world, and with the creation of the world change and movement were also created, as appears clear from the order of the first six or seven days.' Precisely. If an innovative methodology establishes itself in a formal universe, it loses the flavour of materialism and of the creativity of the only creative time, that of the masses. The historical continuum is in this way reduced to elementary series and made to be systemically reorganized. The only real practice of 'now-time' is that of the abstract break, the abstract unity of productive time, and therefore the mechanical and methodical dimension of equilibrium. *Now-time* (*Jetzt-Zeit*) *is a form of time-as-measure*. From this point of view a construction of time like Benjamin's operates perfectly as a mediation between the productive monism of the systemic conceptions of the later Weber and the later Kelsen, and the *socialist practice* of insurrection against the State. Revolutionary reason is grafted onto, and co-inserted into, technocratic rationality; all in all it is a case of the implosion of the development towards zero time that is anticipated by the zero of the insurrectional initiative, of insurrectional time. Recently Erik Olin Wright (1978) has reconstructed the concept of administrative rationality in Weber and Lenin, tracing synoptic correspondences. So wherever we have the negation of real time, in the dimension of administrative measure and reversibility, we find it equally in the path of 'rationality': that formal and atemporal rationality that is sealed in illusory fashion in the original act of the *Grundnorm*, of charisma and *of the* foundational *insurrectional now-time* (*Jetzt-Zeit*). The digression provided ends there where the project of social-ism comes to be identified with the expression of that same nullifying reduction of real time that accompanies the capitalist displacements. The second displacement looks therefore to be also verified in the ideology and the practice of real socialism.

Time zero is completely realized through, and as a result of, real sub-sumption. This is the content of the second displacement, which is under-stood as the form of the series of events. But one must insist on the phenomenological relevance of this definition of time. Aside from the different ideological configurations, capitalist system and socialist system, in the complexity of the relations that envelope work and life, time of work and time of life manifest in an extreme way the irreversibility of a temporal practice with zero valence, one no longer reducible to a concept. *The only way in which capitalist thought (time, measure, system, etc.) can assimi-late real irreversibility is by declaring and treating it as death*. It is a culture, a practice of death that appears here as *absolute now-time* (*Jetzt-Zeit*). All the *now-times* (*Jetzt-Zeit*) elaborated by the bourgeois culture of the past (including that of the first displacement) sought some positive link to the ontological reality of time. And they would put their negative aspect in the service of a constitutive (conjugated) dialectic of a collective and productive time. With subsumption realized, the dialectic completed, the capitalist and bourgeois *now-time* (*Jetzt-Zeit*) is the totality of the sense of death, of a practice of apocalypse. The abduction of time from being, its complete fixation and blockage, which is an expropriation of ontological meaning at the level of the collective that is imploded up to the point of the absolute potentiality of destruction. This occurs across the whole compass of the experience and praxis of the collective. A space that annuls time intoxicates us. From the constitution of the State and from its ever increasing fixed rigidity; to the forms of organization of social time – consumed in ever more evanescent ways; from the great repressive machine that poses the hegemony of the null time of right, to the nuclear State that gathers up the diffusion of the putrefaction of capitalist nature in a decision of death. These are the results and the qualities of the series of events marked 'W' – all of which must be retraced analytically.

To sum up and move beyond: if we take up again Marx's discourse of the working day (breaking, as we have done from the beginning, with the dialectic of value and grasping rather its realization in subsumption), if therefore we take up the dynamic of the working day in terms of the extreme alternative that it presents *literally*, between *death* and *antagonistic liberation of the class*, of its self-awareness in struggle, and we consequently *displace* this antagonism at the level of the contemporary analytic of subsumed labour, that is of realized social capital, well, within this operation of displacement, we find ourselves before a new form of antagonism. It is still *death*, but this time in a *social form*, as *nuclear State*, as accumulation of time reduced to the zero value of a project of total destruction. Total destruction only knows the now-time. Against this, antagonistic *liberation*, understood as the social liberation of the entirety of productive forces. Extended, constitutive, innovative time: revolutionary and subjective time. The displacement is decisive in this finale to the enquiry. (We must continue to insist on the profundity and the heuristic utility of Marx's method of the antagonistic displacement.)

8.2 Endogenous processes and exogenous processes: analytic and catastrophe

The importance of Marx and Lenin in the *theory of knowledge* consists in having definitively set forth the standpoint of the *productive concretion*. The characteristics of the productive concretion – modality irreversibility project – become the characteristics of any theory of knowledge that wants to present itself as science. The red thread that leads from the *Introduction* of 1857 [Marx 1973] to *State and Revolution* of 1917 [Lenin 1977, Vol. 2] (and to Mao's writings 'On contradiction' and 'On practice' [1967]) is a path of the theory of knowledge that grasps the concrete as productive rationality.[63] As rational and productive critique. The central moment is the mechanism of displacement, that is, the conjuncture in which the expressions of the concrete and the products of the collective subject, advancing from threshold to threshold, become conjugated. You do not need Gregory Bateson in order to understand that the structure operates as a whole – Marx and Lenin are enough to determine knowledge as the displacement of the *Umwelt*. Here the process is entirely *endogenous*, that is to say, capable of recuperating *in its interior* the *link with innovation*, without the need for ideological simulations. And this occurs because the matter that weaves together the productivity of being is the collective time of liberation, which is the same as production. The collective process of knowledge determines the regimes productive of the true, of the *practically true*, not through linear projections rationalizing the existent, but by planting itself within the complexity of temporal being and completely reorganizing, each time, the *dispositifs* of the transformation of the real.

Given this, we now come to the formal and problematic characteristics of the displacement as we have studied it so far. We see how in the first place (1) the *displacement* operates in general, and how it articulates itself in the *forms of the exposition*; in the second place (2) we see what the *differences* of expository content are that come to be determined between the first and the second displacement.

Now, keeping to theme *(1)*, it is immediately evident that by displacement we mean a new *Umwelt* of the temporal existence of subjects. A new *being-in-the-world* is determined. And if, as we have seen, the standpoint of critique is that of the productive concretion, to each displacement there corresponds a specific and determinate form of exposition. This has some extremely important consequences – as exemplified on the level of the first displacement we studied, that of the passage to real subsumption. Now, when a collective social organ develops production, it looks at first as though the endogenous mechanism of the qualification of the real peters out in indifference. But the fact that the epistemological validation of knowledge is only given by its link to the concrete means that the indifferent, however real it may be, cannot be taken up in the process of knowledge. Therefore, what characterizes the approach at this point is the insistence on the passage, on the transformation of the framework, on the displacement of the structure. The form of the exposition must make itself adequate to this. The *apparent* indifference of the content of subsumption must be broken by the *expository form*. The eminence of the insertion of productive subjectivity in this passage is fundamental. But this means the posing of a *general principle*: *with each displacement a subjective viewpoint must emerge to discriminate the tendencies of the real.*

In other words, a theory of displacement, and above all a theory of displacement in real subsumption (with the forms of indifference to contents that this involves), does not allow one to maintain a descriptive apparatus of the *type: 'theory of the modes of production'*. By theory of the modes of production I understand a historico-dialectical approach, structural and objectivist and so closed, that excludes the function of the subject as foundational agent of knowledge. The relative validity of the theory of the modes of production *at other levels of* capitalist development falls away definitively when we enter real subsumption. The theory of the modes of production keeps to the contents, but here the contents are indifferent; the theory of the modes of production keeps to the whole, but a mute whole. Only the point of view, only the open transition, only the open expository form that sees the displacement as a complete transcription of the relations of force and of class – and hence poses the decision on the form of the exposition *from within* – can correspond to the intensity of the displacement. The form of the exposition breaks the indifference of the content. The more capitalist development proceeds, the more *antagonism* places itself practically and concretely *at the origin of science*. Feyerabend has understood this. Therefore, from the theory of the modes of production to a theory of the regimes of production of the real as the only route that enables one to grasp the form of the exposition adequate to the intensity of the real displacement.

With that said we come to theme *(2)*, and the *expository differences* between the first and second displacement. In a way we have already seen them. They seemed to us to consist essentially in the fact that, while in the context of the first displacement we find in force a logic of advancing antagonism, on the one hand: of the formal dimension of time-as-measure and of the command of its organization; on the other hand: of the ontological dimension of collective, productive, constitutive time – in the context of the *second displacement*, the asymmetry of the terms that produce the social antagonism dilates to the point of explosion. This dilation is not formal. It can at once be defined with reference to the form of experience and to that of expression. The capitalist innovation of the system of control proceeds in fact beyond the last constitutive threshold proposed in the first displacement, *beyond the subjectification of nullifying command*. Consequently, there *should be no more exposition* here. And in effect there is no longer a *scientific* exposition. The capitalist understanding of command entrusts itself here only to *now-time* (*Jetzt-Zeit*), to aesthetics, to enlightenment – more simply, purely to the *exogenous* mechanisms in force for the reproduction of the system. The capitalist analytic concludes with *catastrophe* as the only possibility for its assemblage of knowledge. Time is not only analytically reduced to zero, but drawn up and exacerbated vertically: from diachrony one passes into *dislocation*.[64] The behavioural axes of the capitalist analytic undergo a definitive hysteresis, they now move in inaccessible regions. Analytic action has reached complete entropy. Therefore, *now-time* (*Jetzt-Zeit*), the messianic and apocalypse are here the only expository form Power can take. Time realizes itself in catastrophe.

The problem of the form of exposition of the other standpoint, the proletarian one, is no less serious. Indeed, as we have frequently underlined, in the expansion of the antagonism one also arrives at a point of no return, and so to a qualitative leap. We call it direct *experience of communism*, of the *collective corporeality of the social proletariat*. But the difficulty of the exposition is no less significant here, because if in the phase of the first displacement the dualistic matrix of the antagonistic relation unfolds its force of recomposition along the line of the dynamics of class, and therefore reorganises, even if only formally, the effects of the pluralistic matrix, when one passes to the second displacement (where the dualistic matrix is completely centrifuged), only the *endogenous solution of the pluralistic matrix*, only the precise reconstitution of the times of subjects can constitute the standpoint. A real standpoint, one that is not catastrophic, but is rather solid and powerful.

This passage from the first to the second displacement leads us to many important considerations. The first concerns what I would call the *overturning* of the asymmetrical *logic of command*. In the whole of the history of political thought *the one* has been pre-eminent and hegemonic over the many. The concept of Power is the concept of the one. The most that can be said is that the many, by coming together, have Power. Our analysis on the other hand shows us the one burning up in *nothingness*, while multiplicity possesses the totality of real time. The higher dignity of the one, that fixes its asymmetrical import over and against the many, is here simply overturned. The second reflection concerns the dynamics of historical innovation, and in particular that of the revolutionary eruptions. Once again the emergence of the one. The wretched Jacobin path of the Revolution, interiorized by the revolutionaries. Enlightenment-terrorism: the innovative link is a blinding light, a *Blitz*. Nor do the theories of continuity, of juridical positivism, alter the framework: the one of voluntarism is substituted with the one of historical profundity, to the Jacobin

Saint-Just responds the institutional and sage Tocqueville. In reality all revolutions have done nothing other than perfect the existing state of things. With Heine we can repeat the three 'R's of *Terrorismus*, of the terrorist equivalence of Richelieu, Robespierre, Rothschild. However, against this and in reality, the real innovation, the real revolution would pass only through the always new social constitution of the time of the exploited multitude, through the continual destruction of the articulations of the one, of command and of abstract unity. Is it possible to definitively affirm this inversion and so point to the overturning of the *asymmetrical practice of innovation?* There will certainly be no revolutionary experience that does not test itself in the practical solution to this hypothesis.

9

Third Displacement: the time of revolution Y

9.1 The time machine

Let us begin by keeping to the results reached so far in our analysis. The series of events that we mark with the letter 'Y' are the ensemble of powers of liberation uncovered in the temporal fabric of life, there where real subsumption is achieved and where the antagonistic alternatives that traverse it explode. Let us take these powers of liberation in the constitutive immediacy, in the productive force and the infinite range – of subjects, of actions – that emanate from them. The method is the rigorous one of materialism where in other words – to the exclusion of any mediation that is not intrinsic to the logic of the subject and of collective action – only the empirical and the a posteriori participate in the category of necessity and only the conventional is universal. How does the time of liberation present itself then? What is its concept?

(a) The concept of liberated time is given as omnilaterality, as universal versatility. Within the massive totality of real subsumption, liberated time is not the residue of exploited time, but is rather the force that breaks up and destroys all the links of capitalist society. It separates them from itself and invests them all. Liberated time is then the concept of a *mass* of versatile, omnilateral, universal relations.

(b) Liberated time is a *productive quality*. It is a productive rationality torn away and isolated from the command that analysed this rationality and extorted it from the time of life. When one says productive quality one is speaking of a surplus, an element of growth, a moment of creation. In Marx all this – though grounded in the foundation of the revolutionary project – constitutes an enigma, one that remains as such only until this creative project is withdrawn from capital's measuring. When this occurs, it then becomes apparent that productive rationality is struggle against work; it is the negative labour that destroys the temporal determinants of 'positive' labour, that is of capital. To the omniversality of liberated time is added the creative characteristic of production: *producing what?* Liberated time, but more – that is against death, against suffering, against the zero of command.

(c) Liberated time is *subjectivity*. Liberation occurs in the form of subjectivity, from the refusal of work to the rediscovery of productive rationality, from self-valorization to auto-determination, from spontaneity to unfolded collective consciousness. The creativity that constituted the hard qualitative core of liberated work is manifested here in the form of imagination and hope. And imagination, integrated with negative labour, is the nature of technico-scientific labour itself – as labour of liberation, as the destruction of unilateral horizons, as polymorphic apparatus of reason, as uprooting of the vile paradigms of reified experience.

(d) Liberated time is *collectivity*. The process of struggle and emancipation, followed by the process of struggle and liberation, have led us to that rational paradox where liberated time is time that cannot be measured, precisely because liberation consists in the destruction of the structural dimensions of time-as-measure. The one schema of organization of liberated time is thus rediscovered in terms of a phenomenology of collective praxis. Love is not of a different nature from collective action, nor from the concept of *productivity* and technico-scientific labour. In the polyvalence and omniversality of liberated labour, only the potentials of collective cohesion change.

(e) Liberated time is a *machine* of constitution. When one says machine one's thoughts race to the idea of physical necessity and to that of fixed capital (= dead labour). Rightly. But that does not take away from the fact that experience and imagination can modify the conceptual relation. Because by machine we here mean *the co-ordinated ensemble* of the characteristics of liberated time signalled under *a, b, c* and *d*, the machine is the *concretion* of the processes of liberation, it is the point at which the substantial trajectories of time converge. The concrete is the subjectivity of social proletarian composition that makes itself the horizon, the surface of totality. All the determinations go on to define the concrete in accordance with the methodological indications of the *1857 Introduction* [Marx 1973], which here, at this second level of displacement, realizes itself completely. Between subjectivity and collectivity, between omniversality and creativity, a strategy of progressively determined relations imposes itself. The dreary de-mystification of God being the thing is not enough for us; we live the project of the thing being God.[65] Our machine of liberated time moves powerfully and with kindness, defining a new world that knows nothing of death.

9.2 Constitution and class struggle

Modern constitutions postulate *peace*. Peace is given as the fundamental value. The Hobbes-Rousseau-Hegel line assumes peace as the foundation: peace as the solution to war. In contractual form in Hobbes; mythical in Rousseau; dialectical in Hegel, peace resolves the state of war that emanates from the multiplicity of interests. But are the concepts of peace and war truly conceptual opposites, so that peace can be considered to be the alternative and the resolution to war? I do not think so. In the tradition of the classics of *materialism* I do not see 'peace' as the opposite and the solution to war, I see life instead.

Peace does not seem to me to be the solution to war but only the mystified value of the victor. If war is violence and destruction of life, the paradox of peace, which appears in the fact that it is taken as the foundation and end of Power, is that in order for it to be efficacious peace ends up confirming war. (It is certainly of no help here to take up the infinite bibliography that concerns the relations of peace/war and the political.) The foundation of the State is peace, in the sense that peace is victory, the legitimated duration of victory given as simulacrum. The foundation of the State is the maintaining of peace as the condition for the legitimate exercise of violence. So *peace is legitimate violence*. Violence is legitimated by the duty of peace. Reactionary thought, in all of its guises, whether bourgeois or socialist, has on these themes given the best proof of itself.

But when we enter into real subsumption, already in the first phase of the displacement, the mystification that makes of peace the fundamental and founding value no longer holds up. The complete socialization of labour and with it of the antagonism, do not allow peace to be considered as lasting horizon and as simulacrum of legitimation. Peace is, at this level of development, war – *simply war*, the everyday solution to a military antagonism. The value 'peace' does not hold up because, like every ideological projection, peace demands to be at least the double, if not a more refined product, of the victory over the enemy. But where is the possibility for this representative (and unitary) duplication in a society completely, *coextensively* involved in antagonism? How is the enemy recognizable when every subject must be partisan? And how is victory recognizable when the relation is stretched across the totality and across the coincidence (coexistence) of antagonism? On the other hand, *in the second displacement*, when separation – even if only as a tendency – begins to be given in physical terms, the word 'peace' rightly ends up having the significance of a symbol on one of the belligerent sides' flags.

The analysis of the time of life and of its ontological paradigms confirms the de-mystification of the concept of peace. The zero time of peace is the homologue of the death time of war. Necessarily. If peace is the consolidation of victory, its time is zero: it is the reproduction of the death of the enemy. The time of the constitutions and the administrations is the execution of the zero time of victory, of pacification. Of course, the valences of constitutional time can vary in intensity: they can go from the constitutional simulation of conflict (in the liturgies of general representation), right up to the legal exercise of warring ferocity (in repressive practices). But the nature of the time lived by the administration and by the constitution is always that of the annihilation of living temporal being.

The time of peace filtered in administration, in constitution, shows itself still in the social organization of work, in the form of time-as-measure of accumulation and of profit. If the bourgeois regimes of yesteryear extolled the ideological form of the time of violence, of pacification and of death, the socialist regimes of times past extolled the material *function* of the empty time of organization and exploitation. But now form and function become one. In this way the barbarity of peace is made essence; the potentiality of death, of destruction of the human race, are intrinsic to the social system as such, and are confronted with the antagonistic proletarian totality in real subsumption. The materialization (and the extension *from* the forms of domestic organization *to* international organization) of this barbarity consists of the *nuclear State*, a force without doubt adequate to the maintaining of peace!

The abolition of the State and of its temporal paradigm (of its values for the organization of the time of life) is the *proletarian constitution*. The proletarian machine of time.

The proletarian constitution of the time of life is to be constructed along two fundamental paths. The first is that which affirms the separation, antagonism and war against the State. This is linked to the *negative force of work*, as the reaffirmation of the value of life, irreducible to that of peace (as its presupposition), and as a continuous definition of strategies of liberation across each juncture, however small, of the events of exploitation. *War* is the reality of the relationship between the proletariat and the State as the exclusive representative of collective capital. Only conventional mechanisms, ones that traverse the entire fabric of society under real subsumption, could determine *paths to a truce*. We cannot speak of peace then, but only of differentiated moments in a permanent civil war. The *bourgeois constitution* is, at best, organization for war: or more correctly, the organization of capitalist development at the highest point of antagonism – the dimension and the control of a permanent civil war. But we have said more than enough about this already.

The second line of construction of *proletarian constitution* is that which takes shape within and from within separation. It sinks its base in the autonomous expression of values: self-valorization, auto-determination, community . . . *Internal mediation follows upon the times of liberation.* Thus it is eminently practical determined liberation – *its necessity is only an a posteriori*. All the definitions of the political as transcendence or as technique, or as simple autonomy, are from this point of view extinct. Mysticism has no place in proletarian constitution. Mediation cannot present itself here other than as constitutive power. The ambit of multiplicity, of difference, which portrays the class context at the level of subsumed society, is anything but undifferentiated or indifferent: it seems banal to repeat it – *it is not*, and everything rests on this. For multiplicity and difference are the *concrete*, and their consistency is *irreversible*. Real mechanisms of composition, structural forms of social composition traverse these differences. (At bottom this is the only sense in which the Gramscian concept of 'hegemony' has still heuristic, if not practical, validity – once it has been subtracted from the ambiguous cultural and representative functions of the party.) It is within this reality that proletarian constitution labours. Prefiguration is *not* then in any sense *utopia*, it is concrete activity. Rigorous materialism brings the tension between actual determination and constitutive project within the fullness of subjects. The time of life, i.e. the ontological practice of lived time, the strategies that traverse it, reveal this prefigurative tension. The temporal machine of proletarian liberation invests the inside and the outside of life, the *soul* and the *body*, and makes them operate – together – collectively, *as collective power*. All transcendence, even logical, is removed. All mediation that is not from the start within the materiality of temporal, collective, productive existence is pure and simple mystification. The problem of mediation within the class is nothing other than the making explicit of the prefigurative tendency, and of its material verification. The practice of negative labour resolves and repudiates the mediatory fixations of the philosophical tradition. The collective imagination constitutes and arranges itself along the trajectories of negative labour.

With this we return to a problem from which the analysis began. That is, to the emergence of the aporia between time-as-measure and time-of-life in relation to the determination of qualified labour, of co-operative and technico-scientific labour. The insolubility of these determinations within the reversible horizon of the theory of value has enabled us to seize upon certain fixed points in order to progress in our analysis, and in order to identify the flow of real time. That which at the start of the analysis was problematic, is now defined. Qualified, complex, co-operative, technico-scientific labour reveals itself to us as collectively constituted real time. But, as we have seen, the collective constitution of real time is negative labour, labour opposed to capitalist time and capitalist command of time. The *time of collective proletarian class struggle* – now dilated to an extraordinary extent by the capitalist subsumption of society and positioned in this extreme dimension as antagonistic coexistence – posited as the *homologation of being itself*. Class constitution is then this same class struggle at the level of ontology. It is the *redounding of war* onto, within and along, the internal lines of the temporal being of the class. It is the demonstration of the constitutive irreversible effects of the activity of negative labour. It is the institutionalization – that is the irreversible concretization – of production in its negative, autonomous, constitutive sense. Institutionality *stands* in the same relation to collective proletarian activity *as* qualified labour, the surplus of valorization linked to co-operation etc., *do* to the working activity of the proletariat. In technico-scientific labour, where frequently a maximum of liberating imagination and a maximum of co-operation are articulated, we can make out the elements of this unfolded proletarian institutionality. Therefore, that which at the beginning was a problematic element (the *surplus-value* which co-operation determines) is now defined as a *constitutive function*. Ontological time, the productive passage of life, is here to be understood as the highest symbol of human dignity: where time is lived constitutively and redeemed in the negativity of class struggle.

Not therefore peace, time-as-measure, the ontological void, but rather life, ontological time and production are constitutional power – living god and not golden calf.

Afterword

For Bruno Valli, Carlo Saronio, Mauro Larghi, Roberto Serafini, Gianmaria Baietta, Toni Liverani: Communist brothers killed within and beyond prison by the functionaries of the dialectic.

When, after many years, replying to the request of old friends/new publishers, I reread these 'Prolegomena on Time', I experienced a variety of feelings. It was, I told myself, both a rich text and a poor one, both learned and incomplete, a 'war machine' fully equipped and defeated. Was it really worth the effort of re-publishing it? It is worthwhile, I replied, if I am able to show, to myself first of all (for I believe my publishers pressed me with some indulgence), that the theoretical blockages of this text are also openings, or rather, that the very theoretical blockage of that period can enable the opening of new outlooks today. It is for this reason that I introduce the new publication of the 'Prolegomena' with a self-critical reflection:[66] it may perhaps help us to translate this incunabulum into everyday language. Others would say: into a revolutionary dialect of postmodernity.

It is first of all a rich text. Though written in prison between 1980 and 1981, it is extraordinarily *switched-on*. That is, it is linked to a contemporary international literature, which, precisely in those years, was interrogating itself on the crisis of the progressive and progressivist conception of time and, at the same time, it comes entirely from within the problems of the movement and is thus linked to the crisis and the re-presentation of its revolutionary expectations and desires. It was then a case of comprehending why the temporal linearity of the socialist outlook was in crisis and how, within the postmodern crisis, communist *desire* [*cupiditas*] (and its 'dystopian' determination) could re-situate itself. Despite the military defeat in Italy, despite the by now definitive collapse of the socialist system in the world, the research path of the movement in 'laboratory Italy' was not yet broken. So that what little of the cultural debate on the concept of time made its way into the prison from outside (the texts of the crisis of French Structuralist Marxism, the journal *Libre*, and those texts of the American Marxist debate which would find their conclusion in Frederic Jameson's *Postmodernism* [1991] some years later, as well as the exceptional contribution to *this* debate of Prigogine and Stengers) was here taken-up and experienced within what was still a coherent research plan in the movement within 'laboratory Italy'.

But what does 'laboratory Italy' mean? It means workshop of theoretical elaboration within the struggles, that is, within the subversive actions of the masses of workers. Naturally, since the workers are placed in a tight relationship with capital (and with the machines and the will which constitute it), the understanding of the struggles, when it is acute – one used to say, *extremely acute* – also describes the movement of capital. An incredible anticipatory capacity in the understanding of capitalist development was then concentrated in antagonistic knowledge. In 'laboratory Italy', the understanding of industry's transition to its post-Fordist forms was being refined; the expectation of the information revolution and its social impact was anticipated; the shift towards the service-led society, towards productive decentralization, was understood in advance and the figure of 'immaterial labour' was elaborated as the hegemonic function of the capitalism to come. But concurrently, the new social activities of productive forces were being analysed with precision and were defined as the 'social worker' and as 'mass intellectuality' – positive achievements which were gathered in the Italian laboratory so as then to be successively verified and theorized on the international level. The strength of struggles is always a surplus of critical intelligence: 'laboratory Italy' was, from the early 1960s to the end of the 1970s, this privileged location.

I am firm in the belief that 'laboratory Italy' was in those years the most important of all those that the worker and subversive point of view had established in the world. If you take into consideration some nevertheless extremely important authors who during that period produced their best analytical works, such as Claus Offe and Jim O'Connor, their analyses were always lacking in that 'second agent' (though considered from the ontological point of view, 'first agent') which is the working class and in general the ensemble of productive labour; so, when looked at as a whole, their analyses appear frighteningly short-sighted in the face of the new configuration of productive subjectivity. Now, it is only *chez nous*, in these 'Prolegomena', but also and above all in other minor and great texts of the many militants of the 'laboratory' of the epoch, that the new subjective reality of the social worker, immaterial, mass intellectual, sprang out from the analysis as the new referent of the materialist analysis, of the antagonistic project.

What I still do not understand is how it was possible, through the cowardliness of the intellectuals, the treachery of the politicians, the self-inflicted harm of the publishers (texts such as these 'Prolegomena' were immediately sent to the pulping plant), to repudiate 'laboratory Italy', that is, to allow that the force of its theoretical results, transfigured into a pitiful image, be expressed, for many years almost entirely, by the 'Censis Reports'.[67] Neutralized, castrated, vulgarized by a political sociology which parodied the literature of the polls. This censorship persists. We have moved from the First to the Second Republic, perhaps, but these effects of intellectual corruption, which are in my opinion much more serious than the 'obvious' effects of the semi-socialist corporative regime of party politics, have not been corrected. Far be it from me to ask the judges of the Republic to deal with this, thereby adding disaster to disaster. And yet there is something that must be rediscovered: intellectual sincerity. It must surely exist somewhere . . .

The richness of the 'Prolegomena on Time' consists simply in its being the summary of the thinking, within the revolutionary movement of the final years of the 1970s, on the transformation of the time of exploitation (no longer reducible to a measure based upon the time of use-value, but) brought into relation with the new forms of social exploitation of labour-power and with the new organization of social temporality. The categories changed, the experience of life changed, the nature of work changed, the quality of exploitation changed, the fight against exploitation changed, the revolutionary project changed, the world and its alternatives changed. Around these changes arose the theoretical problem, and the arborescences of the new temporality were negatively and positively analysed, within a framework that posited antagonism as the fundamental key for the understanding of subjectivities, institutions, and the global structures effected by the transformation. And in the process of constituting itself, the time that qualified the new labour-power was indicated as the time of the constitution of freedom. A constitutive time within which the analytical elements of separation and destruction of the form of life clashed head-on – if the analytic of capital was opposed to the constitutive process of the proletariat, now the analytic of capital was confronted by an 'other time' founded on the constitutive experience of the new movements. They reappropriated the logic (the illogical logic) of development within new dimensions. So many things that today we see in a clear light were, in the half-light of the 'Prolegomena', not only said (the immateriality, the co-operation, the mass intellectuality of labour, etc.), but also constructed as other, as antagonism, as future condition of class struggle. Today that future is present, but 'laboratory Italy' is over. Two great models dominate the world: the service-led society (computerized anarchically and liberalized savagely) of the Anglo-Saxon nations that went through the neoliberal cure; and the 'industrial-info-tech' society which from Japan to Germany seeks to mediate neo-liberalism with some Fordist social equilibrium. Italy and its model, *faute de mieux*, move ever closer to that caricature of the American model that the countries of South East Asia (and now increasingly those of South America) are developing. In Italy, with the disappearance of the balance of forces that define capitalist development when the working class is represented politically, a victorious pseudo-social-democracy seeks violently to efface the memory of the experiences of 'laboratory Italy'. But for the moment these experiences have certainly not been defeated – perhaps only because they are stronger than the control imposed upon them by the politico-formal organization of Power, and without doubt because they extend further than the time of capital.

These things were said in the 'Prolegomena' with a certain degree of clarity (and perhaps with too much impatience with respect to the conditions for a future project). This, however, is what renders this text rich.

But as I said at the beginning, this text is also incomplete. Not so much in its expository framework as in its theoretical development. Certainly this incompleteness is in part due to the history of the text. I worked on it with much effort and dedicated much time to it in the various 'special prisons' in which I found myself living in those years, between 1980 and 1981. Rome, Fossombrone, Palmi, Trani. It was in this last prison that during a fiercely repressed riot all my notebooks were destroyed in the piss and fire of the repressors, for no other reason than that dictated by the revenge of a rabble of cowardly and ignorant prison guards (nevertheless defended by the Public Prosecutors of the Republic who to this day are considered generous and heroic). At that point, stripped of everything, I was again transferred to the special wing of Rebibbia. Here, without any notes other than those fixed in my head, I wrote the 'Prolegomena'. They too risked being pissed on and burnt in that period of prison riots; it did not happen, who knows why. But I do not wish to speak of the text's empirical history so as to diminish its faults, and even less do I wish to justify it from this standpoint. The incompleteness of the text is theoretical.

What does this incompleteness consist in? It consists in the rigidity of the temporal *topoi* identified. The definition of the generic *topos* of 'real subsumption', today we would say of 'postmodernity', was correct. But the rigidity of the antagonistic development of the two tendencies of temporality (capitalist and proletarian) transformed the antagonism into a 'blockage' of the investigation. My concern evidently was to remove any possibility of a dialectical recuperation of the antagonism: to fix the opposition of the temporalities with the aim of breaking with any possible 'synthetic' and 'sublimating' reformist recuperation of the analysis of temporality. But the result became hysterical and led to the blockage of the investigation: indeed, how would it have been possible concretely to open once again the radical *difference* of the subjective and constitutive temporality once it was defined in a sort of symmetry with the analytic temporality of capital? In effect, the only opening left at that point was characterized in ethical terms, and I explored this in my research in the years immediately following (particularly in *Fabbriche del soggetto*, 1987). By that I mean that in the 'Prolegomena', whatever my intentions and the tone of my thinking, I found myself perhaps aping the attitude of *negative dialectics*, a sort of reversed Heideggerianism where the constitutive temporality became *poiesis* which, if not aesthetic, was certainly pitifully ethical. The ontological depth of mass subjective temporality was blocked at the moment in which its *topos* was defined. How is one to explain this drift? Perhaps, in the fullness of defeat and the crushing of all collective logic of struggle, it was a period in which one needed a lot of ethics for resistance.

But is it not too much to affirm the blockage of the investigation when, as underlined above, substantial facts in the new phenomenology of work had been understood or anticipated? But how had this been done? In a sort of symmetry with the development of the temporality of capital. I could repeat as often as I liked that capitalist temporality was destructive and proletarian temporality constitutive – but I failed to demonstrate it other than abstractly, as one would speak of an idea of reason rather than materialistically, by constructing a 'common name',[68] an association – in other words – of constitutive experiences. Yes, the *topos* was identified in a fundamental ontology, but it lacked a *telos*. There was a frame but there was not the figure that animates every representation. There was a geology of temporalities, but there was no genealogy of mass subjectivity. The result was that those same new figures of labour which were identified, from the 'social worker' to 'mass intellectuality', risked a sociological flattening and a quantitative definition – they were incapable of presenting themselves as new paradigms of subjectivity.

So this is what the blockage of the investigation consisted in. But one asks oneself from the start, did not this specific blockage have a positive function? In the end did it not open a new path of investigation?

As far I am concerned the answer is undoubtedly positive. Personally, in the years following this investigation, and particularly after the conclusion of the complementary text mentioned above, *Fabbriche del soggetto*, it is the problematicity internal to the definition of the *topos* of 'real subsumption' (or postmodernity) that motivates the enquiry from *Fine secolo* (Rome, 1989)[69] to *Il Potere Costituente* (Milan 1992),[70] and from *The Labor of Dionysus* (Rome, 1994) to *Empire* (2000) on the one hand; and on the other hand, the work of inquiry into the new technical and political composition of the proletariat conducted essentially around the journal *Futur Antérieur* (which was founded in Paris in 1990).

Each of these investigations dig ever deeper into the ontological radicalism of constitutive time, making it live productively within biopolitics, recomposing brain and affect in the productivity of mass intellectuality and, in general, in the desiring activities of the proletariat in postmodernity. That is to say, they increasingly deepen the constitution of the *telos* within the requalification of the *topos*. That is to say, opening the *topos* to a new 'publicity', which is the action of the multitude, an interlinking and superimposition of social and political struggles, of economic struggles and struggles for rights, and of ethical subversion.

But one can object, why pass through *that* blockage of the investigation which you yourself denounce in order to arrive at these conclusions? Why do you wish to superimpose your personal development on a process of investigation that has independent logical reasons? Why tell stories? The objection is entirely correct and I have no answer to it. With more humility than it is customary to show, I have here made available my personal experience in order to give the reasons for a text of which I am trying to comprehend the utility, and in the light of the republication to which I have been asked to consent. The fact remains that every theoretical encounter has some collective roots and some affinity with the spirit of its era. Also, that that blockage of the investigation, so evident and so serious for me in the 'Prolegomena on Time', represents perhaps the most extreme example of a method of research and political reasoning enduring for thirty years in Italy and perhaps still present today. It is the logic of 'Operaismo', that is to say of the creative Marxism which animated 'laboratory Italy' in which I and a great number of my interlocutors grew up and which still animates what resistance remains to the postmodern tyranny (not only in Italy; on the contrary, increasingly in Europe and elsewhere). My problem today is to work towards (not so much the recording of the blockage of Operaismo, so much as) the expanded reproduction of its power. The critical thinking we are engaged in on the necessity of conjugating a thematics of the *topos* with that of the *telos*, beyond the blockage registered by Operaismo has, therefore, value for general and current proposals. In fact, those old problems are the same as those that are proposed today by: (1) what remains of the old Marxism, and (2) the infinitely more important one, what is reborn on the terrain of class struggle. I mean to say that after *that* blockage there is an epoch. And it is within this epoch that we must move and consciously construct the new temporality. The tension of the blockage is broken and reveals the force the blockage held back. *Thus today it is possible to reconstruct the 'telos' within that 'topos' that presented itself as a blockage.* And if it is not possible, it is desirable. Is there a difference between the possible and the desirable? How is one to measure it without travelling its length?

This path is temporal. It is a discontinuous space that is travelled in a time that has lost all measure, because only linear space can be measured by time. Instead, this space and this time are full of pits, of ravines, of gradients that cannot be explored by Power: they conceal an elusive power of life – one that is constructed. After the symmetrical blockage of split dialectical temporalities, there is the asymmetry of a life that is to be constructed. Jokingly: '*While this Heavenly City is on pilgrimage on earth, it calls out to all peoples and so collects a city of aliens, speaking all languages . . .*' But there is some truth to this: make the logic of Wittgenstein live again in the language of Joyce's *Ulysses* and you will have the same effect. The new temporality here is not therefore 'other' but simply itself. The two temporal series that the 'Prolegomena' describe constitute an explosive paradox: when one lives, only one of the two series remains – making itself autonomous. Benjamin is of interest to us today because he makes the blockage explode. Foucault is of interest to us today because he aims to make his virtual power live, without the need of confronting anything. We like Deleuze and Guattari because they immerse temporality in the autonomy of a thousand plateaus of creativity.

All this finds its place in the great materialist tradition which goes from Machiavelli to Spinoza to Marx and that tells us one thing only: the desire for liberation has an irreducible ontological logic of its own. Immanence is this realm of possibility. Not a classical but an enlightenment *telos*, not renaissance but baroque, not modern but postmodern. A *telos* that literally convulses the *topos* that it traces. And all that surrounds it fades into unreality.

Therefore, if in the 'Prolegomena' presented here there was a blockage of the investigation, this was necessary to liberate it – by pushing it to the limit – from a dialectic of class struggle which, though invigorated by new experiences, resisted the new. Fine, today all this is finished. The necessity has fallen away of confronting the methodologies that, when they did not suffocate, nevertheless impeded the work of construction of a new paradigm of the existent. It is beyond doubt that D'Alema is not Togliatti, nor is Bertinotti[71] an exemplar of the joyous communist left (that of Luxembourg and Durruti): neither the thinking nor the tradition of any of these postmodernists compels us to a confrontation. Credit to the deserving! Salutations to the left! And now let's begin again. We live in the heart of new productive constellations, animated by the articulations of mass intellectuality, shaken in an untimely fashion by the irruption of a new 'publicity'. *The path has been travelled.* The *topos* has itself opened to the *telos*. In order to produce and to express desires and affects of freedom, the immaterial proletariat has no need of either transcendental symmetries, or a machinery opposed to it: it has recovered the tool and has made of language its machine. The sense of constitutive temporality, by disconnecting itself from opposition to the enemy, autonomizes itself and appears here rather as a *medium* between *topos* and *telos*, between a new paradigm and a new practice.

It is to this point that the self-critical consideration of these 'Prolegomena' brings us. In all probability, due to some strange heteronomy of ends that the flavour of time teaches us to appreciate, they have become *prolegomena of something other*. Of what? 'Guess the riddle . . .' In so far as I am competent to speak on this subject, I can only say this: in all probability the virtual is now more powerful than the actual, and the conceptual possible more real than the real. The brain has surpassed the world and, in the antagonistic fashion, is making of it another. One world, one time . . .

May 1997

Kairòs, Alma Venus, Multitudo

Nine lessons to myself

Introduction

This text is born of chance. I was in exile for political reasons. But after more than a decade of peaceful existence I had decided to return to Italy and to prison, faithfully accepting a challenge: I would hand myself over, and the institutions of the Republic would provide an amnesty for all the 'comrades' of the 1970s. (It goes without saying that after I trustingly gave myself up to the law, nothing followed: the republican institutions, and their transcendental foundation are evidently beyond any criteria of loyalty.) I was preparing for this strange event of the return, when a French-American friend of mine suggested I contribute to an issue of his New York magazine on the theme of materialism. He asked me – this at least is how I experienced the situation at that moment in time (what should I call it, a moment of civil passion, or was it suicidal, or delirious?) – to set out the rationale of materialism as the great irreducible 'other' of Power: i.e. as immanent horizon of the tale of the cosmos (Lucretius was my book during this period), but also and above all, as the source of resistance and ethical constitution. An interesting question no doubt, and so topical for me at that moment . . .

So I had begun a lively discussion on materialism with my friend. I know Spinoza; he is well versed in the Enlightenment and Diderot. We were in agreement with the observation that there can be no history of materialism, nor continuity of categories as long as the definition of truth resides in the efficient exercise of a Power founded upon transcendence; in agreement, consequently, that materialism is always repressed because – refusing the transcendental foundation of Power – it is immediately subversive, and therefore, that sustaining it in these conditions (where philosophy is linked to the hangman's sentence, '*he who hides well lives well*') is very difficult. Nevertheless, we also agreed that on the cusp of the twenty-first century, the *dispositifs* of transcendentalism appeared exhausted, the King naked, and his Guard close to a nervous breakdown. We were thus able to repeat the ancient and vigorous incitement: Citizens, one last effort to become materialists! And so to delight in a numinous power: '*. . . delight of men and gods, life-giving Venus* [Alma Venus] . . .'[1]

But how were we to proceed? How was one to invent a history of materialism that went beyond the caricatures that Lange and Bukharin had given it and destroying the interruption that the stake, as well as neo-Kantianism and Diamat had produced? How was one to recompose the theoretical becoming of materialism through the violence of singular events? If only idealism and transcendentalism have a history (given that Power makes history in its image and likeness), how was one to destroy this horrible continuity and overturn this normality? Which is to say: is it possible to array the singular products of the materialist intelligence of the cosmos and of virtue (*virtus*)[2] as a 'war-machine', and project its power against Power?

So that is what was being discussed then, while I was preparing myself to return to prison – and in the meantime, I was carrying out fertile philological incursions into the enchanted islands of materialism with a good dose of irony (that, given the situation, and if what the greatest of materialists said is true, '*Cheerfulness* [hilaritas] *cannot be excessive, but is always good*',[3] did not trouble me).

I was going to prison then, and – in so far as in those places the re-education to virtue is reached through idleness – I asked myself: what is there more idle than to still occupy myself with a little materialism? The old request for an article on 'materialism against Power' tempted me at this point to answer affirmatively to my friend's request. However, I was quite unhappy with the predicament in which I found myself (especially when the loyalty I asked for in return from the republican institutions was not forthcoming); and perhaps, at the start, I was unable to grasp the complex variants of the problem. Working on the subject of 'materialism against Power' I concerned myself with subjects with which I was most familiar, because my habit of reading Spinoza (that I brought with me into my new disciplinary experience) forced them upon me again. That is to say, I saw the materialist ontology of power as the most important thing to be grasped. It was a case then of explaining how today the new ensemble of possibilities established on a postmodern commonality (i.e. on the co-operation and productivity that postmodern individuals experience as the augmentation of their expressive capacity), opened itself at once to an antagonism towards exploitation (which is due to the growing poverty of postmodern Man) and to the constitution of new co-operative constellations (setting out from the postmodern form of loving, that is, from the new form of relationship with the 'other' in the network of production, of social reproduction and of participation in the 'general intellect'). Therefore, I began by writing the three lessons that follow below under the title of '*Alma Venus*'.

But my friend asked more of me, and with persistence he interrogated me as to whether materialism was not above all short of an adequate terminology – indeed, repression renders one aphasic. In other words, should not materialism organize a logic of its own on the same terrain on which its ontology develops. Could materialism be sufficiently logical and logic sufficiently materialist? And so with this programme in mind what will 'concept' mean given the host of idealistic and transcendental reminiscences that characterize it? In materialism the symbol of the common will rather be a 'name', that is, a nominal *dispositif* for the apprehension of the real and the machine of its most general forms – i.e. the 'common name'. But one must construct this name! If materialism recognizes nothing other than a nominalist logical construction, then the 'common name' will be the result of the continual effort of our experience, the fabric of very singular events and acts of will and knowledge proposed in the form of language. Materialist experience is a blade that continually slices through being and assembles it in open arrangements of communication and invention and this is the case in language in particular. In this way any conceptual form that presupposes the whole to the parts and the truth to experience dies, as does every Eleatic fixation of being, and so too every consequent transcendental duplication-mystification of the real which reveals itself to be a logical perversion – a continuous and unbearable tautology. Deleuze has, in the contemporaneity that he opens to the postmodern, banished with enthusiasm and force the abomination of repetition in transcendental logic. For this reason Foucault said, 'this century will be known as Deleuzian' ('Theatrum Philosophicum', in Foucault 2000). But this denunciation is not enough. If indeed the interweaving of logic and transcendentalism reveals itself also as a machination intended to dominate the social, to construct the juridical, fixing a theory of the legitimation of Power in an efficacious practice of execution, then all of this must be gathered up in the refusal. It is once again Foucault who lays the foundations of this critical experience, better still, of this unmasking of that (in our civilization) ancestral Platonism that ignores the right to the real, to the power of the event, and that on the contrary leads everything always back to the 'law' which would come before all other things. I have therefore prefaced '*Alma Venus*' with three lessons on knowing, or rather – better still – on the construction of the common name within the 'immeasurable' of the materialist field.

Here, knowing (an *episteme* and a logic that are within the materialist field) is *kairòs*: the event of knowing, of naming, or rather knowing as singularity, interweaving of logical innovation and ontological creation – *kairòs* is the classical image of the act of releasing the arrow; here in post-modernity, it is the absolutely singular ontological occasion of naming being in the face of the void, anticipating and constructing on the edge of time . . . and so making the name adequate to the event and constructing legitimation, not over or beyond, but within the common. The materialist theory of knowledge is, as occurs in scientific experience, an irreducible construction of being that is both hazardous and absolute. A radical epistemological *displacement*, since the common name, so as to guarantee the conditions of the event, is implanted within the horizon of a fundamental ontology of time, marked by the arrow of time, in the struggle that separates the opening of '*being-to-come*' from the senseless repetition in the void of the 'future'.[4] A new logic then, constructed on/by the will of the common; by its risk, its power, exposed to temporality. In other words, it was a case of forcefully inserting the ontological standpoint into postmodern philosophy, or better still, into the postmodern *experience*. It is for this reason that the reflections on *kairòs*, an extremely singular force of production of temporality, the reverse of the very sad and naked Heideggerian figures of powerlessness, in breaking with every postmodern tautology, renew – on the contrary – Spinoza's desire (*cupiditas*) – *kairòs*, therefore, rediscovered as trace and time of ontological constitution; these reflections became real advances, necessary presuppositions to the argumentation in '*Alma Venus*'.

It is unnecessary to add at this point that a large number of the reflections that I have developed in '*Alma Venus*' and in '*Kairòs*' are directly linked to the theoretical outline and the practical experience of living 'with' and 'beyond Marx' (that is, in the area of historical materialism) that has always guided my philosophical and political thinking, for better and for worse. In particular, the reflections here on temporality and its ontological import, are linked to the work published in 1981 on the constitution of time;[5] and those on the common (and the antinomies of its constitution), to some articles published in 1987 in the book *Fabbriche del soggetto* (a work unknown to most because it appeared at the high point of the repression against the 'real communists', and almost in clandestine form, thanks to comrades from Livorno to whom I owe a fraternal debt of gratitude). In those writings there was a fully developed awareness of the impossibility of retaining, and in any case of defending, the theory of exploitation and of revolution that Marxist orthodoxy imposed in the form of 'value-measure-time'. There was no disgrace in this critique of the theory of value, and it was not an expression of an awareness of defeat: it was an awareness of the temporality turned upside down by the struggles, by the progress of proletarian consciousness and of the military victory of capitalist Power. How could revolutionary passion accompany this rational Marxist spirit? How, taking its lead from the renewal of critique, and its temporal tragedy, could the desire for revolution begin again?

Seeing before me the six lessons in '*Kairòs*' and '*Alma Venus*' finally arranged in order, it seemed at long last possible to tackle this political (and passionate) theme, the importance of which, in metaphysical terms, had provoked and continued to provoke a crisis in all common thought open to the *to-come*. The question was both simple and very difficult to resolve: how is a decision made by the multitude? In materialism this political question is not simply the subjective equivalent of a material and objective *dispositif* that leads to the construction of the 'common name'. It is not that at all: it would be too easy to have this relation there before one, a little angel that watches over us, a 'pineal gland' . . . No, when *Alma Venus* intervenes in *Kairòs* the common will is more than common reason; common decision is more than the common name; the common event is more than any transcendental. If it were not so we would make ourselves the champions of the umpteenth idealist imbroglio and of the falsification of the common in the paper money of 'sovereignty', of its transcendental validation, of the 'general will', along with Hobbes, Rousseau and Hegel: they would present themselves here once again as the unsurpassed limits; the fetishes of the bourgeois conception of Power! No, what is at play here is not the One of the multiple or any other (Straussian) re-exhumation of the ancient; nor, as has been claimed, any reinvention of the modern ideology and miraculous disguise of 'representation'. This game is truly repugnant (and the majority of people, and certainly my readers, understand it as such). On the contrary, here the discussion turns on the formation, the constitution of the common. A necessarily aleatory and savage constitution in the current conditions of Power, but always open, irresistibly open to the arrow of time, always renewed on the edge of being. Here (this is my conjecture in the third group of lessons, '*Multitudo*') the ontological path hooks up again with the political path: because this deciding multitude has a strong resemblance to that which 'in modernity' attempted the adventure of communism and that, for now, 'in postmodernity' expresses itself in 'exodus', the new 'spectral' figure of all communism *to-come*.

From the modern to the postmodern a lot has changed. In the first place the relations of production have changed because labour-power has metamorphosed. In the second place, triumphing over its socialist adversaries and competitors, the capitalist regime has made itself totalitarian and certainly fiercer. And this for the following reason: it no longer produces through factories alone, but makes the whole of society work for its own enrichment; it no longer exploits only workers, but all citizens; it does not pay, but makes others pay it to command and to order society. Capitalism has invested the whole of life; its production is biopolitical; in production, Power is the 'superstructure' of that which stretches out, and is reproduced throughout society. The 'disciplinary system' of social organization has been substituted with the 'system of control' (to use Foucault's terminology).[6] It could not be any other way given that the producer (the worker or proletarian, intellectual or material labour-power) reappropriated the tool of production, which increasingly is called the brain. We said as much above: labour-power has metamorphosed . . . And so how can a revolutionary subjectivity form itself within the multitude of producers? How can this multitude make a decision of resistance and rebellion? How can it develop a strategy of reappropriation? How can the multitude lead a struggle for the self-government of itself? In the biopolitical postmodern, in this phase that sees the transformation and productive enrichment of labour-power, but that on the other hand sees the capitalist exploitation of society as a whole, we thus pose these questions. As for the answers, I certainly do not possess them. But reasoning on '*Multitudo*' after '*Kairòs*' and '*Alma Venus*', probably a few bricks towards the reconstruction of hope (or better, as in '*Alma Venus*', 'dystopia') have been laid.

When I came out of prison ('came out' so to speak, because this story is never ending and hundreds of comrades from the 1970s are still in prison and in exile); when I began once again to frequent (only in the daytime) friends and society (because at night I see only my prison comrades), I did not want to publish this manuscript, the limitations of which I was aware. These 'lessons to myself' seemed to me marked by the inconclusiveness and the sadness of a year inside. I had therefore consigned the manuscript to the shelves . . . Where it would have remained had it not been for something that happened, suddenly, which compelled me to change my mind: a war . . . A war that in one way was like the others, of a terrible banality with its dead from intelligent missiles, the Balkan hatreds provoking ferocious massacres among the poor, the programmed destruction and the spoils of reconstruction. Along with other pretexts . . . But in another way, a war *unlike* all the others: a strange war, they called it a just war, an ethical action, a holy violence . . . I did not understand. One could call it (and so it was called by many western Taliban) transcendentalism in action, war of right. Triumphalist oxymorons. It was enough to leave one speechless. I asked myself how all of this could have happened. Set against the transcendentalist bullying of the western Taliban, the materialist militant failed to understand; even worse, he was unable to explain the 'pre-' modern regression of the political debate and the linguistic barbarism (the rights of man, the justice of the tribunals against the enemy, the beauty of a ground invasion and hand-to-hand combat, etc. etc.) of the refined western Afghans (particularly the Europeans) who were indoctrinating the fighters with the just war rhetoric. I looked back with nostalgia to the Thirty Years War, this oh-so-European tragedy, so rich in consequences, which was so important in determining the vocabulary of modern transcendentalism – I noted: how much more astute had been the seventeenth-century ideologues! Enough, I really had to publish this small text. To give a small contribution to the unmasking of the cruelty and imbecility of the epoch in which we live? Perhaps yes. In any case, that was how I reached the decision to publish this small materialist text, whose premise of struggle is: enough with transcendentalism; and the moral of which, in the end, consists in the answer to the question: will the poor be able to decide the destiny of humanity? That is to say, will the poor be able to decide the common organization that would lead us, not to war, nor to the peace of slaves and the dead, but to the common life of free men and women who produce wealth and who are not tired of living and experiencing eternity? That is, the victory of living labour over every form of dead labour? For materialism, to preach being is to renew it.

In order to draw, from this small book of lessons that I publish here, these conclusions, the reader will surely have to make a big effort. Perhaps someone will reach the end, and these conclusions and be happy. If this happens, this text will not have been begun by chance.

Toni Negri
Rome
6 September 1999

Kairòs

Prolegomena

And I saw a new heaven and a new earth;
for the first heaven and the first earth were passed away;
and there was no more sea.
(*Revelation* 21:1)

The common name

1.1 It is said that: we know concepts, we know through concepts. But the word 'concept' has been abused by too many wars and by very different traditions of interpretation. We substitute the word concept with that of 'name', i.e. with a linguistic sign that we attribute to a thing; and with 'common name' when the things are many and we pretend to represent their common element. Everything has or can have a name, and every set of things, in as much as they are brought together, has or can have a common name.

1.2 Whatever thing I name exists. But it is a case of understanding what form of existence it has. What interests us is that the name calls the thing into existence and that the name and the thing are here. Problems of knowledge are born because my way of naming is chaotic and the things that I call into existence are arrayed confusedly. Being escapes me here. For example, in expressing a name out of the infinite possible ones, my brain gives existence to a thing that is called a 'name'; but at the same time, it does not always bestow existence on a name that calls a thing into existence. And in creating a common name among the infinite possible ones, my brain gives existence to a common thing that is called a 'common name'; but at the same time, it does not always bestow existence on a common name that calls a common *quid* of a set of things into existence. Now, it is precisely that 'at the same time' which provides the name and the common name with its truth, placing name and thing 'precisely here'.

1.3 The name marks something in space. That is the first and most

139

simple experience of naming. At first sight, the common name also appears to emerge from an experience developed in space. The brain *surveys*[7] the world of things and creates the common name for the ensemble of things that are considered, from that height, as common (and frequently are). And yet in both cases, if marking the thing in space (or expressing a common name) did not occur at the same time as the event of the thing (or of the common *quid*), we would not be able to provide the name or the common name with truth.

1.4 Thus, our problem will be that of establishing the conditions of the name (or common name) at the same time as the conditions of the event of the thing named.

2.1 In the transcendental tradition of theories of knowledge that 'at the same time' is not, paradoxically, thought of as a temporal modality. But let us advance beyond this paradox. The idea of time that informs this tradition is completely subjugated by a 'Parmenidean' definition of being; i.e. by the spatial determination of the ontological conditions of the common name. The adequation of the name and thing is certified analytically: the name (and *a fortiori* the common name) is the identity of the thing and of its essence (i.e. that which places the thing outside time). The proposition that establishes the nexus between knowledge and the real, between the act of naming and that which is named, will consequently be true when founded on the identity of subject and predicate. Now 'identity' means that two things are superimposed in space; one thing is placed on top of the other in the same place in space. But there is no 'same place in space'. If there were, every place in space would have to be subtracted from the activity of time.

2.2 This is what occurs in the tradition of classical philosophy, where time is the mobile image of the immobility of being. In this tradition, time is thus an extrinsic modality: it presents itself as illusion or as a measure, never as event, never as a 'this here'.

2.3 The definition of time as an extrinsic modality clashes with the common sense of the moderns. In opposition to the classical tradition, modern transcendental philosophy tries to neutralize the resistance of temporality by pushing the comprehension of the adequate nexus of the thing and the name ('at the same time') towards an originary and fundamental identity that guarantees it, and does so through an infinite process of dialectical inferences. This process is supported by an infinite causality. But this is in turn extrinsic: it removes the thing from being and, on the contrary, would like to drown it in the infinite. That which fails in the Parmenidean hand played is attempted once again by pulling the two aces of causality and the infinite from the sleeves of modern transcendental philosophy.

2.4 Although the subjectivist and phenomenological variants of transcendental philosophy recuperate temporality in internal sense experience, they merely modify the direction of the infinite. From a foundation that precedes and organizes judgement in the form of the infinite, identity projects itself through the force of an indefinite process through which judgement unfolds its pathways.

2.5 From the same perspective, nothing prevents the infinite from being circular. For if the name and the thing are considered adequate only through an infinite referral to identity, and so through an infinite linking of analytic relations, nothing changes if the infinite is represented by the figure of the circle: the tautology will then be assured; or more precisely, it will be reinforced. In postmodernity, in the polar night of a theory of truth founded upon the end of time, the circularity of relations between the name and the thing render the event definitively ephemeral and illusory.

2.6 In whatever way it is thought of, the subordination ('at the same time') of the adequation of the name and the thing to the spatial modality is incapable of capturing the event of the named thing. It removes it, empties it, and annuls it. Considered from the standpoint of classical and transcendental philosophy, and therefore in the guise of analytic judgement, the spatial conditions end up in each case as transcendent, as extrinsic to the event.

3.1 But so what is the 'this here' then? What is the event of adequate naming, i.e. of the real nexus that exists between the act of naming and of the thing named ('at the same time')? It is certainly not the transcendental identity of the subject and the predicate; and it is most definitely not the indefinite projection of this same identity. Both the one and the other bring on a headache. But what is it then?

3.2 In a first realist approach, the 'this here' is the 'this here'. But is this relation not an identity once again? No, it is not: I perceive it as an event. But what is an event? In this first approach to the question, by 'event' I understand the truth (the adequation) of the act of naming and of the thing named when they are produced at the same time. Both are called into existence: in this sense, name and common name constitute an event.

3.3 But does this first realist approach not render us in turn prisoners of a kind of tautology? It will do if, when we analyse the constitution of the common name and when we experience, at the same time, the naming of the thing that appears before us, we fail to recognize that the constitution of the common name is accomplished in the concrete experience itself; at the moment when our temporality (*kairòs*) and the temporality of the thing meet and call a very concrete being into existence (whether it be a case of the name or of the common name). In the name (and *a fortiori* in the common name), this concrete relation between subject and predicate is absolutely singular, that is to say, not ordinary, not repetitive.

3.4 We will see below that the name (and the common name), when generated in temporality (thus presenting itself as a concrete event, as a thing called into existence in the act of naming), takes on corporeal characteristics, for the body is the predicate of any subject that lives in time, i.e. of something that exists in the moment in which it names. When Spinoza defined the 'common notion', when Leibniz constructed the logic of 'contingent truth', there the theory of truth operates in a context of corporeal relations.

3.5 But this first approach, this ensemble of defining experiences, are not yet sufficient to capture the intensity of the 'this here' (of this 'at the same time') that constitutes the event of true[8] knowledge. These experiences, although they possess the consistency of a first form of knowledge, are calm. That is to say static. While the concrete and absolutely singular being of the common name (and of the process that, 'at the same time', generates it), and of its body, are restless.

3.6 From now on we will no longer scrupulously distinguish between the name and the common name, since it is evident that in the common name the characteristics of the event of real knowledge emerge with clarity, and sum up those of the 'name' event.

4.1 Time is restless. The conditions of existence of the event of naming and the thing named, i.e. of the constitution of the common name, are temporal. It is in a temporal context that we establish the relationship between knowledge and being, and their adequation. Thus far we have drawn time into the ontology of knowledge, that is to say, we have made the (temporal) *ratio existendi* resonate within the *ratio cognoscendi*. But we have not yet confronted the central problem of how time establishes itself in the process of knowledge, and that of how the ontology of time participates in the ontology of knowledge.

4.2 We have incorporated into the process of knowledge (of constitution of the common name) a temporal determination: 'at the same time'. That the ontological determination on which the name is established is a *hic temporis* is demonstrated by immediate experience. Yet this immediate experience of time, in so far as it is a simple act of internal awareness of time, does not guarantee knowledge and risks dissolving it; for the immediate apperception of time is a wild state.

4.3 What experience tells us, in as much as it is the immediate witness to the incorporation of knowledge in temporality, is that time is not an envelope or an extrinsic modality of knowledge and, on the contrary, that it plays a part in the constitution of the common name. But how can time and its restless modality incorporate knowledge?

4.4 From the moment the experience of time was integrated into the definition of knowledge, it has been described above all as flux (positively: a vital thrust, a creative force; or negatively: a destiny, an excrement, a corruption). These ontological qualifications, which claim to present themselves as phenomenological forms of the awareness of temporality, demonstrate in each case transcendental stigmata that are incapable of allowing the knowledge of the event. But time is there, in its wild state – because its ambiguity, its evanescence exists as such; the restlessness of time is the real ontological datum. The Augustinian definition of time fits it like a glove.

4.5 What would happen were we to assume the restlessness of time as the ontological fabric of knowledge *in reality*? To do so would mean to take the temporality of being, the sequences of the temporal determinations of knowledge, the *hic temporis* that follow one another savagely in consciousness, as the exclusive fabric of the experience of knowledge – in the ambiguous alternation of consistency and evanescence proper to them, in the intermittent current that illuminates existence. How is one to transform the ontological restlessness of the ontology of temporality into a production of truth?

5.1 In the classical conception of time, *kairòs* is the instant, that is to say, the quality of the time of the instant, the moment of rupture and opening of temporality. It is the present, but a singular and open present. Singular in the decision it expresses with regard to the void it opens upon. *Kairòs* is the modality of time through which being opens itself, attracted by the void at the limit of time, and it thus decides to fill that void. Can it be said that in *kairòs*, naming and the thing named attain existence, 'at the same time', and so are in reality the 'this here'?

5.2 If so *kairòs* will, in the first place, represent that modality of time, that *hic temporis*, that point which excludes absolutely from its definition both the flux and the catastrophe of time. This is a step forward. Better still: if consciousness perceives *kairòs* ambiguously, as 'being on the brink', as 'being on a razor's edge', i.e. as the instant in which the 'archer looses the arrow', then *kairòs* becomes the restlessness of temporality – the name we wanted for that experience. But if it is so, we will then be able to ask ourselves if *kairòs* is not equally real insistence in that point of time defined by the point of the arrow; that is to say, being's act of leaning out over the void of the time *to-come*, i.e. the adventure beyond the edge of time. In third place, we will be able to ask ourselves if *kairòs* is not – *sempliciter* – power to experience temporality.

5.3 I ask myself if this 'at the same time', which qualifies the conditions of existence of the common name and integrates the adequation of the act of naming and the thing named, is not *kairòs*. I ask myself then, whether the event of the common name, in its restless temporality, is not capable of being determined by anything other than the experience of *kairòs*. I ask myself whether the temporality of knowledge is not simply rooted in that modality of the existence in time that is *kairòs*.

5.4 And given that I have until now sought in the ontology of time that moment in which the name calls into existence the named thing, and the thing responds in its concreteness and singularity, I say that the event of real knowledge is produced, in all probability, precisely at the point where the restlessness of time reveals itself as power.

5.5 Thus, if I want to verify my hypothesis, I will have to demonstrate that *kairòs* is power at precisely the moment that the experience of time restlessly observes the edge over which it leans. I will also have to demonstrate that *kairòs* is constitutive at the same moment that the gaze is fixed on the void; that *kairòs* means generation, that it is being (*einai*) in the form of generation (*gignetai*). And I will be certain of it only when, running through the different powers of the common name, I will have demonstrated that knowing the true [*vero*] is watching, expressing, experiencing and living being from the standpoint of *kairòs*, that is, from the standpoint of the instant that finds itself between the accomplishment of time and the opening of the *to-come*.

6.1 First of all: *kairòs* is the instant of verification of the name. For the name presents itself in the vacillation of *kairòs*, and it is through this vacillation that the true is revealed. As Leopardi says, it is in the instant that the young man, vacillating, appropriates the name; and in the same way, he who invents approaches the new; and that the poet, vacillating, fixes the verse. The solution of the vacillation, its necessary decision, is the presentation of the name. This is established from the standpoint of an elementary phenomenology of knowledge, but one that is no less real.

6.2 Every theory of truth has circled around this flash of certainty that is, within *kairòs*, the presentation of the name. But equally, every theory of truth has always avoided placing the mark of the true within this vacillating temporality. It is simply a case of refusing to take time seriously and refusing to submit truth to the ontology of time. (It will be useful to recall that when the phenomenology of internal time consciousness discovers ontology in the vacillation of *kairòs* – in reality, it demands that this vacillation be the precondition of the 'unveiling' of *aletheia*. But the power of truth is not behind, nor in the depth; it is in front, in the risk of vacillation.)

6.3 Secondly: how can one grasp from the ontological standpoint the birth of the name *kairòs*? In the following way. We have said that *kairòs* vacillates between naming and the thing named. But when we observe *kairòs* in this movement, we see that its presence is exposed to that void towards which time makes being precipitate. Why does *kairòs* not precipitate into it? Because it expresses a new being. It is here then, when *kairòs* exposes itself to the void and decides upon it, that the name is born. Through *kairòs*, the ontological affirmation of the name cannot be understood other than as a decision of a new being. In this sense, in *kairòs*, presence is expression. And the name is a product of expression.

6.4 So far we have spoken of the true as adequation of name and thing. How can we now give the 'expression' within *kairòs* a decisive function? It is possible because the ontological perception of *kairòs* poses adequation as an event of generation. The thing, on the edge of being, calls on the act of naming to augment being, in the same way as the name calls the thing to a new singular existence. *Kairòs* is now the arrow that has been released.

6.5 In this sense, our experience of the true has little to do with the static or ecstatic 'intuition' of the spatialized object. The latter is necessarily impotent, because there is no such object. Intuition seeks out essences, it is a game of blindman's buff gone mad, looking agitatedly high and low, always towards the hidden – it is the wandering hand of knowledge. He who wants merely to see, as Max Weber used to say, should go to the cinema.

6.6 On the contrary, here we see how Spinoza's 'common notion' or

Leibniz's 'contingent truth' are endowed with a new light, because here their corporeality can be read in temporal terms when the name is expressed by *kairòs*. These names are full with life.

7.1 In this approach to the theory of truth, contrary to what we find in the classical or modern era, space is subordinated to temporality. To say space is subordinated to time is not to deny the spatial consistency of the name (and of the common name), but rather to define it in its specificity, and in subordination to the modality of time. Therefore the name must have a spatial consistency that cannot be given other than within the constitutive character of time. In other words: if the truth of the name consists in the construction of being beyond the edge of the present, and if its adequation to the thing consists in *generation*, that does not deny a certain spatial form to the name; it will define the truth of the name in the new ontological constitution of time, and not in a static location. But what does this mean exactly? How and where can one grasp the space of the being of temporality, i.e. the location of the truth of the name?

7.2 These observations are essential for the constitution of the common name, which is the central instrument (and operator) of knowledge.

7.3 As we have seen, the truth of a name cannot be given by anything other than its insistence in *kairòs*. Therefore the name has, properly speaking, no place. But a name is said, is heard: it lives in language. In this way it reveals a singular form of spatiality, that of linguistic being. In other words: the name does not ask language for its truth, because it has already asked it of *kairòs*. But in language it finds a place to 'inhabit'.

7.4 But a place to inhabit is always a common place. There is no experience of *kairòs* (that is, from this point of view, the experience of the ontological generation of the name) that is experience of a solitary place. What does the 'common place of the name' mean then? It means that in a place that we call linguistic, an ensemble of names come together. So once it is recalled that the name is an event, the linguistic common place will be defined as the place of the ensemble of events. (But on language and the inhabiting of language we shall speak much more fully in '*Alma Venus*'.)

7.5 *Kairòs* means singularity. But singularities are multiple. So, before a singularity there is always another singularity, and *kairòs* is, so to speak, multiplied in other *kairòs*. When a name is said and heard, when it lives in language, every *kairòs* will be open to other *kairòs* – and all together these events of naming will, in facing one another, in dialogue and perhaps clashing, constitute common names. It is in relation to alterity that the name spills into the common. Here, being reveals itself as *mit-Sein*, as 'being-with'.

7.6 This is the ontological presupposition that enables the move from the name to the common name, from the sign of truth of the name of a thing to the constitution of the common sign of a multiplicity of things. The common name appears here, in a first definition, as the expression of a new spatiality; or better still, as a common territorialization of multiple *kairòs*. But this is only a first definition, one that merely concerns the formal conditions of the constitution of the common name.

8.1 By 'common name' I understand the name that expresses that which is common to many things and so to many names. But in *kairòs*, the name is an event: so the construction of the common name will have to participate in a community of events. These events are given in the present, on the edge of time, that is to say, where temporality opens itself to the *to-come*. The common name is the linguistic event of the community of *kairòs*.

8.2 But the *kairòs* is extended into the *to-come* by definition. The constitution of the common name will thus be carried out in the prolongation of being, in that event of *kairòs* open to the *to-come* that we call 'imagination'. Imagination is not fantasy (which is a modality of memory, as we shall see below). The imagination is a linguistic gesture, hence a common gesture; the gesture which throws a web over the *to-come* so as to know it, construct it, organize it with power.

8.3 The imagination is that power of *kairòs* which has achieved the fullness of its expression. This expression of power is not a foundation, nor something that comes from within, from the deep and the distant; on the contrary, it consists in the recognizing of itself – on the precipice of time – as creator of new being.

8.4 Spinoza has spoken to us of the imagination: he made it function as the power of knowledge that, in vacillating, linked together the forms of knowledge and enabled the passage from one to the other. Consequently, in Spinoza the imagination has the ontological function of recomposing the strata of being.[9] In this way it anticipates from within matter that development of ethical life which leads to the absolute act of knowledge that is love. Modern philosophy from Kant to Heidegger has, in a wretched regression, attempted to translate the ontological imagination into a transcendental imagination, into a schematism that marks out temporal traces of the construction of being. But through the transcendental, the imagination is drowned in the dialectic (whether in its positive or negative form). We must therefore return to Spinoza and rediscover in the imagination not the path that enables us to achieve the synthesis of understanding, but the risk and the love of knowledge, the construction of the common places of the name, of the creative search of the *to-come*. Because being is *kairòs*.

8.5 The common name can therefore be defined as the expression of the common quality of things and, at the same time, as the constructive projection of being into the *to-come*. It is on the one hand a *survey* of the multiplicity of being, and on the other – 'at the same time' – a powerful *kairòs* that constitutes the common in the *to-come*. The *ratio cognoscendi* becomes, through the constitutive imagination that extends into the *to-come*, *ratio fiendi*.

8.6 In Marx the methodology of 'determinate abstraction', which is strictly articulated with the construction of the 'tendency', is linked to this definition of the common name. In Marx the determinations of being can thus be brought to 'abstraction' (to knowledge) only once, through knowledge, determined being is opened to becoming, that is to the power of the 'tendency'. Now my intention in these lessons is to develop a philosophy of *praxis*, a materialism of *praxis*, by insisting on: the dimension of temporality as the ontological fabric of materialism; the affirmative power of being; and the subjectification of becoming (but it should be borne in mind that it will not be referred to as such for much longer). The conception of the common name, innervated by *kairòs*, can already be found within Marx's philosophical project; and it will be precisely through this reference to Marx that we will be driven to search, through the rhythms of the imagination (that we have seen linked to *ratio cognoscendi* and *ratio fiendi*), for the further transition to the *ratio agendi*. Because the imagination is always ethical.

9.1 According to the classical philologists, *kairòs*, after signifying the opening of temporality onto the void, determines its form in relation to the *telos*. But the relation *kairòs/telos* is remarkable, '*auto-teleological*', because *kairòs* cannot but contain within itself its own *telos*. Hence the extension of the definition: in classical thought *kairòs* is the point where *poiesis* and *technè*, by integrating the conscious ends of action within time, constitute *praxis*. In other words: *kairòs* gives practical finality to the common name.

9.2 In the period of *La Grandeur de Marx*,[10] Gilles Deleuze spoke of the common notion (in the case in point, of communism) as the possibility of translating the community of the *episteme* into an ontological common. The common name is the teleological trace (a teleology of the instant, the *telos* of the event) that unites the events in the construction of a community: it is thus the ontological composition of the events that expresses itself as power and imagines itself as reality *to-come*.

9.3 With these two references (to Marx and Deleuze) before us, we find ourselves introduced to the full experience of the power of *kairòs*. *Kairòs* is the power to observe the fullness of temporality at the moment it opens itself onto the void of being, and of seizing this opening as innovation. The common name is situated in the passage (*kairòs*) from fullness to the void: it is a common and imaginative act of production. So the common name is not only the sign of the singular existent in the instant that links the act of naming to the thing named, nor is it solely the seeking of multiplicity in *surveying* over the edge of time. Situated within the power of production of being, it is also the construction of the *telos* of generation. It is this production, that is to say this generation, which we call *praxis*.

9.4 The power of *kairòs*, as the passage from fullness to the void and as production of being on the edge of time, is now the backdrop – better still, the articulation and the schema – of *praxis*. The *ratio agendi* is produced by the *ratio cognoscendi*, and vice versa, only on one condition: it must expose itself within the event. The true rediscovers the connotation of an existence in *praxis*, having recognized itself in the only time in which it can be said: the instant of *kairòs*.

9.5 *Kairòs* is the Christ that empties itself so as to produce new being, it is temporality augmented by expression, it is *praxis* of the common name.

9.6 It is possible to transform the world at the same time as it is interpreted. Here *episteme* and ethics are recomposed once again. Because *kairòs* is, as Aristotle says, 'the virtue of time'.

The immeasurable

1.1 That *kairòs* releases an arrow and that its trajectory is given irreversibly (that is to say that time is traced by the tip of the arrow), everyone seems to admit. But transcendental philosophy denies that the common name also follows the arrow of time. While on the contrary, this is precisely what we lay claim to. But if time, as ontological power, is an arrow, how is the common name articulated with it? What does it mean to say that the act of naming corresponds to the thing named in accordance with the direction of the arrow of time and in relation to its irreversibility?

1.2 The preceding argumentation, in positing the common name as the product of *kairòs*, insisted on the instant that made of the common name the act of a specific production of being. However, one cannot forget (and we have frequently underlined it) that in the production of an always-new reality there reverberates a sort of restlessness in the power of temporality. Even when the common name appears as a *survey* and a search (as we have seen in the analysis of common becoming in knowledge), when it is the product of the imagination, the restless vacillation of its production continues to make itself felt. Restlessness cannot be placated.

1.3 The restless state that the creation of the common name displays through *kairòs* is still more evident if we look at this production from the psychological standpoint. Here, restlessness presents itself as the impossibility of discerning the instants of consciousness one from the other. It follows from this that temporality, broken and rendered creative by *kairòs* in accordance with the arrow of time, appears instead to present itself as the duration between a past and a future. The common name, even as it achieves its reality in *kairòs*, is brought back to testify to a sort of continuous fabric of the *before* and *after*, and not to the creativity of *kairòs*-time and of its irreversible power.

1.4 But if the common name was not shown to be the tip of the arrow of time; if then (with its power left intact) we were to consider the instant of *kairòs* in a kind of continuity with the *before* and the *after*, and made of it the restless bridge of duration, then there would be no possibility of determining the singularity of the common name; and together with the common name, time also would be conceived of as flux and not as power, that is to say, it would be reconstituted as destiny outside the arrow of power. But this definition is refuted by the experience of *kairòs*.

1.5 On the other hand if – as occurs in classical thought – the instant is removed from the definition of time and considered as an element definable only by the ephemeral intuition of a vacillation of becoming (between being and nothingness), all experience determined by the adequacy of the act of naming and the thing named would be rendered inadequate and inconclusive.

1.6 If we wish to give to the common name the direction of the arrow of time and place it in relation to its irreversibility without losing its singularity, it is necessary then that the common name is grasped as an act or *praxis* of temporality. Only in this way will ontology escape the restlessness that traverses it and will knowledge escape from the perception of the ambiguity that makes it vacillate.

2.1 Seen from the perspective of the arrow of time, that is to say of its consistency, *kairòs* is the only real [*vero*] point of ontological irreversibility. It is so because *kairòs* is the force [*vis*] that advances.

2.2 Were we to try and think the 'reversibility' of the arrow of time, we would have to pass by way of the *kairòs* in order to then go back; but this cannot be done. We can thus see the falsity of Zeno's argument, because his argument demands the co-presence of the force of *kairòs* (that advances) and of the sophistic reasoning (that on the other hand moves backwards, and in doing so divides *kairòs*); but equally, we can grasp the aspect of truth of the Eleatic argument, which consists in the destruction of the transcendental idea of the *temps-durée*, in as much as it affirms that only the instant is ontologically real.

2.3 Thus, in *kairòs* the name and the thing named are presented as one and the same reality, which are both expressed by the force of temporality on the edge of time. The expression of *kairòs* is an ontological force. We find ourselves here in the parallelism of Spinoza, where being presents the thing and the idea in the form of a mould (that desire [*conatus*] produces together).

2.4 The common name is therefore a mode of affirmation of being; that is to say, the common name is a force of being, something that constructs new being. For example, if we pass from the adequation of the name and thing to the imaginative expression of the common name, we witness a truly constitutive operation that situates its creative power on the edge of being (in other words, at the tip of the irreversible arrow of time).

2.5 We call this process – that is expression of *kairòs* – 'ontological *praxis* of truth'. To say *praxis* is to say force (*vis*) that constructs, or transforms the thing into the name and the name into the thing.

2.6 In Marx one finds the formula the '*praxis* of truth'.[11] It consists in fixing the truth of that which *praxis* constructs, setting out from the determined (and tendential) expression of a resistance. The true [*vero*] will appear as the affirmation of being that rises up in revolt from within the struggle. Already before Marx, Machiavelli had considered the '*praxis* of truth' as the power to make the virtue (*virtus*) constitutive of the political emerge from the temporal grasping of the moment. It is within this double perspective that we define the *praxis* of truth as the development of the force of *kairòs*.

3.1 The most obvious thing when speaking of time is to divide it into past, present and future. But as soon as we begin to look at time from the point of view of the temporality of *kairòs*, past and future are anything but obvious. Because the only certain ontological consistency is at the tip of the arrow of time, when it buries itself between name and thing (as though they were one and the same), the consistency of that which 'comes before' and that which 'comes after' must be carefully analysed before including the names 'past' and 'future' in our lexicon. Perhaps we will discover we have something different before us from what is commonly intended by these terms.

3.2 Outside of the illumination of *kairòs* and of the force that, by continuously opening up time, constructs new being, the past appears to be that which is 'finished [*finito*] here', while the future appears to be that which from here onwards is 'un-finished' [*in-finito*]. But this first defin-ition of past and future is entirely without consistency. It makes no sense to call that enormous irreversible mass of being that precedes us finished [*finito*], or to call un-finished [*in-finito*] what is not yet. This first definition (and this first error) persists thanks to a kind of obtuse tendency to con-sider past and future not in accordance with the arrow of time but on a homogenous plane. There is a failure to see that, by doing so, time loses its character of irreversibility and *kairòs* its creative force. From this errone-ous perspective, time is reduced to a single extension without gaps that is traversable in every direction – which contradicts the common experience of the irreversibility of the arrow of time. Further, from the perspective we are criticizing, *kairòs* no longer exists as such, because in this time made of extension no creative event can be discovered.

3.3 In the conception of time as *res extensa*, all rests on the Power of a transcendent being who takes away all ontological consistency from time and so any consistency from past and future. One would do well to remember the 'homicidal God' that the mystic Geulincx theorized against Spinozism: God understood as absolute despot, within whose arms there rests the illusion of a well-ordered world, where everything, even horror, is pacifically necessary, and where the past and the future are entirely inscrutable within the constitutive act of the absolute.

3.4 From the point of view of *kairòs*, what is the being that has already been and the being that has not yet come? Which, and what are the names that we give to that which, in the arrow of time, is before *kairòs* and that which is not yet *kairòs*?

4.1 Many see in the name of the 'future' the identical repetition of what has already happened. From this point of view the future means that which persists. And even when others see the future as a progression that modifies the conditions of arrival in comparison to those of departure, it is still the case (with greater or lesser variations) that the future will be a positive or negative – but continuous – reproduction of itself. On the other hand, all the forms in which predictions of the future are attempted are in some manner statistical, which is to say that they are the study of the repetitions and of the constants to which (or to whose measure) any exception is reduced. The same can be said for all forms of future-orientated normative prescriptions (those of the form: 'you must, therefore you have to') that are always the result of the hypostasis of the principles derived from what has already happened. For the most part, therefore, the future is future duration. The restlessness of time is subjected to the continuity of space.

4.2 In so far as it is future duration, the future is the vision that lies at the base of technologies, whether those of the hard science, or of the human or normative sciences. In this case also, the temporal a posteriori is reduced to the norms of the a priori spatial calculus. The progress of technologies is translated into the ever-increasing presumption of the prefiguration of the future. But that is not the way things are, and indeed the foreseeing of that which will be is only valid when it springs from the *praxis* of *kairòs* and constitutes itself – as we shall see – in the temporality of its tool.

4.3 Desire also invests the future: we call it utopia. But it invests the *to-come* in an ambiguous manner: in fact, on the one hand, it proposes the spatial homology of the past; on the other hand, it overtakes it in the imaginative expression of desire. In general, however, utopia cannot present itself as the name of the *to-come*, because (even when it does not repeat the continuity of the spatial figure) desire presents itself here as spatial distance (non-*topos*, but still place).

4.4 In all and each of these cases what is missing is the apperception of the creative moment that establishes that which is yet to arrive. In the perspective we are criticizing (and which seems to us to be the most widely held), 'future' is a mystified, erroneous name. On the contrary, we give the name of '*to-come*' to the horizon of experimentation of the adequation of the name and the thing, and to the imaginative perspective that – in realizing itself – presents itself as new being. The passage to the *to-come* is always a difference, a creative leap. Repetition, and with it duration, are de-structured by the current experience of the *to-come*, and the real is in this way comprehended in a new manner in the making of *kairòs*.

4.5 We will define the time that is coming as the *to-come*; and the *to-come* as ontological constitution in action; and the common name *'to-come'* we will define as the expression of the force of invention (that is to say, as the *vis* of *kairòs*).

4.6 The everyday sense of life confirms the definition of that 'which is coming' as *to-come*, rather than as future. It is indeed in the struggle for the free appropriation of the present that life opens itself to the *to-come*; and desire perceives – against the empty and homogenous time in which all is equal (including, and in particular, the future) – the creative power of *praxis*. If life is not based on this active experience of the *to-come*, it cannot be called life. The same goes for technologies and sciences: it is not a case of little spatial machines made to dominate the future; on the contrary, they are placed in being and innovated in their efficacy by the activity of the common name as *praxis* (by the *vis* of *kairòs*). Sciences and technologies are the tools of *kairòs*, they are born and develop within life and produce the *to-come* on the edge of time (but we will discuss all this in later lessons).

5.1 In the same way, when I consider the name 'past', I also usually find myself before the erroneous idea of time past as extension, and that is in the image of a dead, finite time distended in duration. I therefore understand why 'past' is, for the majority of people, only the name of destruction and death. When understood as such, the past is – in effect – the enemy of *kairòs*-time. From the moment Aristotle said: 'Time is in itself above all cause of corruption, because it is the number of movement and movement puts the existent outside of itself', the philosophers have been able to lead us into error concerning that which has been, because in such a way time would be considered – *simpliciter* – as a duration that comes to an end through corruption, as a number that expels existence from being. On the contrary, I cannot conceive of time other than as *kairòs*, and so never as corruption and death. In other words: the past is normally conceived of as the accumulation of the destruction of physical events. But to think that temporality could have 'destruction' as its name is meaningless, because the temporality that we experience and that we live through is that of *kairòs* and of the creative act that constitutes it – and only that. In being, 'all is created and nothing is destroyed' within the immediacy of the present.

5.2 The 'past' of man constitutes his history. When I consider the name 'past' in this acceptation, I normally find myself before the erroneous idea of a continuous genesis of the present, extended along an – ordered or not, it changes nothing – sedimentation of concluded human events. But to consider what has occurred before us as the sedimentation of time traversed without recuperating – moment by moment, point by point – the vitality which created it, and of the monads of *kairòs* that are expressed in it, goes against our experience of temporality, which is precisely that of it as creative force.

5.3 Men and women amuse themselves in making history (historiography), interpreting (they say) the past, falsely imagining the time that went before them as accumulated according to a cemetery-like order. But there is no possibility of immersing oneself in that being which comes before, if not by illuminating it with the present, reconstructing it and feeling it live in the present. In other words, the common name of historical *praxis* cannot but be a 'genealogy of the present', that is, an imagination that brings to being that which 'came before' in the same manner as it constitutes the *to-come*. One does not interpret the past; one tests it out.

5.4 It is the innovation brought about by *kairòs* that produces the world, that is to say, that produces the being that comes 'before' as it produces that which comes 'after'. (Every instant of life, of that which has been and of that which will be, is a creative act.) Innovation, i.e. the creative force of the name, is always singular and determinate; considered from the point of view of this being and of its intensity there is no first and no last, no past and no future. Consequently, there is no 'becoming' in the past or in the future, but only the act of naming what has been and that which is yet to come. When we use the erroneous name 'becoming', we lose the sense of temporality, of its living pulsation: not transformation (i.e. becoming) as a bad infinite, as indetermination – before or after – but as the emergence of differences, of determinate moments of *kairòs* and of the power to name them.

5.5 We will then give the name 'eternal' to the time that is 'before'. Eternity is the time that comes 'before'. It is indeed the power of accumulated life, of an irreversible and indestructible temporality; it is the common name of the being that is. Every *kairòs* is installed in this eternity.

5.6 What we are saying – i.e. that *kairòs* is installed in the eternal, that is in the time that comes 'before' – does not push *kairòs* into the past, but rather it renders the eternal present to the present of *kairòs*. The 'here' of *kairòs* is not detached from the 'here' of the eternal; there is no order by which its temporal distance can be measured; neither is it possible to think a sort of contemporaneity of *kairòs* and of the eternal: for the eternal is a consisting in the place of *kairòs*, a simultaneous consisting.[12]

6.1 How can the common name of the eternal be expressed? In what way are we in the eternal? In the first place: we cannot think of that indestructible being which precedes us in 'equivocal' terms, i.e. as though it were different in nature from that which we express. The eternal is not different from *kairòs*-being: *kairòs* is difference, but only in as much as it prolongs the eternal, increases and innovates it on the edge of lived temporality. If eternal being were ontologically other, it would present itself as an envelope of a different nature, a 'container' of present temporality (i.e. of the temporality that possesses expressive power). But that is contrary to our perception of what has been, as the genealogy of that which is. And we are in the eternal and we perceive it as the power of that which is.

6.2 In the second place: the indestructible being that precedes us cannot even be thought of in 'analogical' terms, as though it were a first foundation, an eternal temporal substance of which our experience of time simply carries a trace. For we have already seen that our relation to that which was is not a relation to something other. But neither is it a climbing back up an infinite chain of relations at the end of which – precisely because it is infinite – our reason is forced to postulate something other simply to get its bearings. On the contrary, thinking the eternal means simply to install *kairòs* in an indestructible mass of life, that is to say, in the mass of being that has in turn realized itself under the aegis of *kairòs*, and that only the genealogy of the present – through *kairòs* – has been able to actualize.

6.3 From the ontological standpoint, the analogy of being (a key procedure of theological thought) is a 'weak' form of the transcendental 'dialectic'. In effect, while the dialectic, by operating on the infinite in a discontinuous manner (which is modelled on the discontinuity of the world), produces a hierarchy of consistencies of being that are sublimated in the eternal (in the absolute), the analogical procedure, by separating immediately the infinite and the eternal from the finite and time, gives a weak consistency to time ('time is the mobile image of eternity') and gives the world a degree ontologically subordinate to that of the absolute.

Therefore, the dialectic and *analogia entis* operate on the same level (analogy is a static dialectic, dialectic is analogy in movement), but analogy gives weaker answers to the insatiable transcendental hunger of the absolute. It remains the case that by concentrating on the absolute none of these conceptions can accept the simplest thing: that it is the finite that augments the absolute and it is *kairòs* that enables the power of the eternal to breath.

6.4 To be in the eternal means to be in 'production'. The majority of philosophers have considered time in relation to movement; and the definition of time was always tied to that of becoming and to the idea of the infinite, which together constitute the principle of the spatial modality of understanding being. On the other hand, experience enables us to think the eternal not in accordance with the modality of space, but in accordance with that of temporality; not on the basis of the infinite, but on that of the presence of *kairòs*; not as the 'movement that places the existent outside of itself', but as production that places existence within itself. So, on the basis of this consistency, we can construct a *praxis* of truth that produces the eternal.

6.5 *Kairòs* rests then in the eternal. Better still: *kairòs* is the eternal that creates. This eternal is prior to us, because it is at its edge that we create and that we augment being, that is to say, eternity. All that *kairòs* opens is eternal. And so we are at once responsible for eternity and for producing it.

7.1 If the 'before' is eternal and the 'after' is *to-come*, time – in the arrow that constitutes it – is the immeasurableness of production between this 'before' and this 'after'.

7.2 When one says immeasurable, one is saying neither indefinite, nor indeterminate. We have already seen why the construction of the common name cannot have at its foundation an undefined process of knowing, because the adequation of the name and of the thing is fixed by the expression 'at the same time', of a 'this here'. For the same reason the construction of a common name cannot be indeterminate: the product of the expression of *kairòs* is indeed always singular (the *hæcceitas*).

7.3 The following problem thus becomes increasingly pressing: how can the ontology of expression (when *kairòs* opens itself to the void that exposes the eternal power of invention of the *to-come*) configure itself as finite and determined production in the immeasurable? If the creative act of *kairòs*, which qualifies being each time ('at the same time'), is a leap into the new, and if this leap is immeasurable, the definition is without question problematic. (Nor can its problematic character be attenuated through the analysis of the *praxis* of *kairòs* as 'auto-teleological' activity. This would merely serve to displace the problem.) It is a case then of deepening our understanding, within the modes of temporality, of the relationship that exists between the vertiginous *topos* in which being is created, and the *telos* that self-organizes this production. This 'deepening' can only be carried further and reach a conclusion in the next group of these lessons: in the chapter '*Alma Venus*' we will try and grasp the force that constitutes the common form of the common name.

7.4 In the remainder of this chapter we need to understand how it is possible to construct an ontological enquiry within this immeasurable passage, or rather, how its presuppositions can be guaranteed. Where does he who describes the immeasurable place himself? What stage of things corresponds to the regime of definition of the immeasurable? What, then, is the terrain of ontological enquiry of materialism?

The materialist field

1.1 The problem is to define the field in which the enunciations of knowledge correspond to states of things (or events). That this determination is problematic is amply demonstrated by the restless vacillation that characterizes the constitutive relationship of the common name in the immeasurable opening of *kairòs*. What then is the body of the common truths when the names, in making themselves common, expose themselves to the risk of the *to-come*? That is, when the consistency of that which has been opens itself, through *kairòs*, to an always new experimentation?

1.2 The problem is posed in a paradoxical manner by the theory of scientific mutations when they observe the crises and transformations of the great scientific paradigms. When an old scientific paradigm breaks up and a new paradigm comes to light, the enunciations proper to the first paradigm are incommensurable with the second. This is obvious because it relates to that which has been. Only in the action of *kairòs*, in the genealogy of that which is present, will the preceding state of things become comprehensible once again. But this historical problematic of knowledge and its eventual solution becomes less clear when, instead of to that which was, one looks to that which is about to be. When one looks forward rather than back, it is innovation itself, that which is about to be, that appears incommensurable with the preceding dimensions of being. The novelty of the new state of things produced by 'action on the edge of being' reveals itself, in itself, to be irreducible to every previous enunciation. That is to say that knowledge exhibits the immeasurability of its self-affirmation in the experience of innovation; or better still, it exhibits the immeasurability in which it is given, between the eternal and innovation. And this signals the restlessness of knowing.

1.3 The logicians tell us that there is no fact of importance capable of establishing what any linguistic term refers to. They also tell us that the only way to translate language and things, and to give a determination to this translation, is by means of an 'existential quantifier' (i.e. through the affirmation that 'something exists such that a name' is adequate to a state of affairs, a regime of enunciation to a field of a state of things). It is therefore necessary to say it 'exists'. Paradoxically, the logicians must then accept the truth of *kairòs* in the form of ontology. This fact, far from suppressing the restless vacillation of *kairòs*, renders it even more evident.

1.4 If we were to continue to consider the ontological determination solely within the trajectories of different *kairòs* (of the monads of *kairòs*), we would not have the possibility of *positively undergoing* the restless vacillation of *kairòs*, despite knowing that it is within it that truth is determined. In the rupture of temporality between the eternal and innovation it is therefore necessary to take into consideration the ensemble of events and define it as the material field of *kairòs*. This field is the only 'place' (but always 'place of temporality') where univocal being presents itself as productive; it is the materialist field, where to formulate the predicates of being is to innovate it.

1.5 In order to affirm the common name within the immeasurable, we must seize the ever-new emergence of a force of predication of being that is materially able to say: 'this is here'. This does not suppress restlessness, the 'Pyrrhonist temptation' and the consequent vacillation of phenomenological consciousness, but it permits one to resist it. The materialist field is this field of resistance.

2.1 The material field of the production of being is corporeal. We have in fact defined the body as the predicate of any subject that is (or affirms itself to be) in time; that is to say, that exists at the moment in which it names. The ensemble of bodies is the world, i.e. the material field of the production of being.

2.2 There is no reason, however, to consider the ensemble of bodies as less restless than the different *kairòs*, the monads of *kairòs*. In itself, the corporeal constitution of the material field of *kairòs* takes nothing away from the restless vacillation of knowledge; on the contrary, it returns it fully to the immeasurable. In order to overcome this situation (that seems to be a logical brain-teaser), the analysis will have to penetrate into the mode of production of the world in so far as it is the expression of the common name, which is what we shall attempt to do in the following group of lessons ('*Alma Venus*'). Here, however, it seems important for us to try and get accustomed to considering the corporeality of *kairòs* within the immeasurability of the world. To proceed in this way is to begin to employ that materialist ascesis that enables one to perceive the unity of the subject and the predicate within the body.

2.3 The analytic/synthetic distinction rightly fell under the blows of the contemporary critique of language (and of scientific understanding). A conceptually valid enquiry is just as fallible as are all other (empirical) affirmations that change with time. The construction of knowledge in the materialist field thus considers the name and common name in accordance with the restlessness of temporality. And if this most certainly dissolves the illusion that there exists, in absolute terms, correct sequences of thought, it does not remove from the affirmation of *kairòs* the corporeal intensity of being true. Pascal's 'reed' is the best metaphor of the materialist field and of the truth that lives within it.

2.4 Pascal's reed bends under the wind of the eternal but, in so far as it recognizes its fragile existence, it affirms the dignity of knowledge. Leopardi's *broom* vacillates, interpreting the same character in the *theatrum mundi*. But these citations would be without interest were we not to relate them to that common paradigm represented by Machiavelli's *The Prince*, in which the dignity of resisting the world and destiny take on the form of a virtue [*virtus*]. That is to say, it appears as constitutive power of the world: once one has escaped the transcendental chimeras, there is no other way to affirm the consistency of being than by posing its powerful insistence in the shade of the eternal. This, and only this, is materialism (certainly not those philosophies that apologize for the empirical, nor those that paradoxically conceive of matter as a great transcendental 'envelope'). From another point of view, Spinoza's common notions and Leibniz's contingent truths also undergo this same transfiguration: indeed, in accordance with the overcoming of the division between analytic and synthetic judgement, they propose a productive qualification of univocal being.

2.5 The materialist field is productive. Its production traverses flesh, desire, and the generation of the common name expressed by *kairòs*. We are within this production because we cannot be anywhere else but in the body. But at the same time, we measure ourselves against an enormous expressive power. Retracing our steps we ask: where can we situate ourselves in order to reflect upon this immersion of ours in constitutive material being? How is it possible to recognize oneself in the corporeal consistency of being, by conducting an ontological enquiry that brings us back continually to the power of *kairòs* intended as *praxis* of the true and as production of subjectivity? In the materialist field, where does he who conducts the ontological enquiry situate himself?

3.1 When the question of the ontological enquiry into the materialist field is posed, it is necessary to bear in mind that certain paths open up that cannot be followed because they propose a forceful distinction between the corporeal field of knowledge and the reflection that operates within this field. We will discuss some of these errors below. Consequently, in order to legitimize our enquiry into the materialist field, we must on the one hand confront reflection, in its autonomy, with the world; and on the other hand we must guarantee that, by this action, reflection does not lose the intensity of its insertion in *kairòs* that gives reflection its form. It is nonetheless difficult to accomplish this exercise of reflection, even when we act with all the necessary precautions, because the materialist field of knowledge is always restless. If we want to succeed, we must then call upon the reverse ascesis of which we have spoken, and to which we may perhaps become accustomed: it enables one to lift one's head higher, to see better, but only, paradoxically, through the corporeal immersion in the materialist field.

3.2 From this perspective, the pure and simple verification of a name through its presentation in *kairòs* does not appear to allow one to establish the conditions for a reflection that opens itself to the whole materialist field in a productive manner. I will here once again pick up the paradox of the logicians who say: when I affirm that something is here, thus when I verify a name, I have no adequate criteria to establish if I am speaking of this thing here or if I am speaking of the rest of the world excluding this particular thing here. It is evident then that, in order to fix the 'here' in relation to the field (and vice versa), in order to give meaning to the name, I need to identify a way of passing from the 'here' to the field (and vice versa), and that to this end, the sole experience of verification of the name through *kairòs* is not sufficient.

3.3 The philosophies of the subject place the determination of the meaning 'here' (in the materialist field) in the act of knowing that perceives and reflects. But this epistemological pre-eminence of the subject, this ontological supremacy of the subject, is the product of a transcendental illusion and is immediately in contradiction with the ontological experience of *kairòs*. For subjectivity is not something that subsists: it is – on the contrary – produced by *kairòs*, and (as we shall see) depends on the connection of monads of *kairòs*. Subjectivity is not before but after *kairòs*. Subjectivity, should one attempt to construct it, is not identifiable other than through the path that leads from the 'here' to the materialist field, and it is precisely on this route that it is produced. Thus, the recourse to subjectivity cannot enable one to locate the production of reflective sense in the materialist field.

3.4 Can we accord to 'good sense' the capacity to follow the path of reflection along the line of separation of *kairòs* and the corporeal field of knowledge, when we know that it is a case of an immeasurable separation? Good sense could indeed represent a useful tool for epistemological enquiry, if it were not for the fact that it is, as is well known, the most equally distributed of things among men.[13] But, precisely because it is so distributed, you will not find a single good sense that corresponds to another. What's more (with the passing of the centuries, from Descartes to today) it is a virtue that has become increasingly less popular: good sense has today become bourgeois popular opinion, and as such it fears above all else the void and the immeasurable, which are the conditions in which the truth of being is created.

3.5 Therefore, one must dig deeper in order to situate reflection within the materialist field of *kairòs*. But to dig deeper is to advance further. One must situate the definition of the field of reflection (that the paradoxical turning upside down of the figures of determination by the logicians, the pretentious adoption of subjectivity of the transcendentalists, the timid aporias of good sense are unable to understand) within that process which constitutes the body of the immeasurable.

4.1 If ontological reflection on the materialist field is posed by *kairòs*, and if it is the body that carries out this reflection, it will have to first accept the immeasurability that exists between the eternal and the *to-come*. In fact, the corporeal field of ontological reflection is eternal and the field that is determined by *kairòs* is absolutely open. But if the body is the 'bearer' (*Träger*) of *kairòs*, it will not be easy for it to sustain this relationship. Yet it does so because the body, in so far as it is power of determination that lives in the singularity of the materialist field, is as though nourished by the gap that generates the immeasurable. As we have seen, the key to the production of new being is indeed located in the gap of ontological temporality. The body reacts to the gap by producing new being. Given that the body is inserted in the materialist field of the eternal, it leads the eternal itself – the eternal in its entirety and entirely in the single instant – to the gap and regenerates it, testing itself out – itself, as body – in the form of a *praxis* of time. In the first place, the corporeal reflection is thus an ontological immersion that activates the eternal through its opening on the edge of being, on the point of the *to-come*.

4.2 We can thus say that: when the body reflects, it is on the one hand immersed in a material field (the 'before'), and on the other hand that it is open to innovation (the 'after'). If the before is the eternal and the after is the *to-come*, the body reflects the eternal by putting it in contact with the *to-come*, because even if this relationship is immeasurable, it is still, at the same time, production.

4.3 Through the analysis of the genesis of the common name, we have come to define it in terms of expression and imagination. We have considered expression as the constructive experience of that which is common to many things, and imagination as the gesture of that which, as power, throws a net over the *to-come* so as to construct it. In this way we have underlined the co-presence of expression and imagination in the action of *kairòs*. If we bring this ensemble of power back to a reflection on the body in the materialist field, we give *kairòs* a corporeal form, we give it weight and colour, that is to say we consider the body as the incarnation of *kairòs*. Expression and imagination are elements of the body because they are elements of the common name.

4.4 Spinoza said, 'No one has yet determined the power of the body' (*Ethics*, Part III, P2, Scholium).[14] The Dutch philosopher attributed to the body the power of the idea, and affirmed of the idea and of the body the ability to exist together, as parallels that overlie one another in the play of expression and imagination. If expression creates, it is the imagination that gives to the body the strength to go beyond, up to the highest level of knowledge. In Spinoza bodily experience finds itself living the process of the totality of being through the imagination. In such a way Spinoza demonstrates that the body is always positive, because it is the form of the affirmative power of being. What would materialism consist in if not in this primacy of the body in the field of being?

4.5 It is by following Spinoza that we become able to give to reflection (and to the material field to which it is applied, and to the *to-come* that it opens) the consistency of an act of passion, where reason and affect are joined together. In effect, the corporeal *kairòs* is production of being and of bodies, but when it is the body that produces, it does so through love, which is the father of all passions and is in turn knowledge. So that love is reason itself that produces through the common name, and reflection (that corresponds to the ontological conditions that permit the power of the common name) is always amorous.

4.6 So through the body, and without losing any of its power to construct in the instant, *kairòs* buries itself in the materialist field. So through the body, the common name finds itself in the materialist field without losing any of its power to throw a net of knowledge over the *to-come*. And so through the body, reflection, which is hoisted up to a point that is always situated on the edge of time, has the capacity to seize the materialist field, and to illuminate it with passion (as we shall see in '*Alma Venus*').

5.1 To the question as to where he who conducts the ontological enquiry situates himself, we have so far elaborated the following answer: within the force of predication that nourishes and regenerates the ontological field, opening itself to the *to-come*. The act of reflection presents itself as follows: it is corporeal, a singular incarnation; it suffers from the immeasurbility of production that lies between what has been and what will be, and that, for this reason, creates the material field of reflection.

5.2 The act of reflection is *praxis*, a production of bodies. However, this opening to the materialist field is not a pragmatism; or rather, it is also 'pragmatism', that is to say the practice (and theory) of a reflective act that realizes itself in production, that renews the past in the present through a projection of practical sense, and finally, that charges production with utility and value with affectivity. But it is not only pragmatism, because, even in its richest traditions (those of Dewey and Peirce), it did not dare to confront explicitly the *praxis* of the true, to confront the creative power of being. On the contrary, here we have advanced a definition of the materialist field that, constructing itself in accordance with the arrow of time, always reveals the immeasurable that breaks the tranquillity of that which has been (of the mass of events, of the eternal) and offers it up to the hazardous production of the *to-come*. Materialism is revolutionary because truth 'without ornament' is an engagement in being. On the other hand, pragmatism, in its tranquil moderation, retains its ornaments.

5.3 Marx established the distinction between constant capital and variable capital. The first is the ensemble of material and technical elements accumulated by production and conserved in its development; the second is the living labour that regenerates that which has been accumulated (existing as latent in accumulation) and makes of this the basis of a new valorization. But this distinction does not only concern the capitalist mode of production. Rather, it concerns the materialist field in its entirety, that is to say, the world. Production constructs the world following a trace of which temporality is the substance. Dead labour, the finished time of creation, continues to accumulate on the 'before' of this process; the 'after' is represented by living labour, that is, by the *kairòs* of bodies that create truths through *praxis*. On the edge of being, living labour is thus the power of the world, of that which has already been (and that remains there in a constant manner), and which is now regenerated by that which will appear from the work of creative living labour. It is here that the metaphysics of materialism finds its basis as well as its centre: in recognizing that the capitalist process has subsumed the world, turning it into a dead creature, and that on the contrary living labour is *kairòs*, the restless creator of the *to-come*. And as we shall see in the chapter '*Multitudo*', living labour takes the world in hand, transforming and innovating it radically in the common.

5.4 Thus, in the materialist field, the ontological enquiry is entirely within the productive dynamic. Here there is no name that is not adequate to the event, nor event that is not creative within the arrow of time. And this act of birth of creative materialism turns back to what came 'before', to that which it created earlier, so as to give it life. Reflection *surveys* that which has been (and eternally is), opening itself to a time *to-come* – new being, constructed each instant, and that augments and enriches the eternal. The materialist field is all this at once; and reflection (the point of view of he who carries out the enquiry) is given where the immeasurable that exists between what was accumulated before us and what is created by us for the *to-come* is revealed. He who conducts the ontological enquiry expresses living labour, new power of temporality.

5.5 But why are we so keen to define this field as materialist? Is not materialism fundamentally a philosophical tradition that has always been bewitched by spatiality and has been a prisoner of extension, and so has little to do with the act constitutive of a materialism of time or of a temporality of matter? Certainly modern philosophy, from Machiavelli to Spinoza to Marx, constructed the premises for a new definition of materialism, but what utility is there in presenting once again this minoritarian thread of modernity? And yet it is of great importance to us that we fix this birth of a creative materialism as well as the definition of a new materialist field, even if for the moment it only allows us one point of view to reflect on the world – one that is nonetheless compatible with the constructive power of *kairòs*.

6.1 Why is there no history of materialism? Because, in the history of thought, materialism has always been defined by its adversary, which – in the history of Power – always triumphed over it. Transcendence and transcendentalism have a history because they have always been the philosophy of the victors and hence of those who command. There is no space, no tradition, nor any duration for those who lose. The philosophy of those in Power always leaves a string of catastrophes before the eyes of materialism. Yet it is forced to allow materialism to present itself as a problem. In effect, he who rebels poses a problem, and *kairòs* loves those who rebel.

6.2 In classical philosophy, matter 'is not'. That is how the heritage of Platonism defines it. In modern philosophy matter is defined as the limit of phenomenal knowledge: it is like saying of matter, 'if it existed, it would not be knowable'. Finally, in postmodern thought, the very possibility of its being expressed in language is removed from matter. It is like saying of matter, 'if it were knowable, it would not be communicable'. The old materialist sophism has thus been distorted and turned into a historiographical refrain of idealist metaphysics.

6.3 But the most ignoble thing is when materialism is plundered and violated by idealism from within the materialist field itself. Then, instead of making it live as immeasurable creativity, the philosophers, as good geometers of Power, do their utmost to stake out and measure the materialist field and make matter dance to the rhythm of their logics. The extreme case of this brutalism was in the wretched time in which materialism was taught as 'dialectical materialism'.

6.4 Materialism always rises anew and penetrates the history of thought in the most underhand (from the point of view of the academic Inquisition) and subversive ways (from the point of view of the science of Policing). In this new resurgence, materialism continuously breaks with the thinking of Power: it is Machiavelli, Spinoza, Marx, the common thought of the struggles. The history of materialism as *kairòs* defines the genealogy of a present that opens itself to the *to-come*, it is a history of resistances and insurgences. *Kairòs* places the hardness of matter against all transcendence, and against all dialectics of thought and Power.

6.5 The hardness of matter is grasped in the immeasurable (difference) that exists between the eternal and the void over which innovation extends itself. Matter is neither a nothing, nor a phenomenon, nor the incommunicable. Matter discovers its hardness there where temporality decides of being, to create new being at the edge of time, in defiance of the immeasurable that exists between the 'before' and 'after'. Whoever is able to construct the history of materialism will have given voice to the immeasurable within which every monad of *kairòs* exists at the moment in which it decides to produce. Here is where the *Angelus Novus* is also presented to us – the angel does not look back, but ahead, proceeding in the storm.

6.6 The hardness of matter is the hardness of the eternal that is not solicited by the decision of *kairòs*. Classical and modern materialism, when they have had a chance to express themselves on this subject, have frequently defined matter only as hardness, emphasizing this static condition, this constant capital of matter. In the face of this we can now proceed because, knowing that matter is temporality and that we can regenerate on the open limit of *kairòs*, we have brought the hardness of being towards a constitutive moment of passage.

6.7 Thus, to the prohibition against materialism there responds a hardness of matter that increasingly presents itself as an irrepressible resistance and revolt at the edge of being. This is what *kairòs* reveals within the materialist field. In other words, in so far as the hardness of matter revealed itself through *kairòs* as resistance, the materialist field has been radically innovated: resistance made a weapon of the hardness of matter, which previously constituted the limit of materialism. For this reason resistance is always positive affirmation of being.

7.1 There is no difference between the materialist field and the predication of being, because the reflective point of view is born of the monads of *kairòs*. The existential quantifier of the propositions (i.e. the ontological indicator of enunciations), that which materially supports name and common name, is thus rooted in the materialist field. Of course this rootedness is vacillating, because only the immeasurable creates a link between what has been and what is, and in the immeasurable the monads of *kairòs* lean out, anxiously, over the opening of new being. So the materialist field is always projected forwards; it consists in the arrow of time and it insists in the tip of the arrow. The production of time is the predication of the being of the world, for it is only here that each instant of being consists (and/or is renewed, regenerated).

7.2 Each enunciation (name and common name) is only verifiable pragmatically. The meaning of the names (and *a fortiori* of common names) is never determined if it is not sustained by the predication (affirmation) of the being of *kairòs*. Which is to say: among the many meanings that the names themselves indicate for the enunciations, only those which are qualified by the point of view of *kairòs* can count as true. Which is also to say: only that which reaches out to construct new being verifies what has already been. Therefore, in the materialist field, reflection is radically pragmatic, because *kairòs* is the praxis of the true [*vero*].

7.3 The pragmatic radicalism that *kairòs* imposes on reflection in the materialist field does not sadden thought (by flattening it onto the principle of utility, as so often happens in pragmatism). On the contrary, it enables it to advance in its search for truth (or the denunciation of falsity), which lies in the association [*comunanza*] of the monads of *kairòs*.

7.4 The extraordinary importance of the linguistic turn in contemporary philosophy, which aims to make all verification of knowledge pass through language, demonstrates its materialist basis here. Because language is in no instance a pure instrument, just any implement, but is a tool, a prosthesis, and a *praxis* of truth. It is not a senseless surface made up of noises, but rather a plane of association [*comunanza*] of monads of *kairòs*, the material fabric of forces of the common predication of the being of the world. As Burroughs says, language is not a cannon that fires missiles, but a spaceship in which we live and with which we construct trajectories of truth in the void. But we will explore this more fully later.

7.5 We can draw some not unimportant consequences from the preceding considerations that define the standpoint of the ontological enquiry in the materialist field. That is, the possibility of thinking the reversibility of time in the materialist field, when we consider it, not only as the arrow that traces the thread of an indestructible temporality (which is what we have done so far), but also as a network of instants or monads of *kairòs*. The latter, in their autonomous insistence, we can imagine developing – there where they existed – in every direction. In this way we can think the freedom of the eternal. It is a difficult exercise frequently attempted by geometers and physicists. We are forced to think again of matter as eternity (with its aporias and alternatives) in the manner in which the ancients have at times thought of it: as *Alma Venus*.

7.6 The materialist field is the field of common truths created in the immeasurability of production between the eternal and the *to-come*. And we are its actors.

Alma Venus

Prolegomena

Judith, God speaks at last during the ultimate oppressions.

(Pascal, *Pensées*)

The common

1.1 The guiding light of materialism is the eternity of matter. The eternal is the common name of the materialist experience of time. From the ethical point of view, the problem faced by materialism is that of holding singularity responsible for the eternal. These truths of the materialist tradition find their confirmation in the experience of *kairòs*.

2.1 Among the other meanings that could be attributed to the eternal in the materialist tradition, one sometimes finds the name of the infinite, as though the two were synonymous. Is matter infinite then? We can concede this only if, breaking the synonymy, we subsume the infinite under the eternal, in as much as the materialist production and the course of the eternal are infinite. But each production is singular and finite: the course of the eternal may be less today, more tomorrow. This finitude and this singularity can only be called 'infinite' when the presence of the eternal and its power take charge of them. Outside of the name of the eternal, the infinite would consist in nothing other than the idea of temporal transcendence, and as such, could not be a quality of materialism (i.e. of materialist production).

2.2 In as much as the infinite is an ambiguous name, comprehensible only if subsumed under the eternal, it would be better not to use it.

2.3 Ethical experience has nothing to do with the infinite. Ethical experience establishes itself in the presence of the eternal.

3.1 Although transcendental philosophy has assumed the infinite as the ground of all its manoeuvres, it has in reality paid very little attention to it. Like a suit that is only worn on special occasions, the idea of the infinite is useful to poetry, theology, mysticism and all confused reasoning. For everyday use, transcendental philosophy attires itself rather in the idea of the indefinite. What is the indefinite? It is the idea of a measurable infinite. But the eternal, eternal matter, is not measurable, it is immeasurable. It is so because the eternal always confronts the *to-come*, and this relationship is itself immeasurable. Therefore the indefinite is an illusion. But it becomes an effective illusion when it introduces transcendence as the measure of immanence. In this case illusion becomes transcendental mystification: it is the continuously repeated attempt to subordinate the present to the infinite and not to the eternal, and so to subordinate the singular to a measure.

3.2 In materialism ethical experience is always faced with the immeasurable and the opening of the eternal to the *to-come*.

4.1 The eternity of matter reveals itself as temporal intensity, as innovative presence; and the full present of eternal time is singularity. 'Singular' and 'eternal' are interchangeable terms; their relationship is tautological. Whatever has happened is eternal; it is eternal here and now. The eternal is the singular present.

4.2 In materialism ethical experience is the responsibility for the present.

5.1 *Kairòs* is present to us itself as irreducible singularity. Nevertheless, in the production of the eternal, we have seen that the monads of *kairòs* link themselves to one another and become common events that are driven to transform themselves into a common name. That is to say: we are immersed in the common because *kairòs* is a fine dust of interwoven and interlinked monads that expose themselves to the void indicated by the arrow of time, thus constructing the *to-come*. For this reason the singular is the experience of the common.

5.2 This common is irreducible to essence or to any preconceived notion. There is no presupposed *das Gemeinste*, no presupposed element that is 'the most common', as Kant would have it, unless one were to understand this as mere concatenation. (For Colli the primary meaning of 'common', *Xunòs*, corresponds precisely to 'that which is concatenated', which the materialist tradition has handed down to us through Heraclitus.) The monads of *kairòs* are common in that they produce and reproduce life, exposing themselves on the edge of the present edge of the eternal: it is the immeasurable *to-come* that creates the common.

5.3 The common is the form that singularity assumes in the production of the eternal. The production of the world (of Man and his *Umwelt*) renders the elements that constitute singularity all the more common. Therefore the experience of the common is the mark of a teleological process. But what teleology?

5.4 In materialism, ethics is the responsibility for the present in as much as it is innovation of being. But if innovation is common, ethics is the responsibility for the common. And if the common is teleological, materialist ethics must confront teleology. But which teleology?

6.1 'Teleology' is the name that suits materialism in so far as it is the name that suits the common. Materialist teleology knows no final cause from which and/or towards which it advances. On the contrary, it is the form through which the eternity of matter, that is to say the horizon of the world, progressively constitutes itself without any axiomatic qualification. 'Constitutes itself': i.e. the present forms, establishes and innovates itself, through singular common figures. 'Progressively': in accordance with the direction of time fixed by the arrow of temporality. Time progresses. The regress in time does not depend upon time but on the human activity of time (the fixing of time, the accumulation of its moments, memory). Consequently, the singular horizon of life is increasingly the common form of being in time. It is all of time realized in the actuality of the common.

6.2 Ethics, assuming the direction of the arrow of time, posits the common as teleological, that is to say, it considers matter to be increasingly common.

7.1 When materialism follows a teleological progression in its definition of the common, then it proceeds in the opposite direction to that proposed by the metaphysical tradition. In the metaphysics of Plato and Aristotle, the effects of which run right through to the final avatars of Hegelianism, teleology is not progressive. In fact it presupposes an *arché*[15] that operates in teleology so as to place being in action within a hierarchy pre-constituted by the *arché*. The clearest demonstration of the teleological fiction in the metaphysical tradition is that *archein* means at one and the same time 'to begin' and 'to command'. In this way teleology becomes the theoretical praxis that subordinates the principle to command and thereby defines the limit prior to development and order prior to production. The tradition of classical metaphysics finds its confirmation in the procedures of modern transcendentalism. The Hegelian *Geist* is a transvestite that dances to the rhythm of the Platonic-Aristotelian flute; and in as much as every transvestite caricatures the original, here the original is the State, that is to say, the most explicit and violent limit that the development of the common is confronted by.

7.2 In materialism ethics installs itself in the unlimited production of the common.

8.1 In materialism the *telos* is the product of common existence. It is not then a pre-constituted value, but the perpetually progressive production of the eternal, in the same way as a boy matures and becomes a man, or as death follows from birth after life has run its course. In the same way that the adult does not represent a greater value than the young boy, so death is not the negation of the value of life. On the contrary, all is eternal. I am, that is all: this and only this is the *Da-sein* of the eternal.

8.2 The common produced that the movement of the human and its produce, *Umwelt* is not a value, it is a destiny. The word 'destiny' must be torn away from the blindness of chance as well as from all pre-determination; it should rather be redefined from the constitutive perspective of the common. We will call 'destiny' the ensemble of Man's actions considered as generic multitude, to which nothing is presupposed other than the environmental conditions that Man continually modifies and that, in so far as they are modified, affect the existence of the common. From the ethical standpoint, 'destiny' is the common name of 'Man' in so far as he materially constitutes himself.

8.3 From the destiny of the 'centaur' (Man merged with nature), Man arrives at the destiny of 'man-man' (Man constructed through *praxis*), through to the emergence of the destiny of 'machine-man' (Man transfigured in production, developing his being artificially): second, third, nth natures . . . In each of these epochs the common progressively assumes different forms. Different but not metaphysical, nor axiological, nor historicist, nor eschatological. 'Being-centaur', 'being-man-man' and 'being-machine-man' is as progressive as the progress in time from life to death.

9.1 From Democritus to Epicurus, from Lucretius to Giordano Bruno, from Spinoza to Nietzsche, from Leopardi to Deleuze, from Hölderlin to Dino Campana, this production of the common between life and death was considered a sign of eternity. Once again, this sign was not axiological; on the contrary, it reveals the ontological intensity of production in time. If the direction imposed by time to the actuality of production is increasingly common, that means that the experience of the singularity has an ever-stronger grasp on eternity. Eternity is rewarded by the actuality of production and the common decides upon time in so far as it reveals time as eternity.

9.2 The world is not a practico-inert backdrop but a context of activities, a fabric of *kairòs*. With each instant the world is created anew in its totality, in a movement of dilation of the common. In this context, human *praxis* in its destinality cannot be represented as that which is already constituted; rather, it is that which constitutes, i.e. it constitutes an ever more common context.

9.3 In this movement, the more the common constructs itself, the more the world becomes immeasurable.

9.4 If in materialism ethical experience is forever confronted by the immeasurable, then resistance is action 'outside measure' and constituent power is action 'beyond measure'.

10.1 In the teleology of the materialist tradition, the relation that exists between eternity and existence has always been expounded in an adequate and sufficient manner. However, materialism runs into aporias when it confronts eternity with the time of innovation; that is, when, on the edge of being, the eternal confronts the *to-come*.

10.2 The crisis experienced by materialism surfaces on the terrain of ethics. At present, the eternal is confronted by the immeasurable of singular action in the present, and it appears unable to contain it. But must it really contain it?

10.3 From what has already been said, it is clear that when we say 'at present' we mean 'the present'. In this way the ambiguity of the metaphysical 'actuality' is dissolved, and meaning is given to the common name *in reality*. '*In reality*', because here, now, in the time that is at once that of the name and of the event, the common name exists. And this is *apodictic*.

11.1 In classical materialism the theme of innovation is both central and unresolved. From Democritus to Epicurus the atomistic construction of the world is immersed in eternity. As for freedom, it is the conduct of life played out in terms of the metaphor of the cosmos. In this flattening-out, freedom is extinguished and innovation is incomprehensible. Only in Lucretius does freedom strive to break this meaningless metaphor so as to act autonomously in the physical ensemble of atomism, that is to say, to inflict a tear in the eternal. Nevertheless Lucretius poses his *clinamen* only furtively, in a whisper, as though he were trying to annul the violence of the tear that comes from the imperceptible deviation (*clinamen*) that allows the world to be renewed; that permits one to grasp the singular and, along with it, the meaning of freedom. The shower of atoms is traversed by a minuscule – but nonetheless – immense glow: poetry is exalted by it, philosophy humiliated, the problem posed. Modernity will inherit this problem unresolved.

12.1 Only with Spinoza is the problem transformed. With Spinoza the ontology of materialism is not touched by the *clinamen*, it is rather invested and founded anew by desire. The rhythm of the constitution of the world is sustained – in a confusion of forms – by a living force that unfolds in the world so as to constitute itself as divine. Freedom constructs itself in this development and interprets its continuity within the absolute productive immanence of a *vis viva*, a living force, that unfolds from a physical *conatus* to a human *cupiditas* on to a divine *amor*. Before interpreting the human world and sublimating itself in the divine world, ethics constitutes the physical world itself. Eternity is lived as presence, and the common is brought back in its entirety within the development of ontology. The composition of bodies is common; the object of *cupiditas* is common; the divine form is common. The common is ontology considered from the point of view of passion, of the force that agitates and constitutes both world and divinity.

13.1 The problem undergoes a powerful displacement in the shift from classical to Spinozist materialism. The problem of innovation is no longer thought of as a deviation in the course of life; it is now posed within the horizon of eternity. Absolute immanence is the dynamism of life, and it gives life its power. Singularity begins to take form within the sea of being, or if you like, it reveals itself within the overall dynamic of materialist teleology. But however radical this *displacement* is, is it sufficient to resolve the problem? Is a physics of desire enough to endow eternity with the form of freedom? Is it enough to imprint the world with the discontinuity of innovation in order to bypass the aporias of materialism and of the crisis of the common? Spinoza's asceticism brings to mind a forceful edict that imposes immanence as the proper plane of materialist discourse, and through which the force of life is established within it. In this way the common is affirmed. But that said, despite this, one is forced to add that Spinoza's asceticism is incapable of providing a full account of its progression. For it forms an image of beatitude that, in separating itself from the production of desire, touches upon the notion of beatitude without appropriating it. As we have already seen with the *clinamen* in the atomic turbulence of Lucretius, in Spinoza we witness a series of imperceptible qualitative leaps within the continuity of ontological experience, which attempt to break with the monolithic materialist metaphysical framework by dividing it into a physics, an ethics and a teleology. But within the merciless grip of the necessity of traditional materialism, this modification is still too cautious, when it is not altogether meaningless. So once again a creative sense cannot be given to the progression of the common, that is to say, to the unity of eternity and innovation. Because this is the problem: that of producing freedom in the same way as eternity, making the common not the flat result but the active key of the construction/reconstruction of the world. Moreover, an axiological element is surreptitiously reintroduced into these philosophies of immanence. Classical and idealist teleology, with their idea of the infinite, spew their transcendental poison against the radicality of the materialist procedure. Thus the eternal is still broken by an 'external' determination of value.

14.1 In modernity, that is to say with the advent of the man-man, axiological transcendence even insinuated itself into the most powerful of materialist teleologies. This can be explained by the conditions under which the progression of the ontologies of the common was given at the time. The relation between experience and the common was indeed contradictory on the very terrain on which it was positioned, i.e. on the terrain of *praxis*. If the attempt was to bring transcendence back within experience, this reduction (presented in a revolutionary, that is to say, open manner) was – nevertheless – limited by the unsustainable weight of the indefinite (which always characterizes the *praxis* of asceticism), and was thus still transcendent. The fabric of immanence could not therefore become common if not through the hypostasis of the common. Philosophy wanted the common but, precisely because of this desire, it made it transcendent. Thus a hiatus, or worse, an opposition was formed between the experience of the common and the teleological tension of materialism.

14.2 It is within this tension that an aporia was created – an imbalance that the metaphysical tradition reproposed in modernity at the heart of social and political philosophy in the shape of the thinking of individualism and of the State. But the individual is only an aporia of the singular, and the State a mystification of the common.

15.1 In postmodernity, that is, in the epoch that began with the revolutionary events of the 1960s, and in which we continue to live, the ethical and ascetic illusion of modernity seems to have reached an end; and with it so too the metaphysical folly of transcendence and command. The common is now able to appear in the fullness of its definition.

16.1 The qualifications of being have now become entirely common: we live in the common. Experience furnishes us with clear proof of this: for common being appears under the three determinations of 'linguistic-being', 'being as production of subjectivity' and 'biopolitical-being'. These three determinations are absolutely equivalent to one another, so that the sequence in which they will be discussed is solely for the purposes of exposition.

16.2 Language is common. The tool in the relation between man and nature and man and man is completely transformed. We no longer need tools to transform nature (and tame the centaur) or to place ourselves in relation to the historical world (perfecting the ascesis of the man-man); we only require language. The tool is language. More correctly, the tool is the brain, in so far as it is a common instrument. Making the tool immanent to the brain removes the foundation from the metaphysical illusion. When the only tool is language, one can no longer properly speak of a tool – because the tool, that had up until then been something other than the agent, gives way to a set of prostheses that have been added one to the other (and in accumulating they have multiplied their productive power). Their power is common. Language is not born and does not develop other than in the common and from the common. Nothing is produced that is not produced through the common: all commodities have become services, all services have become relations, all relations have become brains, and all brains form part of the common. Language is no longer only a form of expression; it is the only form of production of the human and its environment. Language is thus the mode of being of common being.

16.3 The common is production, and all that is produced must be related back to the common. But production is made up of a multitude of linguistic acts, of monads of *kairòs* which, because they expose themselves on the edge of being, constitute new being within the common name. The production of subjectivity gives meaning to this network of singular innovations. For the experience of subjectivity consists in recognizing that if being is language, linguistic production can be nothing other than productive power of language, that is to say, a production of productive force. But if productive force springs from the common network of actions and relations of monads of *kairòs* at the very moment that they hurl themselves against the void, there is always an instant that corresponds to a moment of imputation of production: that is subjectivity. Subjectivity assumes the responsibility for the production of a productive force that, in turn, can be nothing other than subjective. Therefore, subjectivity brings together the linguistic acts that create the innovation of being into one. It does not stop the movement of production but, in slowing its progress, it identifies it as productive force. This reasoning enables us to say that subjectivity is nothing other than the imputation of common experiences, that is to say, of a common productive force that identifies, or rather names, the agent of linguistic productions. It follows that subjectivity is not something interior placed before an 'exterior' that we define as language; on the contrary, like language, it is another mode of common being and nothing more. The production of subjectivity, i.e. of needs, affects, desire, action, *techné*, is carried out through language, better still it is language in the same way that language is subjectivity. This density of productive relations is always in motion, and this common movement is eternal, but it is always inscribed in the subjectivities that innovate the eternal.

16.4 Making life common constitutes the third mode of common being. It is nothing but the consequence or, if you like, the tautology, of what has been said so far. Common being is tautological. It is a strange tautology, however, in as much as it is powerful and shows us that language and the production of subjectivity, in so far as they are modes of the common, together recompose the multitude of linguistic acts and the production of life. This recomposition (that is to say, the productive tautology seen from another perspective) is *polis* (in other words, the political). But if common being invests the political with such intensity, it redefines it as the common name of a multitude of linguistic acts and of productions of subjectivity. But life and politics, these old fetishes separated by the disciplinary technologies of transcendental understanding of modernity, here become indistinguishable from one another. There are no longer political domains, just as there are no longer domains of nature or of production that are not already recomposed, as a multitude, within the production of the being of the common name. Therefore, the political presents itself as a mode of being indistinguishable from language and from the production of subjectivity. And the world is this ensemble; it is the biopolitical.

16.5 It is under these conditions that the destiny of the 'man-machine' appears. The production of man as multitude, gathered up in the common name, becomes indistinguishable from that of the production of the natural and historical *Umwelt*. The *polis* is not therefore an *arché* but a biopolitical production. The world is invested by the teleology of the linguistic and subjective prostheses. This is what we call 'machine': i.e. the production of the world which man carries out through a thoroughly material production of artefacts that adhere to his nature: biopolitical artefacts. Eternity is at present developed by machinic power. The common organizes itself as a machine, as a biopolitical machine.

16.6 Have we in this way overcome the traditional aporias of materialism and of the crisis of the common that follows from it? In some respects, yes. Nevertheless, later on, after this first phenomenological approach to the common has been completed, we will have to return to the aporias and the crisis, and take up again the demonstration that until now has barely touched upon the materiality of the processes. For the present it is enough to bear in mind that, if production is communication, the world of nature and of artefacts must be related back entirely to the production of subjectivity, and that subjectivity establishes production in the biopolitical.

17.1 Through these modes of material being we are now able to observe the materialist horizon progressively constitute itself in the form of a common horizon. The *telos* of this progress is in no way external to the movement of the constitution of the common itself, nor is it the force of something preconceived realizing itself; it is simply the common name of a material action. This *telos* could only have not occurred if time were an unnecessary dimension of material being. But in as much as it is necessary, it is also necessary that the intrinsic finality of action in time be realized. We verify the fact that it is realized, and that therefore the living constitutive force has reached the formal fulfilment of its common expression.

17.2 In following this progress of the common, we asked ourselves if we had not reached a crucial turning point, one where eternity and innovation come to be joined together (which was never achieved in earlier forms of materialist thinking), and we admitted that we were indeed faced by the formal conditions of this conjunction. But the formal conditions of the expression of the common, in order to become real, must be put to the test on the ethical and the political terrain; i.e. they must be verified on the eternal edge of being.

18.1 Let us return once again to the problematic of the conditions of the common materialist *telos* as it is expressed in the various forms of post-1968 thinking, i.e. of postmodern thinking. Do they satisfy the questions posed on the terrain of ethics and politics?

18.2 The postmodern philosophers that take communication to be the exclusive horizon of being declare the reality of the common. It is nevertheless difficult to take their assertion positively. For they presuppose a completed teleology – and nothing else. They bring their search to a halt on the edge of current being, and go no further. The result is the exhaustion of the ontological sphere, the end of history and an omnivorous tautology of the exposition. If the common submits to these conditions it will present itself as the end of the common.

18.3 Some postmodern authors look for an opening on the margins of the model that is emerging. But the margin is a liminal transcendence – an immanence that is almost a transcendence, an ambiguous location where materialist realism must bow to mysticism. Some endlessly peruse this margin (Derrida); others fix on it as though it were a case of gathering up the power of the negative that has at last been seized (Agamben). This thinking of the common, in the anxiety of awaiting the other (as in Levinas), results in mysticism.

18.4 Lastly, there are those thinkers who have attempted to traverse this completed teleology by projecting it over a thousand plateaus of singular power: it is here that the physical and psychic tensions of worldliness are released. But although this approach allows for innovation and the eternal to be articulated according to a genealogical rhythm, it nevertheless presents the common in the form of a circle from which there is no exit. The edge of being is broken, and duration takes the opportunity to appear again (Deleuze and Guattari).

18.5 Thus, each and every one of these figures of materialist teleology interprets the exuberant richness of the postmodern experience of the common, but they remain somehow imprisoned by it. In this way the eternity of matter is traversed by teleology, but the visibility of innovation, and the ethical and political standpoints themselves, are eliminated. We have returned to the splendours of a Democriteanism or an Epicureanism.

19.1 We grasp here the 'aporetic' element around which the theories of the eternity of matter clash with those of innovation (that is, they have rendered innovation aporetic). This element is the immeasurableness of the world. Although materialism has always been a theory of the immeasurableness of the world, the materialist experience has always failed to satisfy the dimension of the immeasurable. The renewal of materialism must thus include the recognition that, through innovation, the eternal looks out over the immeasurable.

19.2 And what of the common? It also becomes increasingly common, on the condition that it is understood as immeasurable opening. Only the immeasurableness of the eternal constitutes the common and ensures the progression to the constitution of the common. The immeasurable is there, beyond the threshold that the materialist teleology opens at each singular present.

19.3 Ethical experience is a liberation, because it is a creative communication, a production of common subjectivity, and the constitution of biopolitical temporality in the immeasurableness of the *to-come*.

20.1 In the immeasurableness of the world, innovation and the eternal are expressed by love. It is love that brings together the eternal and innovation in the multitude of singular thresholds that are presented to the teleology of the common.

20.2 It then becomes clear why the eternal is not the same as the infinite. Indeed, love is not infinite but eternal, not measure but immeasurable, not individual but singular, not universal but common, not the substance of temporality but the arrow of time itself.

20.3 *Alma Venus*: there where the materialist discourse began, there it should be taken up again.

Poverty

1.1 There is, however, another experience that comes before that of love on our path through the phenomenology of the common, one that is rooted in the present and is exposed to the immeasurable: it is the experience of poverty. We must now reflect on this experience.

1.2 Those most exposed to the immeasurable are the poor. When he appears before us, the poor person is naked on the edge of being, without any alternative. The misery, ignorance and disease that defines poverty, along with the experience of the indigent condition of the body, of the needy biopolitical situation, of the desirous disposition of the soul – that together form the shape of the arc of the bow – nevertheless constitute a point from which the arrow constitutive of time is released with increased strength.

1.3 But is this not an easy rhetorical game that is characteristic of negative dialectics, which aims to give to absolute nudity the privilege of an eminent valorization? It would doubtless be so had we not some time ago cut any links with the dialectic, insisting on the contrary on a subjectivity (understood from the standpoint of materialism), which finds itself on the edge of being and represents the exclusive power of giving sense to the *to-come*. The poor person is then not someone constituted by pain, but is *in reality* the biopolitical subject. He is not an existential trembling (or a painful dialectical differentiation): he is the naked eternity of the power of being.

1.4 If you are not poor you cannot philosophize. For poverty is an immeasurable place where the biopolitical question is posed in an absolute way. It is there that the body in its nakedness is confined to the experience of innovation on the edge of being; that language is opened to hybridization by the pressing recognition of the common; in short, it is here that the biopolitical, becoming immeasurable between the eternal and the *to-come*, finds its definition. So where in humanist thought it was ignorance that was at the basis of philosophical questioning, in the biopolitical it is poverty that forms that ground. To the 'learned ignorance' of the humanists, corresponds the 'powerful poverty' that makes us amazed at the world.

2.1 Naked and exposed to the immeasurable, the poor shatter the postmodern aporia of production and confer meaning on the materialist teleology of the common. For poverty cannot turn in the void, it can only go forward, and to go forward means to go forward in common. Were we not to start out from poverty, we would not start out at all; that is to say, in this situation the production of being could occur or not occur, because the force that sustains and propels it would not be necessary. Indeed, no teleological process would be given (and neither would a teleology of the common), were it not posited by poverty; because poverty puts the immeasurable production of the arrow of time in motion necessarily, one instant after another (there, where *kairòs* becomes a biopolitical event).

So, if the power of poverty were not given, one would not have a tele-ology of material being either, and therefore eternal being itself would also not be produced.

2.2 If as we have seen, the common name is the event of the multitude, then the common is the product of the multitude. But it is only when poverty presents itself as the *topos* (location and motor) of the opening of the multitude within the teleological process of common being, that all the (postmodern) tautologies of the common are dissolved. In this way the common 'doings' of the multitude of the poor necessarily intro-duce the immeasurableness of the eternal, and imprints on this immeasurable becoming the seal of the common. This is what we mean when we say 'the poor are the common of the common'.

2.3 It is not wealth – which is forever a *quantitate signata* – but poverty that has always represented the common name of the human. From Christ to Saint Francis, from the Anabaptists to the Sans-culottes, from the communists to the Third-World militants, the needy, the idiots, the unhappy (i.e. the exploited, the excluded, the oppressed), it is they who exist under the sign of the eternal. Their resistance and their struggles have opened the eternal to the immeasurableness of the *to-come*. The teleology and the ethics of materialism have always been related to this naked and powerful community whose name is 'poverty'.

2.4 He who is born is a naked and poor being. Generation is the event of the common.

3.1 On the contrary, poverty is ostracized by transcendental axiology (and in the same way it is banned from the history of the political). The name of the poor is defined by the determinations of wealth, i.e. by the presupposition of hierarchy and limit.

3.2 In classical civilizations and philosophies, the poor person is the slave. Hence, where man is centaur, the slave is the beast of burden, a 'quasi-animal' excluded from the human species. The most profound truth of Plato's and Aristotle's philosophies are to be found in this exclu-sion of the poor, where slavery is fixed within the presupposed hierarchy of nature. The ontological *archein* predetermines and orders slavery in the necessary rationality of life. The teleology of the common is broken at its most basic level so as to expel the slave from human nature, and so from the common. Yet he is a beast that is able to draw near to the human, can give birth to men and must reproduce the common: the slave is nonethe-less an inferior beast to the centaur (to the man who, through the noble families [*gens*], through the hierarchy of biological heredity [*eugenia*], built the city). The slave who reproduces the common is excluded from it by force; the hierarchy of nature provides the ontological legitimation for this exclusion.

3.3 The thinking of modernity conceives of poverty as exploitation. The community of man-man is productive: it is thus in relation to production that the hierarchy of grounds must be reimposed. A new form of subjugation accompanies this becoming immanent of the concept 'man': exploitation is the enslaving of man within the 'second nature'[16] produced by man. But the more the common is intensified, the more violent appears the dwindling of one of the two elements whose destiny is to be put into the productive service of the other. The teleology of the common is interrupted when it begins to show its greatest efficacy. The man-man commune becomes the common exploitation of man by man.

3.4 In modernity, the formal idea of the common serves as the basis for its real break-up; and the world of the Rights of Man is both proclaimed and shattered by the productive use and political subjugation of the poor.

3.5 A natural measure is imposed upon the slave; a measure of the exploitation of work is imposed on the proletariat: everywhere measure, against the immeasurableness of the practice of the eternal by the poor; a hierarchy, against the common; the rationale of wealth, against those of creativity. In other words: misery must let exploitation through work be imposed upon it; ignorance must submit to the rules of understanding; sadness must reveal that man is-for-death. Economic, humanist, moral and religious – these are the measures that the transcendental imposes upon poverty.

3.6 The concept of poverty excludes that of death in as much as, in order to live, the poor have already overcome death. The poor have put death behind themselves: the common is exalted by this realization.

4.1 The more the poor produce the common, the more violent is the transcendental exclusion of the poor from the common. From the era of the centaur to that of the man-man, this violence increases in line with the emancipation of the proletariat from slavery. The more the exploited proletariat (i.e. the poor of modernity) are inserted into production and are determined by it in turn, the more they are absorbed within consumption (in contrast to the slave), and all the greater is the violence they must suffer.

4.2 Can we thus define the poor as the product of violence? A naked creature defined simply by violence? No, because this definition overlooks the fact that violence is exercised 'within' the common. And it is the exploited proletariat that creates the common. The creature that lies at the basis of exploitation and of Power is not naked: it is powerful, capable of the productivity of the common. Once again we are able to confirm just how far the experience of poverty has taken us from the dialectical conceptions – even the negative ones – of the production of being.

4.3 The violence that the citizen of the *polis* exercises over the slave and that the modern capitalist exercises over the worker are negations of the power that the poor possess: the power of the poor to open themselves to the immeasurableness of time. This violence is envy of the eternal.

4.4 On the contrary, the violence of the poor person is the affirmation of the eternal.

5.1 The poor, the producers of the common from which they are – nonetheless – excluded, are the motor of materialist teleology, because only the multitude of the poor can construct the world under the sign of the common, pressing forth relentlessly beyond the limit of the present.

5.2 It is precisely this that is erased in the ideology (and historiography) of the transcendental. It establishes a philosophy of history – in the two forms of an apologia and of an eschatology – that presents itself as a 'negative' teleology of the common. In the apologia of the rationality of history, transcendental teleology denies the presence itself of the multitude of the poor as producers of the world; in its eschatological version, on the other hand, transcendental teleology postpones the recognition of this fundamental destiny to the 'ends of time'.

5.3 There is, however, 'another history', which fuses with the teleological constitution of the common, and where the poor become the engine of teleology. From the ontological standpoint the path unfolds in linear fashion, although it is interrupted by innovative leaps that the multitude of the poor impose on history: these break the 'order' of the world so as to launch life beyond the limits of time, in order to render it radically immeasurable, through a search for and a reconstruction of the common. Ontologically this 'other history' presupposes the eternal to the arrow of time; historically it provides a new articulation of the eternal and the arrow of time. But this 'other history' is only grasped from the instants of *kairòs*.

5.4 When the poor begin to advance and to destroy the hierarchies and measures, wealth and domination, then that 'other history' leaves its mark. The history of the poor is always revolutionary, because the eternal (i.e. the being that produces) is the refusal of work, of understanding and of the limit.

6.1 In the present era, the experience of poverty is shaped in a dimension of the common that recognizes no 'outside'; in a compact dimension of the common that no longer consists in spatial fissures or temporal suspensions. In the postmodern era the poor are excluded, and this exclusion occurs 'within' the production of the world.

6.2 But from the point of view of the consistency of the common, the excluded are a logical paradox: from the standpoint of a linguistic community, the excluded can only be a pathological factor; from the point of view of biopolitical productivity, a material impossibility. So here, in postmodernity, the first traits of the scandalous experience of poverty are presented (to the eyes of a superficial phenomenology). In the present, the poor are the poorest of the poor, because they are the most integrated in the common – in the common of life, of language, of production and of consumption. The poor are excluded from within the biopolitical itself – in that same biopolitical in which the poor person produces and in which his subjectivity is in turn produced.

6.3 In the postmodern era, poverty is defined spatially and/or temporally within the intense confines of the common: if illness, unemployment and misery (which are only the superficial figures of poverty) are located in the interdependence of an extremely tight biopolitical relation, then the content of the violent postmodern exclusion is enormous, because it breaks the tension of the common at its core.

6.4 But in a biopolitical society, where all existence is a relation and every productive act is language, the tension of the common is exercised through the cohesion of a network of singularities. Consequently, the rupture of the tension of the common determines an infinity of sequences that deploy themselves everywhere. In other words, since within the postmodern network the singularity is rich in effects provoked by the production of subjectivity in the core of the common, the exclusion produces a variety of biopolitical effects, all of which are scandalous.

7.1 This scandal is ontological. Poverty has always been the salt of the earth, but here poverty directly illuminates the common, i.e. the power productive of subjectivity, weighing it down with suffering and pain.

7.2 Here, in the conflict between this negativity and the material tele-ology of the production of the common, we see dissipate the saccharine and illusory utopias according to which the postmodern development of production by way of language would create a world of pure circulation of goods, services, and of increasingly perfect languages. Faced with what these illusions would have us believe, the conflict becomes ontological. The conflict produces effects of crisis that denounce the crumbling away of appearances and then announce their radical de-mystification, not only in the face of the eternal, but also in the pain of singularity. But equally these effects of crisis can endow the common with a multiplicity of possible creative meanings.

8.1 My question is thus the following: in the postmodern era, how can one grasp – through the ontological scandal of poverty – the meaning of the crisis of the common? How, within an experience that has no exter-iority, is one able to sketch a line of flight out from the crisis of the common?

8.2 To answer the question one must deepen the analysis of the experi-ence of postmodern poverty, i.e. one must identify the reactions, the counterblasts, the violence, but at the same time the effects of production and of construction of meaning which, in the experience of poverty and in the paradoxes it implies, are thereby freed up. We must try to do so from within the *topos* of poverty (i.e. within poverty as the *topos* of the com-mon), because it is here that the *to-come* is produced. And if this experi-ence is still insufficient to link production of subjectivity to the teleology of the common, we will nevertheless have consolidated the basis for a further stage in our enquiry (one that passes through love).

9.1 The experience of poverty is given on the edge of time, in the innovation of the eternal; it is thus a practice of the immeasurable. This practice presents itself as 'outside measure', i.e. as resistance; or it presents itself as 'beyond measure', i.e. as constituent power. In every case it gives ethical meaning to life by making it escape the dominion of the axiomatic of the limit, of measure and of wealth.

9.2 In the postmodern era, that is to say, when the teleology of the common is absolutely immanent, these practices of poverty are before us *in reality*. They can only be recognized clearly in the postmodern era, i.e. from the moment that materialist teleology is reborn in the tautology of the common that it interrupts.

10.1 How much the concept of 'resistance' has changed in postmodernity, and how its practices are transformed! If we attempted to identify it in accordance with the categories and experiences of modernity, we would now be incapable of understanding it. In modernity, resistance is an accumulation of forces against exploitation that come to be given a subjective determination through a *'pris de coscience'*. In postmodernity, none of all this. Resistance appears as a diffusion of singular behaviours of resistance. If resistance accumulates, it accumulates extensively, in circulation, mobility, flight, exodus, desertion: it is a case of multitudes that resist in a diffuse manner and that escape the increasingly confining enclosures of misery and Power. And there is no need for a collective *pris de coscience* for this: the sense of rebellion is endemic and it traverses every consciousness and renders it proud. The effect of the common, which attaches itself to each singularity as an anthropological quality, consists precisely in this. So rebellion is neither a punctual event nor is it uniform; on the contrary, it traverses the expanse of the common and defuses itself in the shape of an explosion of behaviours of singularities that it is impossible to contain. In this way one can define the resistance of the multitude.

10.2 Therefore, in the first place, poverty is given as resistance. There exists no experience of poverty that is not at the same time one of resistance against the repression of the desire to live. 'Resistance' should be understood here as the affirmation of self as common and against exclusion: a 'self-valorization' that rises up from naked poverty against the enemy.

10.3 A gigantic cultural revolution is underway. Free expression and the joy of bodies, the autonomy, hybridization and the reconstruction of languages, the creation of new, singular and mobile modes of production – all this emerges, everywhere and continually. Transcendental perversion opposes exercise and fashion to bodies; disinformation and censorship to languages; an untouchable command over the world to the new modes of organizing production; and rigidly defined frontiers and global tourism to stateless movement.

10.4 In other words, since resistance produces new spaces of creation and circulation, it follows that new institutions of measure will try to control them and bring them under their rule, while new enterprises will attempt to exploit them. In this way the world market of parasitical transcendentalism is constructed. In this way the *to-come* is opposed to the future, statistics to *kairòs*, and repetition to difference.

10.5 But the leap imposed by poverty is irreversible. When, in the postmodern age, production becomes production of subjectivity (starting from, through and for subjectivity), subjectivity is formed within the resistant singularity. The resistance of the poor person produces new subjective forms of life and widens its markets, invests new assemblages and expressive machines without interruption, and creates new linguistic spaces. For this reason we can say that it produces *in reality*. When, as occurs in the postmodern era, poverty is marked by the exclusion from the common, resistance becomes a reaffirmation of the common, and plays itself out in – and against – the space of exclusion. Resistance is the indeterminate negation of the limit that exclusion imposes on the common. It is the unlimited (*apeiron*), against the limit (*peras*) of exclusion and of measure; it is an absolute opening, against the closure of the common and the perversion of its teleology.

11.1 In the second place, poverty is given as singularity. For it is evident that every affirmation expressed by the resistance of the poor (even when it is undetermined) is singular. The expression of the poor is always singular because the interweaving of resistance and the new opening on the edge of the *to-come* (which constitutes the ontological figure of the poor) is always immeasurable. It is the singularity that brings the 'outside measure' of resistance to exclusion into relation with the 'beyond measure' of the power that constitutes a new common.

11.2 Transcendental thinking affirms that it is necessary to exclude for order to be provided, and that it is not possible to dispose of being in an ordered fashion if the common is not withdrawn from the immeasurable. But the common is the immeasurable. And so singularity is the power of the immeasurable.

11.3 The postmodern philosophers, in order to try and identify the crisis that the singularity provokes in the core of the order of the world – which is presupposed by transcendental ideology – and so as to have a point of leverage to overturn its pretensions, have looked at the margins of the world and have fooled themselves into believing they have found an outside or a 'bare life'. No, the moment of crisis is rooted in the body of the postmodern common, there where poverty, in the shape of expressive *apeiron*, resists in the face of all order and every limit; and – at the same time – presents itself as the 'fount' of all expression, as a poor yet powerful singularity.

11.4 The highest form of the definition of the singular is to be found in the common name of poverty; a common name which recognizes no 'outside'.

12.1 Therefore, in this way, the common name of poverty presents itself as productive force. For what is production today for postmodern thinking, if not the valorization – in the biopolitical – of the singular acts that, interweaving and forming a multitude, produce the world and reproduce it? Or in other words: valorization of relations of affect, of language and communication that, while each is entirely singular, begin to form subjectivity by virtue of their interweaving? And where is this 'generation' to be found if not in the poor, understood as the common singularity of existence, of resistance and expression? More than in any other constellation of the magical postmodern circle, it is poverty that can be identified as the salt of the earth. Poverty is the opposite of wealth because it is the singular possibility of all wealth.

12.2 The beautiful is lived as joy of the multitude; it is imagination and expression of all wealth in that absolutely singular moment when the poor lean over the edge of time. Aesthetic delight lies always in the perception of the immeasurable and there is no artistic creation that is not (or that could not be) delight of the poor as multitude. Consequently the monuments erected by the Powerful to the divinity of measure must be destroyed, just as the museums, veritable temples fashioned by the measure of Power, must be deserted. What is beautiful is the generation of subjectivity.

13.1 Finally, resistance and singularity find a third power in poverty: the capacity to give being meaning, that is to say, to construct common meanings for being. In this way poverty is experienced as action in the teleology of the common; action that marks the constitution of the common at each instant with the seal of resistance and of singularity, and so produces generation and innovation. By constructing common events, poverty endows being with teleological meaning.

13.2 To give meaning to languages and to innovate in the course of the circulation of meaning: these are the gifts that only poverty can bring. Every limit is overcome by *dispositifs* that are all characterized by a single teleological necessity: to remove and annul Power and misery, and so to make poverty – as the expression of the desire for life – triumph. One must thus return to the common the fullness of productive power and suppress all exclusions. The only rationality (were we to still amuse ourselves with fetishes of this sort) of the historical process (were we to still venerate teleological illusions of this type) is poverty!

13.3 The heart of common being beats to the rhythm of poverty and in its name; thanks to its power it leads into the heart of its vital circulation. In other words the poor, as the form of resistance and of the affirmation of singularity, open themselves to the power that consists in giving meaning to the common.

13.4 Therefore, it seems that we must admit that this is the place where ethics is born.

13.5 And so in the present, the immeasurable is traversed by lines of force that are equally lines of power that trace creative *dispositifs* on the edges of time. And in so doing, project the eternal.

14.1 With this affirmed in principle, in what way precisely can one seize the productive key of common being – when considered from the standpoint of poverty – from within the teleology of the common? An attentive critic will always be able to point out that it does not follow from the recognition that poverty has the form and the power of resistance, that this power is able to constitute the determinations of meaning in a linear fashion. For the same reason, those who recognize in poverty the signature of singularity and of an indeterminate power of production cannot, on that basis alone, relate it back in linear fashion to the common. Unless one introduces surreptitiously a *deus ex machina*, or one assumes, as occurs in the 'theologies of poverty', the miracle of the untimely and extremely radical appearance of something that illuminates (and redeems) the ontology of the common. But we consider all illuminations to be illusory.

14.2 The ontological enquiry must thus be carried further. And although we can now assume that the answers we shall give will prove insufficient to overcome the difficulty that we have before us (which is still that of exhibiting the common *dispositifs* of innovation and of the eternal), the analysis will at least enable us to sketch out a more comprehensive scenario.

14.3 On the terrain of materialism, a conclusive answer to the questions we are posing can only be provided by a deeper reflection on the force of love, taking up the theme of *Alma Venus* again. But the experience of poverty shows us the 'location' of the ontological recomposition of innovation and of the eternal.

15.1 If the body is the 'location' of poverty, in conditions of poverty, the power of the body is exposed to the immeasurable. For in conditions of poverty, the body is affected by the exclusion from the common that it constructs. Nevertheless, in conditions of poverty, that same body shows itself able to act, that is, as we have seen, of expressing resistance, defining singularity and bestowing meaning. And this is all the more the case the more the body is faced with poverty.

15.2 The Body, in opening itself to the immeasurable within the biopolitical, is affected by it; but its being affected is power. For if the body is the capacity to express affects, the body, when it shows itself as 'being affected' (i.e. able to undergo affect) by the productive relations of singularity, finds itself – on the contrary – augmented in its power. And this is all the more the case the more poverty spurs it on.

15.3 'No one has yet determined the power of the body', said Spinoza,[17] taking up the experience of the revolution of bodies carried out in the Renaissance. This revolution, exalted by the new science and art, found its origin in the joyfulness of the body of the poor, in their laughter in the face of Power, in the free carnivals of *eros*, in the productive disenchantment of the bodies in struggle. This is the signal for the passage to that 'other history': in modernity transcendental discipline will no longer be able to contain this 'other history', but only to mystify or ape it.

15.4 In the postmodern context of our analysis, the power of the body is equally the power of knowledge. Reason, as we have already amply observed, by becoming common, by integrating the tool, becomes ever more corporeal; in the same way, the body becomes increasingly intellectual. Affect and knowledge, immersed in language (i.e. the most common form of the common), recompose themselves in the body and in opposition to all transcendental divisions. In other words, the affect integrates the common force of knowledge that traverses the production of life; and passion and reason together inhabit productive language. In other words, the common intellect (that is, the *General Intellect*)[18] discovers *eros*, and love is intelligent.

15.5 When we say 'general intellect', we are speaking of the productive conditions of the postmodern era, in which intellectual and affective productive forces have become hegemonic and the primary fount of the valorization of the world. The general intellect is a machinic productive force, constituted by the multitude of corporeal singularities that form the *topos* of the common event of the general intellect. With the generation of the general intellect we enter the epoch of the man-machine.

15.6 When poverty encounters the new revolution of bodies represented by the general intellect, the poor desire the machine in so far as the
machine (tool or language) augments the productivity of bodies. That the
poor have hated and resisted the machine, that they have at times proclaimed themselves General Ludd, has been because the capitalistic use of
machines impoverished and destroyed the common productivity of the
bodies of the poor. But in the epoch of the man-machine, when the productive machine is reappropriated by the body through language,
machinic desire becomes fused with the desire [*cupidità*] that seeks to
generate new life, new bodies and new machines from poverty.

15.7 Therefore, in the biopolitical postmodern, when the poverty of
bodies undergoes the most extreme violence, the power of the poor on
the edge of time projects itself – despite everything – beyond measure; it is
as though the immeasurable opens up within the bodies of the poor themselves. There are no linear presuppositions behind this production, and
there is no linearity characterizing its course: it is in this that we recognize
poverty. In as much as the power to act of the poor is corporeal, it is at
once the expression of affects and of being affected, being worker and
machine, living in pain and in joy, the production and reproduction of the
man-machine and of the machinic body. Thus, in the postmodern era, we
can situate the 'location' of the teleological movement of the common
within the body of the poor.

16.1 If poverty represents the 'location' of the teleological movement
of the common; if it is not only a matter of resistance, but of poverty's
surging up, through resistance, as singularity; and if it presents itself,
through the construction of meaning, as common constitutive power –
then are we also able to identify, in the 'location' of poverty, the seat of
responsibility of a *dispositif* that leads from the common name to its ontological materialization, i.e. the setting in motion of materialist teleology?
Can we once again take up the constitutive teleology of common being,
but this time from 'below', from a reversed perspective than that given in
the transcendental position on the common, the latest example of which
is to be found in postmodernism?

16.2 In order to answer these questions we shall return to the analysis
of the process characterized by the tool's new nature, by the constructiveness of language, by the biopolitical materiality through which the postmodern common has come to be realized. This production repeated the
characteristics of the physics of materialism in its chaotic linearity, in its

powerful and eternal turbulence. The backdrop to this process was eternity. But, as we have seen, the common advances and innovates. The materialist physics of the *clinamen*, and following this modern asceticism, were both unable to explain this innovation. Therefore, the common appears as the product of an eternal agglomeration of elements, as a great shower of matter – or rather, as a linear constructive process, as an architectonic of ethical power. Finally, in the postmodern era, the common becomes the product of singular *dispositifs* of the multitude. An imaginary product. But what remains unclear in all of these cases, and paradoxically, this is all the more the case the more we approximate to ontological materiality, is the element in movement, i.e. innovation. We only begin to grasp it once we begin to seek it in poverty.

16.3 But if we situate it in poverty, can we really say that the aporia of materialism and the crisis of the common are resolved? That the circular character of this movement is definitively broken through the path of innovation? That innovation is expressed on a plane of immanence? That the eternal has really found a creative *clinamen*? And that the meaning – not the meaning marked by the inertia of physical movement, nor the ethical one of linear passion, but the creative one of innovation – is finally returned to the common?

16.4 If it were so, the power of poverty would – in itself (and *in reality*) – be not only the possibility of all things, but would be their determinate realization – the decision of the biopolitical, the immeasurable corporeal innovation. But one cannot draw this conclusion, because our premises have not yet been developed sufficiently. In effect, resistance, singularity and the production of meaning are not yet able to produce the autonomous imputation of action that we call 'subjectivity' (in the full sense of the term). So far we have only touched upon it.

17.1 We must be more careful. For the epistemological and ontological conditions of the innovation of the common – carried out through a materialist teleology that originates from the 'below' of poverty – appear to have been constituted. But if one stops at this initial determination, the confrontation between the physical and circular teleology of postmodern thinking and the power of poverty (this power that goes 'beyond' measure) still risks appearing as a confrontation between structurally fixed positions – one which would therefore necessarily call for a dialectical solution.

17.2 This is what occurs in the most careful, critical, and attentive postmodern readings, as we have repeatedly underlined. In order to grasp the movement, they are forced to construct a structural dialectic that surreptitiously recuperates the margin or reinserts bare alterity within totality.

17.3 That is not the case here. Our insistence on poverty enables us to grasp it as a power that cannot be recuperated in any synthesis. Nevertheless this first position is insufficient. For what is missing from the beginning is something that renders the opening of power onto the plane of immanence not only corporeal (i.e. biopolitical), but also creative. Without this move the reasoning is open to crisis once again: a crisis that not only affects the epistemological and ontological consistency of the common name of poverty, but also the possibility of orientating oneself in the common itself.

17.4 But is this crisis real or apparent? In order to overcome it, if it is possible to do so, what other transitions are we in need of – while avoiding any structuralist deviation and every dialectical shortcut?

18.1 What is certain is that this crisis is no longer played out around the recognition of the opening of common time to the immeasurable, as was the case at the end of the prolegomena to 'The Common'. Here the crisis is transferred from poverty to power itself as the 'location' of corporeal singularization and, at the same time, as 'location' of the common.

18.2 In placing itself on the limit of time, between plenitude and the void, between the eternal and innovation, poverty demands love.

Love

1.1 Poverty and love are tightly interlinked. Not because *eros* is the son of misery (and of wealth, in that tension between animality and virtue embodied in the classical centaur) – on the contrary, because from the start it represents, ontologically, the location from which the power of the whole of the possible is generated. When, having experienced it, we located the power of poverty through the rupture that resistance opened and, at the same time, through the meaning it bestowed on the common, we – in that way – exposed it to a creative and indestructible relation with all the possible *to-come*. But we also pointed out that this relation was uncertain, hazardous, and that once again it could flow back into the insignificance of the postmodern tautology. We must therefore once again analyse the experience of poverty as the ontologically constitutive location. But how are we to do this? The common name of love will be our guide.

1.2 That love is the constitutive *praxis* of the common has been a truth since antiquity. Love is the desire of the common, the desire (*cupiditas*) that traverses physics and ethics – Spinoza said as much. Knowing that desire (*cupiditas*) buries its roots in the eternity of being, we have still to demonstrate that the experience of love constitutes the dynamic of the innovation of being; but further, that love re-invents the relation between poverty and the common, and lays bare its absolute teleology; i.e. if poverty re-embodies the teleology of common action, then love makes a subject of it.

2.1 Without poverty there is no love. To speak of poverty is in some sense to speak of love. This appears evident even to the most elementary phenomenology: for it is beginning with poverty that love is set in motion. The poor person is the subject of love, even (and above all) when he is absolutely naked or is crushed by misery. It is the poor person who renders love real.

2.2 One of the greatest evils perpetrated by Christian philosophy consists in considering the poor person not as the subject but as the object of love. It is of course true that Christ's mysticism and theology overturns this proposition, such that in each poor person one discovers the figure of Christ. But in common usage, traditionally and in the triumphal history of Christianity, the hegemonic affirmation is that of the object-like status of the poor. The very name of the poor is rendered unusable by pity. On the contrary, the corporeality of the poor, their immediate reality (contrary to what is sustained by the dominant philosophies, 'which cannot claim not to be Christian', in the words of Benedetto Croce), is given a subjective determination in love. The latter, after being animated by poverty, puts poverty in relation to the common.

2.3 The experience of poverty introduces one to the constitution of the common; the experience of love is an activity of construction of the common. If the common is the incarnation of love, then poverty provides the corporeal basis of this relation.

2.4 From this perspective one can say without any doubt that the relation between poverty and love is configured as an eternal return of the power of love to the location of poverty. And it is a creative return that installs itself in the physical and ethical context of the fall of the atoms of life, yet it breaks the linearity of their fall and so generates the common. It is the figure of the *clinamen*, but in subjective form; it is the chaos of the eternal cosmos, but brought back to subjectivity.

2.5 The common is animated and given subjective determination when born of the creative relation between poverty and love. It is for this reason that, in order to nourish the desire of the common, one must be or one must make oneself poor; and if one wishes to construct the common, one must love.

3.1 In materialism, love is the ontological power that constructs being. But being is not a given, but a constructed product. From the standpoint of *kairòs*, we have seen in the first part of these lessons how this construction of being occurs when the arrow of time precipitates into the void of the *to-come*. Further, we have also seen that love has the effect of making the relation between the eternal and the *to-come* immeasurable. From the ontological point of view we are confronted by the 'being that is there'; but this being is there in its quality as artefact, as a contradictory determination of the common that is always exposed to the immeasurability of the *to-come*. Materialist teleology exhibits an aleatory history of the construction of being and, through it, of the common. And it cannot but exhibit this since it is a construction, an artefact (and the fact that in the biopolitical, nature and artefact can be used as interchangeable names, does not change the substance of the problem); but all that which is constructed is aleatory, i.e. is born of the necessity of exposing itself to the void; and the multitude is made common by nothing other than this necessity.

3.2 How, then, can we demonstrate that love is the key to the dynamic of the construction of being? We have already answered this question: because poverty and love construct the common name of the common, they consequently call the common into being. But if it is so, and it is indeed so, we must nevertheless deepen our exposition in order to shine a light on the entirety of the power of the ontological construction that love is capable of. To do so *in reality*, we must grasp this power in terms of the constitution of the ontological parameters, that is to say, of the production of the temporal and spatial dimensions of the world.

4.1 The first fundamental dimension of the experience of the world is that of time: love must therefore become the temporal construction of the world. Now, being is indeed constructed in accordance with the arrow of time that advances without conclusion. But temporality is unable to emancipate itself from the eternal and open itself to production – i.e. to augment the eternal, opening it constitutively to the *to-come* – except for when it is sustained by love. It is 'generation' that augments the eternal, that innovates being.

4.2 What do we mean then by 'generation'? 'Generation' is love that follows the thread of time from its beginning and so weaves its fabric in the common. Through generation love gives subjective determination to time by projecting it in the common. There is no solitary love: love constructs tools, languages and politics of being within the common; and in generating, it creates being, i.e. it renews the eternal. But in the common, generation is always singular because it is characterized by poverty. Common being is generated setting out from a multitude of singular existences, and the eternity of the common is a sky whose stars are singularities. Love continuously illuminates the stars of this common sky.

4.3 The Lucretian hymn to *Alma Venus* no longer resounds like a desperate song in the night, representing the triumph of the cosmic turbulence of a tempest of atoms that repeat the blind eternity of the world; it is not a pathetic comet in the immobility of the skies. No, *Alma Venus* is here something entirely creative, it is a hymn that sings the continuous creation of the eternal. Generation is irreducible: the horrible fairy-tale that considers corruption and destruction as its necessary complements is merely the illusion of an immobile world, of a cosmos that adds up to zero, of a being deprived of love. Against this, once generated, being is no longer inclined towards death, and generation holds for eternity. Nothingness and death are prior to love, before the experience of the generation of being; then being is regenerated in the common and in the eternal.

4.4 Love thus embraces the arrow of time, making it creative, and it prolongs its trajectory within the tension of the generation of the *to-come*. Time is the offspring of love because only generation prolongs the temporality of the *to-come*. The time of the eternal is made immeasurable, through generation, within the *to-come*.

5.1 The second fundamental dimension of the experience of the world is that of space: love must therefore become the spatial constitution of the world. But spatial being is made and remade in the common, as we have repeatedly underlined from the standpoint of *kairòs*. It is only when love constructs the common name of space that it is called into existence. Or rather, love constructs space only in so far as space is constitutive of the common. But why does love construct space? Because love seeks the common, both the eternity of the common (i.e. the already generated) and the *to-come* of the common (i.e. that which is to be constituted on the edge of time). Space is the projection of the accumulation of the experience constitutive of being produced by love within the temporality that is rendered immeasurable between eternity and the *to-come*. This constitutive experience is proper to the multitude of temporality, i.e. to the ontological subjective determinations of time when – urged on by poverty – they extend themselves over the edge of being. Space is born from this experience; from this point the arrows of time, driven on by love, constitute while projecting themselves into the void in order to go on perpetually constructing common being in the modality of space.

5.2 That which, in time, is generation (i.e. a formidable innovation of the eternal) is, in space, co-operation. Co-operation is love that proceeds by making itself common among multiplicities. Consequently, it is the power of love multiplied. Co-operation is the space constituted by the common and so is multiplied in its productivity – productivity: nothing other than the capacity of the common to become increasingly common. Co-operation is a common generation of space. And the co-operation of singularities is more productive than any singular existence, because it expresses communally the striving of the multitude of singularities that attempt to endow being with meaning. But this striving would not in turn exist if co-operation were not an amorous force, i.e. the exploration by the poor singularity of the common as the expression of power.

6.1 The common name of love is thus the constitutive ontological power in the true sense – constitutive of time and space, adequate representation of common being and, above all, the establishment of the foundation of the biopolitical.

6.2 If generation and co-operation, i.e. love, augment the eternal, better still, render it ever more productive, the dilemma of materialism between eternity and innovation is resolved; and the fact that the eternal can be rendered more powerful disengages it from the paradox of classical metaphysics which, every time it spoke of the eternal, spoke of the global invariability of being. But resolving this dilemma also means arriving at the awareness that the common is a biopolitical production. In other words: all the temporal and spatial powers of love, in their precipitation towards and beyond the edge of being, make the common into a vital force that brings together – almost as though it were set in a natural context – the resistance and the power of the multitude.

6.3 From the standpoint of the epistemology of *kairòs*, it also means that in the biopolitical common, the power of knowledge is defined by the interweaving of intelligence and affect, of brain and body, that becomes concrete in the ontology of love announced by the phenomenology of poverty.

6.4 Love as biopolitical power is the name of absolute immanence, but of an immanence that generates. To insist on the biopolitical figure of the constitutive force of love means not only to offer elements towards a solution of the enigma of ancient materialism but also to those of modern materialism, and more precisely still, to that of Spinoza's materialism. For the immanence of love to the ontological process was certainly formulated in terms of constitution and production in Spinoza; but the constitutive *praxis* was unable to unfold its generative potential by bringing together the logics of constitution in a biopolitical epistemology. Inhibited by the difficulties of modern rationalism, of the ideology of the man-man, Spinozism resorted to mysticism, and through mysticism there reemerged the old and always repeated pantheist illusion of the immobility of being.

6.5 Only love produced by poverty constitutes the common in the biopolitical, i.e. puts the process of constitutive *praxis* back on its material feet. Therefore, absolute immanence presents itself not only as 'absolute democracy' – which is still merely a repetition of the typology of forms of government proscribed by the classical tradition, but rather as a constitutive *praxis* of the multitude and of all its powers of life brought into relation with a new virtue (*virtus*) of the common. When this virtue (*virtus*) is developed, the political is dissolved into the forms of life, so that we can here look back over ontology through the meshes and practices of the biopolitical. With no residues.

7.1 Thus in the biopolitical, the name of politics understood as command is dispelled. And if politics presents itself as command again, it is simply a matter of violent mystification. The self-government of the forms of life becomes the only possible horizon for the teleology of the common. If constitutive *praxis* proceeds through a common language and biopolitical *praxis* of the common, it is within this movement that we live and construct the common at the same time as we construct being. In the biopolitical traversed by love, politics also becomes common, along with the production and reproduction of life. Who doubts that these tasks of the *vita activa* constitute the specificity of our daily engagement? For politics is a daily task revealed by love as the productive power of the present. It is the quotidian responsibility for the generation of the eternal. In the common name of that which is productive and political one discovers one of the keys to the understanding of common being. Politics as command is thus the mystification of being that violently subtracts being from the common.

7.2 Every shortcut, every mystery, every hypostasis in the definition of Power is thus swept away by the simple sense of the common construction of being. In this way the cynical fables of the autonomy of the political, the perversions of Machiavellianism and the vulgarities of the Raison d'État are subjected to the destructive critique of the biopolitical, and thereby lose any credibility. And all this despite the massive and spectacular instrumentalization that is played out around them so as to hide their violent and parasitical character. But the real is stubborn. The real takes another course, traversed as it is by love that inclines poverty towards the common, that is to say within the teleological *praxis* of the common.

7.3 The materialist teleology of the common is revealed here as practical force, because its finality rests on the necessity (for production) of constructing, within the *vita activa*, its conditions of reproduction, and consequently of activating the singularities in view of the construction of the common – which is what the finality of the singularities themselves consists in. And what, therefore, is politics, if not the common transcription of this production of life and the interpretation of these material finalities? We shall return to this later, when we tackle the topic of the biopolitical not only from the standpoint of the teleological substance, but also from the point of view of the practical *kairòs*, that is to say, of the decision of the singularities that project it.

8.1 Let us return now to an observation we have made on more than one occasion, that is, to the fact that the revolution of the common presupposes postmodernity. Materialist critique (i.e. the teleology of the common) discovers in the postmodern era the emergence of the common name of the common in forms that are frequently contorted and mystified, but which are nevertheless strong and effective. To clarify this frequently reiterated observation, let us compare the (generic) postmodern perception of the common with the definition given it by modernity. Modernity constitutes the common as public space, as cultural and/or sociological and/or transcendental ensemble of individual interests. This constitution of the common is therefore understood as a transcendental (general and abstract) of the interests of individuals, and not as the product of the *vita activa* of singularities. It should also be borne in mind that, in modernity, interests are not individual only in their social form; modernity expresses them in this way because it formulates them on the basis of a corresponding anthropology. Man and citizen, society and market, are derived from one and the same genealogy, which is that of individuality. Now, postmodernism, in as much as it is the philosophy of our epoch and the (generic) perception of the common, rejects the genealogy of modernity and rather poses citizenship (Man) and market (society) in a relation of uninterrupted circulation, almost as an equivalent tautology, and does so against the backdrop of a decisive attenuation of the progressive characteristics of history and of the exclusion of any prophetic destiny, going so far as to speak of an 'end of history'. Postmodernism radically de-substantializes the categories of modernity. It follows that the categories of the private (individual) and of the public (juridical abstraction, or socio-institutional concretization of a general norm of work, language and the *bios*) are now proposed as interchangeable functions in time and space. Postmodernism thus correctly registers the mutation that the organization of work, the structures of the markets and the order of the world have undergone, and enables us to subsume them in theory. Up until the present, perception, although generic, has been common; but it is equally from this point that the differing points of view emerge. The retainers of Power (as well as the philosophers who applaud their hegemony) do not, however, draw adequate consequences from the new perception of the world, from this revolution that has radically overturned the relations of production and the forms of life. If this perception of mutation has enabled one to move away from the ideologies of modern philosophy, this point of view repeats them in the evaluation of the situation, for it once again posits, in the present case, the modern measure of the transcendental (of the private, of capitalist appropriation, etc.) above and against the mutation which has taken place. The mutation reveals that the common is not an abstraction of individual interests, but is the circulation of singular needs; that the public is not a juridical category, but is biopolitical; that politics (law, government, etc.) are not above, but within life. Postmodern philosophy, inspired by Power, takes no account of all of this, if not so as to better adapt the old measures to the new immeasurable. Incredibly, postmodern philosophy, inspired by Power, seems here to realize (in relation to the categories of political thought and of juridical practice, to not speak of other areas) that sort of 'communism of capital' of which Marx spoke when prophetically analysing the emergence of 'stock-companies'.[19] But in the face of the generic perception of the common in the postmodern era there emerges another standpoint, and it is precisely to this that our critical analysis of postmodern philosophy refers. This standpoint denounces the mystification of the new relation that Power attempts to establish between the singularity and the common. And it insists on the necessity of providing the revolutionary mutation with revolutionary consequences.

9.1 This internal relation of the singular and the common must thus be explored so as to understand how love constructs being. And in order for us to begin to perceive this, let us recall that in the history of human *praxis*, love has always sought to become a technology of constitution and, it goes without saying, of the transformation of being. Love is rooted in that 'way up' that passes from the singular to the common and that determines, in each epoch, the specific materialist teleology of the common. Outside the maturation of this technology, the 'technologies of love' are incomplete and unsatisfied. They seek transcendence, instead of interpreting and developing immanence. They live the transcendental illusion itself, instead of innovating the world.

10.1 In this way Christian *caritas* (but this is already the case with the pagan *virtus* or *pietas*), in fighting against slavery, sweetens its contours but puts off the solution until the kingdom of God. What power is to be observed in that *caritas*! And what a revolution it sets in motion! But it is a subterranean power, which is never able to give a name to the real, which in other words is unable to recognize the common name of poverty without making reference to transcendence. This power comes to a standstill before the State, acknowledging its autonomous and necessary consistency. The illusion gives the heart power and, when necessary, nourishes martyrdom. The revolution is implicit, whispered to spirits, entrusted to angels. But in the age of the centaur, *caritas* can never – by means of the soul – redeem the bare matter that constitutes the body of the poor.

11.1 In the modern age the technology of love is ascetic. *Amor*, on the one hand reaches the lofty heights of metaphysical expression constructed by the philosophies of immanence (from Bruno and Campanella up until Spinoza), on the other hand searches for a worldly course in the protestant theories of predestination – but it is unable to get a hold on the teleology of the common other than by insisting on the passion of the individual and entrusting itself to an improbable community of ends. A sort of providence has moved from the transcendent to the transcendental so as to bring together the ethical ends and the ascetic individual, linking itself to the genealogy of the social, but always understood exclusively in terms of individuals. It comes to a standstill before the law, which is the law that extols the contract and exploitation in the hypothetical perspective of the community of ends and of progress. Love and its technologies become historical, they attach themselves to an object-subject to be constructed historically, but are always closed in the indecent circle of individualities. What formidable powers and illusions are expressed there! And what pride is revealed in the affirmation of the historical power of the man-man! The asceticism of work, wherein resides the ethicality of modern Man, is here the centre of the genealogy of the common. The man who dominates this tableau is the man who works hard and with a civic sense pays the price, the man who from being a worker becomes a citizen. But all this unfolds within a horrible secret: of the one who, in sacrificing himself, wants Power; of the private sphere that, through a juridical framework, constitutes the public in its image and only elevates itself through exploitation.

12.1 'Militancy' is the third technology of love to offer us the experience of the common. It corresponds to the highest maturation of the technology of the common. It was anticipated ambiguously (and was pre-constituted in an almost vicious manner) in the tradition of revolutionary social movements of the nineteenth and twentieth centuries. Anticipated and pre-constituted because, in this history, singularity and the common effectively become, within the experience of the multitude, a form of co-operation; ambiguously and viciously, because this process of the co-production of the common has been broken by prophetic and consequently bureaucratic moments that overlay the movement of the multitude; but also because the definition of the common has, with increasing frequency, been confused with the achievement of modernity and has been subjected to its construction. In that tradition to which we refer, instead of speaking of 'the multitude', one would speak of 'the masses'. But in the concept of 'the masses' there lived the shadow of the transcendental – when one did not go to the extreme of configuring the term as a dialectical moment. Today, against this, outside every preconception and all prefiguration, can love constitute an adequate technology in the heart of militancy? And what would it consist in? As we have already said, it could consist in co-operation, i.e. in the co-production of singularities and of the multitude. Therefore, in place of the 'masses' we now have the 'multitude' – which is precisely the always open striving of the multiple singularities within the constitution of the common. Militancy, as the *praxis* of love, reveals the coexistence of the dynamics of poverty and of the constitution of the common.

12.2 But why do we continue to refer to this technology of love with the old name of 'militancy'? Has not this old name been completely discarded (and objectively displaced) following the crisis of real socialism? Perhaps. But who will ever forget the virtuous energy of those movements, of those men and those multitudes that in the course of more than a century rebuilt hope? And who invented, in new forms, the common name of the common in revolutionary practice?

12.3 Another objection to the use of the old name of 'militancy' seems more pertinent. Given the new biopolitical dimensions (within which the definition of the technology of love is about to be provided), the name of militancy lacks the entrepreneurial and constitutive qualities that give birth to linguistic, productive and political networks that define its novelty. But what should take the place of 'militancy'? 'Entrepreneur', 'political entrepeneur' or 'social entrepreneur'? What contradictions would be provoked by such a linguistic contamination! (Should we use the anodyne name of the 'voluntary sector'? But does this not bring us back to a transcendental culture from which we are now far away?)

12.4 So, despite these reservations, let us for now keep to the terrain of militancy. And let us insist on the material dimension of the common name rather than on a linguistic formula. Militancy is therefore resistance, rupture, the discovery of singularity (of itself and of the event), and the production of the common name. These are the essential moments of this experience, which are what render it irreducible to any other. The intensity of the common that it comprises is precisely what defines it. 'Militancy of the common'. Therefore, it is an experience that develops within the complex totality of the biopolitical. It does not create superstructures that hold it back or sustain it in illusory form; this experience expresses itself as constituent power across every articulation of the biopolitical experience. It traverses the reproduction of life, just as it works on the production of relations and of the social relations through which values are formed; at each moment it is affective energy and rational passion. It is the construction of the multitude through the production of subjectivity. It is at once the capacity to command oneself and the common in command.

13.1 But if we wish to deepen further our concept of the militancy of the common understood as practice of poverty and love, we must turn our attention to the radical transformation of the relationship between anthropology and ontology that is presupposed by the practice of the common. The construction of the common does indeed take into account the modifications of the ensemble of anthropological conditions. And this is possible today not only because the revolution of the tool and of language completely transform sensoriality and affectivity, but also because the limits of the human being are extended and now comprise the environmental context. These anthropological qualifications cannot be considered purely extensively; this is only the case – at least in part – in modernity. In postmodernity, the transformation of the tool, the productive hegemony of linguistic practices and the formation of a biopolitical context within the production of subjectivity, metamorphose the human being and realize its hybridization across all pre-established boundaries.

13.2 All this is well known. What we want to underline in this transformation is the power of love, i.e. the technology of loving and the militancy of the common, which develops into the capacity to meaningfully arrange the diagrams of the common through metamorphosis. Overcoming the 'natural' limits, the contamination of languages, mixing of genera and races and the general hybridization of being are all constitutive elements of the common in postmodernity. The only problem is that of endowing the interweaving of languages and of bodies with the meaning of the common; and it is indeed love that takes up this task by referring back and verifying once again the teleology of the common understood as an experiment in metamorphosis. In postmodernity the common presents itself as metamorphosis. The materialist teleology is a teleology of metamorphosis. Anthropology and ontology live in this *milieu* of hybridization, in the heart of this process of love that the new technologies of love are able to endow with meaning – and that thereby become indistinguishable, because the one has become the prosthesis of the other.

13.3 One final remark regarding these reflections on anthropology and ontology concerns the question of poverty. If we look at it attentively, this experience includes a first definition of the new relationship that we are describing – in as much as it is the possibility of all positivity, because it is lacking in all determination of wealth, of inclusion and of liberty. This lack is total. Therefore it places poverty (as anthropological experience) in relation to the ontological totality. The experience of love, when it comes to maturity through militant activity, exalts this constitutive relationship and reshapes the general fabric of experience. It is from this standpoint that we can best define that same concept of metamorphosis. It is no more a concept designating the transformation from one natural or human form to another, as in the epoch of the centaur, any more than it desig-nates the metamorphosis of work, of commodities and of capital (that is followed by the metamorphoses of spirit, whether individual or absolute), as in the epoch of the man-man. Here the concept of metamorphosis designates the creation of new forms – *tout court* – in and by the common. The completely open possibility that is given in poverty shows itself here as creative plenitude. The ancient and modern enigma of the relation between eternity and innovation is resolved, once again, thanks to the determination of poverty-love as the energy that constitutes the new forms of the common.

14.1 The requalification of the nexus between anthropology and ontology leads us on to ask ourselves about the procedures of that tech-nology of love that we have called the 'militancy of the common'; and in particular to that dimension of the procedure that is immediately com-mon, and that tradition has handed down to us under the name of polit-ics. If politics is given to us in this way, we must settle our accounts with it as such. We must do so radically, entirely destructively, because tradition-ally the political is the opposite of love. And yet it is a form of the com-mon; up until the entry into postmodernity, it has even represented its highest form. The role that mythology and teleology played in the centre and at the margins of the epoch of the centaur was taken up by politics in the age of the man-man. But today it is no longer so. And when it still presents itself as such, politics (and with it all the other fetishes that lay claim to the form of the common: property, right, civil society and its various institutions) represents a ghastly anachronism. Closed in this anachronism that tears it from what it wants to represent, politics becomes spectacle and violence. The parasitical character of the political has become total. The technology of love thus denounces this figure of Power. It goes against it with that same naturalness with which the lion tears the lamb to pieces. But what else do you expect when the most intelligent political scientists define politics as the practice of systemic compatibility? This definition is sufficient to justify the contempt, and often the disgust, with which even the most intelligent politicians are effectively considered.

15.1 The common is anything but accountancy, compatibility and systematization. Today, the militancy of the common takes the place of politics. What does it consist in, how does it operate? Militancy, this construction of the common, acts in the common by producing meaning. Will it still be possible to call it 'politics' and consider it as an activity that takes up the same space occupied by modern politics? It acts on a different terrain, that of the totality of life. From this point of view 'biopolitics' is already a more plausible approximation to the common name. For biopolitics brings to the forefront the constitutive movement, the productive force and the procedures of love understood as energies that traverse common matter and transform it. But this is still only an approximation. In reality we will only be able to construct a common name in a definitive manner once love, as technology of the common, has invested the entire political context, destroying and replacing it.

15.2 That is precisely what is happening: since 1968 the history of humanity has taken this course; the materialist teleology of the common is engaged in this task. And it is precisely at the moment when Power celebrated its most propagandized success – that is, postmodern globalization – that the genealogy of the common transformed itself into a technology of love and began to emerge. The destruction of the separation between public and private, nomadism and the flexibility of labour-power, the new configuration of the social as the structure of the common (in all its biopolitical dimensions), the emergence of mass intellectuality – here are just some of the powerful prefigurations of the common animated by love. Every attempt by Power, by 'politics', to throw new nets over this powerful production of subjectivity, determines new resistances, new communities, new programmes on the side of poverty; but also movements and powers that go against, that trace new horizons and create 'another' order of life: the common. It is politics in its entirety that is assailed by the common movement of poverty and of the militancy of the common – it is 'another common', other than politics, to which love gives meaning.

15.3 So what is 'politics' today? It is the activity of production of the common name between poverty and love. But how? And then?

Multitudo

Prolegomena

> I had stood up. Under the impassive stars,
> on the earth infinitely deserted and
> mysterious, from his tent free man
> extended his arms toward the infinite sky undefiled
> by the shadow of Any God".
>
> > (Dino Campana, *Orphic Songs* ('Pampa'))

Politics

1.1 The postmodern multitude is an ensemble of singularities whose life-tool is the brain and whose productive force consists in co-operation. In other words, if the singularities that constitute the multitude are plural, the manner in which they enter into relations is co-operative.

1.2 Our question is the following: how can this biopolitical (intellectual and co-operative) mass, which we call 'multitude', exert 'governance over itself'? How can the plurality and the co-operation of singularities express governance of the common, in so far as they form the constitutive power of the world?

1.3 The transcendental metaphors of Power (that once again take up the teleological ones) deny that, within the horizon of singularities, co-operation can be elevated (in itself) to the efficacy of Power, and deny further that mass intellectuality is capable of a united decision over it. Modern sovereignty is the generic name of these negations.

1.4 Adding the following proviso, however: unless co-operation and intellectuality are mediated by and/or directed towards a destined end; in other words: unless they are surreptitiously sustained by a finalistic and/ or eschatological plan. But this is nothing other than a liminal conception of sovereignty.

1.5 On the basis of what has been said so far, our enquiry takes the name of sovereignty to be illusory. We thus, on the contrary, consider the common to be the exclusive criterion of the political. But how is one to provide the common with government?

2.1 In the course of the development of revolutionary political thought, the fundamental perception of the revolution as ontological transformation has always recuperated and integrated the thought of sovereignty. Political ontology has paid for this original sin. Within the teleology of the common, on the contrary, ontological transformation frees us from sovereignty.

2.2 From the diachronic perspective, the 'reformist' conception of ontological transformation has always been subjected to a powerful critique that sought to show the impossibility of transforming the parts without transforming the whole. But once outside the transcendental illusion, the whole is nothing other than the ensemble of the parts. Therefore, the ontological grounds of reformism have a real consistency.

2.3 From the synchronic perspective, the 'reformist' deliberations on ontological transformation have been accused of relinquishing the (rational) decision of the reappropriation of Power within the political system, i.e. of refusing the rational character of insurrection. But Power cannot decide upon the ontological transformation, just as insurrection is not the negative face of Power (for on the contrary, it expresses ontological innovation).

2.4 In freeing itself from the transcendental character of sovereignty, political philosophy (particularly in its materialist form, and the ontological *praxis* of the political that follows from it) transforms the meaning of the thematic of the decision. Contrary to what occurred when the decision represented the 'eminent' sign of the political, and insurrection represented the matrix of a fantastical 'taking Power', decision and insurrection, once situated within the horizon of mass intellectuality and co-operation, will have to be absorbed and worked through by the singularities that constitute the multitude.

2.5 Decision and insurrection are neither rational nor irrational, neither systemic nor spontaneous; they participate in the teleology of the common, that is, in that teleology that at each instant is opened in a creative manner to the immeasurability of the *to-come*.

3.1 The teleology of the common, in so far as it is the motor of ontological transformation of the world, cannot be subjected to the theory of sovereign mediation. For sovereign mediation is always the foundation of a unit of measure, while ontological transformation is always immeasurable.

3.2 The modern State-form articulates the unit of measure through a process of composition and 'organic' distribution of 'representative' functions. Measure subordinates the plurality of singular powers to a schema of organic mediations and distributes them in a hierarchy of functions. Modern representative democracy is a practice of measure and a glorification of the limit.

3.3 'Leninism', when it poses itself the problem of the recomposition of the multitude, failed in its task in the instant that it defined dictatorship as the highest form of democracy. From this perspective it participates in the history of modern sovereignty. All this becomes evident when, independently of the genesis and the formidable success of the October Revolution, one considers that the industrial development (taken as the unit of measure) is the skeleton in the cupboard of the Leninist theory of revolution.[20]

4.1 In the materialist teleology of the common, political philosophy has nothing to do with 'direct democracy'. On the contrary, direct democracy does not free itself from the form of modern sovereignty; rather, it extols it through the transcendental illusion of the community (of singularities).

4.2 That is perfectly clear in that thread of political thought that reaches (despite the enormous differences) from Rousseau and Hegel, to Bakunin and Nozick. In this tradition, the hypostasis of the totality (general will, general class, the glorious eve of anarchism, individualist logic of the political market) is presupposed to the temporal production of the multitude and to its exposure to the immeasurable.

4.3 The only real existing form of direct democracy is that of corporatism. It has existed in two forms: the fascist one, which recuperates the mediation of social groups within the ethical State (that is eventually capable of annihilating difference); and the New Dealist/Keynsian one, that subjugates the accord between *big business*, *big labour* and *big government* to the measure of imperialist development. The constitutional project of democratic corporatism is the destruction of the multitude.

4.4 The pluralistic theories of democracy of Proudhonian inspiration, those, in other words, that imagine plural measures and differential social development, can also be brought back to the model of modern sovereignty. Indeed, mediation is fundamental here as well; and although the intervention of sovereign Power is modest in this case, this is only because one imagines its functions and its units of measure to be absorbed by and in the social. This broth is only a little more insipid than that of corporatism. It remains, however, a variant of it, since it knows nothing of the immeasurability of the *to-come*.

5.1 In the postmodern era, a weak theory of sovereignty requires a form of pluralization and of 'syndicalism' (or corporatism) of the social, as the condition of Power over the multitude. Once one has recognized the social organization of diffuse webs of communication, whose consistency is autonomous and that are subjected to a strong tension between territorial rootedness and the global market (of production, reproduction and circulation of values), this theory formulates the project of a process of re-centralization founded on the globally valid unit of (monetary, financial, etc.) measure. The articulation of the entrepreneurial territorialized forces, and the reduction to a common measure of the global market, must, however, arise through a dialectic of sovereignty that finds its guarantee in a supranational and/or imperial force. But at this point sovereignty, from being weak, becomes strong once again; and the pluralization (or syndicalism) of the social, which was a sociological figure, is torn away from this terrain and is redirected towards representative functions that are intimately related to imperial Power. In order to respond to the power of the multitude, sovereignty extends its centre of gravity within deterritorialized horizons. Although this conceptual and practical somersault alters the form of sovereignty, it does not alter its reality.

5.2 Even when in the postmodern era we have reached this level of systemic complexity and of dialectical neutralization of singularities, it is clear that the continuity of the transcendental conception of sovereignty remains intact. In the extension and accentuation of its efficacy, not only the reformist but also the revolutionary conceptions of Power end up being subsumed. This is the *dispositif* of imperial sovereignty.

5.3 But within the context of the sovereign organization of globality, Empire is directly confronted by the multitude, and the multitude by Empire. In this context, all mediations tend to disintegrate.

5.4 So far all reforms and all revolutions have only strengthened the political philosophy of measure and unity, i.e. the transcendental illusion of the unit of measure. For the articulation that brings together society and State, in modernity, cannot be either severed or realized differently. But the postmodern multitude can make it explode by affirming a commonality that does not bow to any equation of sovereignty, exposing it rather to the immeasurability of time.

6.1 To say that the political order of postmodernity is exposed destructively to the immeasurability of time means that the multitude produces life by taking out an option on the *to-come*. It is not Power but the constituent power of the multitude that creates the common existence of the world. This common existence is presupposed to any order, because it renders any order immeasurable.

6.2 It is the biopolitical that determines all production of the world by affirming the consistency of being in constituent power and by opening the constitutive arrow of time to the innovation of the eternal.

6.3 The teleology of the common lives through its exposure to the *to-come*. If the biopolitical is the matter of the teleology of the common, poverty and love are its keystones. But poverty and love are also open to the immeasurability of the time *to-come*. Consequently the teleology of the common is exposed to this immeasurability. It follows at the same time that:

6.4 The production of the (physical and political) world and of its riches *to-come* is a 'superstructure' of the common. I say this as a paradox, because it is evident that in the biopolitical there is no up and no down, no inside and no outside. But it is important to insist, even paradoxically, on this – against all the mystifications of economism, against all the illusions of the 'superstructure' – thereby demonstrating that only the common is foundational *in reality*.

6.5 Every biopolitical genealogy is determined by the opening to the beyond measure.

7.1 The biopolitical horizon of the world is plural. The multitude is an irreducible ensemble of singularities, and singularity (as an instance of exposure to the beyond measure) is the production of new pluralities, of new multitudes.

7.2 Situated on the edge of time, every productive nexus between singularities in the core of the multitude, and between singular multitudes, is a communicative nexus. In this context, production is the production of subjectivity.

7.3 But if production is production of subjectivity, that is, if the producer and the product are subjective, and if the productive process coincides with the linguistic sphere of the general biopolitical intellect, then we can explain the common name of co-operation as that force that brings together the producers by increasing their productive capacity; this, therefore, allows the singular production of subjectivity to become productive power. That is to say, there would be no production if there were no co-operation.

7.4 If the plurality is co-operative, the multitude is an ensemble of constellations productive of subjectivity.

8.1 Our current problem is that of analysing how the constellations productive of subjectivity are formed and how they intersect (or in other words, the way in which they situate themselves in relations of co-operation).

8.2 This is a crucial point in our analysis, in as much as here the theme of the generation of the eternal, i.e. of its innovation, is taken up once again. Co-operation is a constellation of differences in the heart of the multitude; it is that *clinamen* that productively organizes the chaos of the multitude of singularities. We speak here of constellations, where others have spoken of *dispositifs* or assemblages.[21] This is evidently still only a first step in our enquiry. There will be other steps in which we will seek the reason and/or the dynamic force of this process, that is, in which we shall return to the analysis of love as the constitutive power of every constellation.

9.1 A 'productive constellation' is formed where the power-differences of the multitude co-operate, creating new power. A constellation is more productive than the sum of the productive singularities (taken separately) that co-operate within them. It is thus for this reason that the singularities endeavour to co-operate and the singular multitudes form constellations, because in that way they may produce more; or better still, they can continuously move beyond the singular measure of productivity and can open themselves increasingly to the immeasurable.

9.2 The genealogy of the co-operative constellations seems, therefore, to be defined by its result: the concluding surplus-value. But this quantitative determination should not deceive us: the constellations are formed when, on the edge of being, the singularities ask themselves how to productively advance their labour. This question is sustained by poverty and love, and consequently the co-operative constellations are a teleological advancing of the common.

9.3 In modernity, productive co-operation was imposed through capitalist and/or state appropriation. Here one recognizes the revolution of the man-man that made exploitation the foundation of the common.

9.4 In the postmodern era, productive co-operation was imposed by the hegemony of mass intellectuality. Without co-operation (or more precisely, without linguistic co-operation) it cannot produce: it is thus the character of (intellectual) productive labour itself that constructs and imposes co-operation on the singularities. In postmodernity, the singularities themselves would not exist without co-operation.

9.5 Linguistic co-operation conveys co-operation from the outside to the inside of the social organization of work, thereby changing it; that is, it annuls the 'outside' and transvaluates co-operation, making it a power *in reality*.

9.6 If in modernity the multitude (the masses) was produced from the outside, in postmodernity the multitude is formed spontaneously. Which is to say, the multitude is the power of the singularities that are brought together within co-operative constellations; and the common precedes production.

9.7 The epochal break between modernity and postmodernity is 1968. For in 1968 mass intellectuality presented itself for the first time in hegemonic form, that is, as a hegemonic constellation in and of the multitude.

10.1 In becoming power, the multitude generates. Generation is not something that precedes the multitude, but on the contrary is something that belongs to it, i.e. that defines it in constituting it. Generation proceeds from the multitude.

10.2 The value produced by the multitude is the immeasurable. It is the power of the multitude projected beyond the edge of being.

10.3 The generation of the multitude innovates being.

11.1 How the productive multitudes intersect is not a problem that presents itself *after* that of the formation of the constellations, but at the same time. The complex genealogy of sequences of co-operation is in fact an interweaving of singularities and multitudes. It is a Tower of Babel of languages that has become productive. It is the primordial physics in which every *to-come* is installed.

11.2 The genealogy of productive power is a free interweaving, as is the development of the teleology of the common, because it has no beginning and no end, but is eternal. It knows no commandments other than its own free *telos*, following the arrow of time that it looses at each instant, so as to create new being.

11.3 Everything flows and everything hybridizes on the edge of time. On all sides, in the face of the void, the singularities mount assaults on the limit so as to construct in common another plenitude for life. That is what the biopolitical production of the multitude consists in: stretching itself out from fullness to emptiness so as to fill the void.

11.4 Obviously, every formation (and every interweaving) of constellations can and must be considered in its specific determination.

12.1 In modernity, the biopolitical is the product of productive *Welfare*. In postmodernity, *Welfare* is extended across the whole space of biopolitics, to the point of merging with it. It is under these conditions of formal extinction and real irreversibility of *Welfare* that the biopolitical becomes the base, and production a superstructure.

12.2 In the genealogy of postmodern thought, Marx's notion of the extraction of surplus-value from production is exhausted (even when one makes the process of exploitation adhere to the totality of the social). The conditions for Marx's notion of exploitation are over, because industrial production is no longer fundamental and has become only a simple consequence of the productive activity of the biopolitical base. In other words, in postmodernity, work has become intellectual and immaterial; it has installed itself in biopolitical co-operation; how can it be exploited?

12.3 In postmodernity, what we call surplus-value in the economy of modernity is no longer simply the extortion of labour (beyond the value necessary for its reproduction, which is modified in all cases). In postmodernity, surplus-value is above all a blockage of the teleology of the common, that is, it is the attempt to render it tautological and to render the common name of the common meaningless. What in the economy of modernity is called exploitation is, in postmodernity, defined by the barriers set up against the attempt, by the poor, to pass beyond the limit of being by means of the immeasurable. Exploitation is deflation; it is a thwarting and a reduction to measure of the power of biopolitics open to the *to-come*.

13.1 In postmodernity, 'constituent power' is no longer that creative and instantaneous concentration of the multitude (or of poverty in revolt) that, through insurrection (and its successive ensuing Thermidors), constructs a new order, as is the case in modernity. In the present, constituent power has become the political dimension that corresponds to the development of the teleology of the common; that is, it is the constitutive force that proceeds from a biopolitical base, extends itself across all horizons of being, and so to every instant of temporality.

13.2 The formation and interweaving of productive constellations are manifestations of constituent power.

13.3 The critiques of constitutive power that play on the 'instituting-instituted' opposition, whether they are of dialectical or vitalistic inspiration, are false. For in postmodernity, constituent power knows nothing of that opposition, in as much as it exists in accordance with the direction that urges the common to constitute itself against the void, on the edge of time. Because it is always present in this exposure to the eternal, constituent power denies that something constituted could be simply presupposed.

13.4 One must give credit to the critics of 'Jacobinism' (understood as a generic concept which can be identified with the historically existing practice constituted by Heinrich Heine's threee Rs: Richelieu, Robespierre and Rothschild) for having correctly defined ontology as more fundamental than politics in the history of modernity. The idea that the reactionary philosophers of modern politics have been wiser than the revolutionary is not new. In postmodern philosophy this ontological priority is absolute, because ontology has absorbed the political.[22]

13.5 All that which is political is biopolitical. The concept of the 'autonomy of the political' is in consequence a perfidious and morbid ideology. In postmodernity, its impotence (i.e. its uselessness) is total.

Living labour

1.1 We must now analyse the transvaluation of values (or rather of the sense of languages and decisions) that biopolitical production creates, and pursue it through the innovations it determines and that unfold in the constellations of the real.

1.2 This analysis is necessary in as much as, once it has been established that in biopolitics ontology precedes both the sphere of production and that of the political, one still has to show how the ontological determinations reveal a transvaluated power within production and politics. Nevertheless, such a transvaluation is given.

1.3 When we install constituent power within ontology, we do not thereby define the constituent powers that are in action in the constellations of the real. We know that co-operation determines a transvaluation; now the work of co-operation, in its new ontological determinations, must reveal the modalities of its new and singular productivity.

1.4 From the methodological standpoint, the ontology of the biopolitical is considered as a pre-condition for the production of the political, as the basis of the singularization of political events and as motor of transvaluation.

2.1 But what do we mean by transvaluation? Transvaluation is the point where the eternal and innovation meet; it is the *trigger* that innovates the eternal. Transvaluation emerges at precisely the point where the tradition of classical and modern materialism breaks down.

2.2 In transvaluation the eternal and innovation are united indissolubly, becoming co-substantial in the creation of new being. Consequently transvaluation is recognizable by the fact that it has no model. It is neither repetition nor imitation, and we cannot provide an example of it on the basis of pre-constituted values and realities. Transvaluation situates itself in a radical manner on the edge of time, and only there. Transvaluation is the productive event.

2.3 It is for this reason that transvaluation is observable everywhere, because the edge of time is everywhere. Transvaluation is power diffused on all sides, and it emerges here as irreducible plurality. (It is at once the simplest and most difficult thing. Transvaluation does not see the world as an adolescent, but is in itself an adolescent.)

2.4 This plurality is the sign of singularity. In other words, transvaluation pertains to the singularity, in as much as the innovation of the eternal is proper to the singularity.

2.5 Nevertheless, transvaluation is always an omniversal machine open on all sides – better still, it is a virtual factory – because it is nothing other than the teleology of the common. Which is like saying that transvaluation proceeds from the multitude.

3.1 The City of Man, i.e. the world of everyday life, is the teleological machine of the common.

3.2 The mark of this teleological machination is the eternal exposure on the edge of time and the necessity to innovate (to create new being). Given that ontology augments anthropology, the machines of teleological transvaluation are on the one hand the power of the poor, and on the other the creativity of love.

3.3 The City of Man is the city of the teleology of the common. It stands in opposition to the City of God (and reveals its unfoundedness), because materialist teleology poses the eternity of finitude against the transcendental or eschatological infinite. The City of Man realizes itself by imposing, through its aleatory process, within its constitution – step by step, singularity after singularity (but always as multitude) – the creative machinations of a common language.

3.4 The common language of the materialist teleology is dystopia. That is to say, while utopia appropriates a future fully determined, the common language of dystopia invests a *to-come* that remains empty. But dystopia is vigorous because it projects the power of innovation into the void. Dystopia is the virtue (*virtus*) of poverty.

4.1 The analysis must define how the machine of transvaluation operates within the macrocosm of the City of Man. The microcosm of the act of transvaluation (which has the same power as that experienced in the macrocosm) is, and can only be, the body. Only the body participates in a singular manner in the world, and so represents the perspective from which innovation can be viewed.

4.2 Or more precisely: when the problem of the transvaluation of decisions and hence of the teleological machine is posed, one also presupposes that a substrate, an *upokeimenon*, be given: i.e. something which inscribes this variety of activities, of *dispositifs*, of productive constellations and constituent powers that lie at the base of every innovation of being effected by the multitude, in a singular and irreducible presence. But without wishing to express a judgement on this presupposition, we note that the body is not only the location of the power of transvaluation, but it is that power itself. The substrate (*upokeimenon*) is absolutely singular.

4.3 When we distinguish between transvaluation and innovation, we do so because 'innovation' is an ontological name, while 'transvaluation' is a (productive, economic, etc.) common name. 'Transvaluation' is the name whose merit is that of carrying within itself the weight of the process, and hence the life of the body. Transvaluation tends towards singularity and event.

4.4 Further progress in our analysis can only be envisaged in terms of a microphysics/micropolitics of bodies. What is meant precisely by a microphysics/micropolitics of bodies? It means that bodies present themselves as plurality and as relation (internal and external to each body), that is, as a continued tension between parts and/or totality of a body and between bodies themselves. (From Spinoza to Foucault the definition of microphysics/micropolitics has not changed. From this standpoint the ancient and the modern are transvaluated into the postmodern. But this is a materialist exception.) Here, the multitude reveals itself as an ensemble and an interweaving of corporeal singularities agitated in the teleological crucible of the common. Here the machine becomes a factory, and the bodies, rather than being the cogs of the machine, are the workers of the factory. This tension is always singular because it is located on the edge of time, and it is creative because it is prepared to lean out over this edge (so why seek elsewhere for the epistemic mark of '*dispositifs*'?).

4.5 It is around this tension that the transvaluation machine is formed. It is a machine that weaves together the *dispositifs* of the singular possibilities of bodies, constructing within the multitude a rich and common texture that fills the void of being, i.e. innovating the eternal.

4.6 The world has always constituted itself in this way. But the process of constitution only becomes apparent in the age of the man-machine, when the body makes itself language and language becomes productive. This transformation constitutes the present form in which the tensions between bodies, in the heart of the multitude, are translated into a new productive force. The linguistic production of the world of everyday life is thus the first ontological configuration through which transvaluation appears as the product of the power of bodies, and where the bodies completely reappropriate the teleology of the common.

4.7 But the full power of transvaluation will only become manifest once we are able to consider the bodily machine in terms of poverty, and once its heaviness is made lighter by love.

5.1 From the political standpoint, transvaluation encounters the problem of the decision. In modernity this problem was considered a central, if not a crucial moment in the definition of political Power. From the ontological standpoint, it is a case of playing down this centrality and relating the political decision back to that which it is in reality, a variety of the transvaluation of bodies.

5.2 The theme of the decision is extremely difficult to grasp when placed – as it is in modernity – in a rational context: it cannot indeed be contained, nor can it be described in terms of rational choice. It immediately reveals an impasse that we have already found in the rationalist tradition: the political singularization of judgement cannot be deduced from the general (universal and abstract) premises of regulative order. Brought to a standstill by the conundrum, the theorists draw the conclusion (worthy of Baron Münchausen's theorems) that the only way to resolve the problem of the political decision is to anchor its effective character 'outside' the rational. The writers and poets of one particular Italian publishing house of excellence, have tragically and pathetically glorified this 'outside', identifying it as political instinct or Zen wisdom, as empathy or cynicism . . . The more sophisticated logicians have tried to find support for a rational explanation of that 'outside' in the performativeness of language or in the latent schematism of transcendental judgement. It is evidently another example of the fraudulence of modern rationalism. Pascal was not wrong when, looking to the perfection of the rationalist Cartesian world, he underlined ironically that, in any case, it always had the need of a divine 'nudge' in order to work.

5.3 The space for the irrational character of the decision is reduced to a minimum in sociological thought and in the political science of modernity (as it is in the understanding of the constitutional law and in rational ethics). In order to exorcize the irrational, one locks it away in a cupboard, sometimes bigger sometimes smaller than the political society and the legal constitution. The whole of the rest of the social world will then be subjected to a functional rationality. According to Max Weber, there is very little in mature capitalist society that is left to the irrational, but what is, is decisive.

5.4 The only way to remove the impasses and the contradictions of the decision is by subtracting it from the rational/irrational dichotomy, and considering instead the 'choice' as a decisive element for the articulation and the movement of bodies, in as much as it is the product of the brain in a body in movement. The decision becomes an element of bodies, and is thus implicated in the ontological conditions of action. If bodies are a free productivity on the edge of time, then the autonomy (rational or irrational) of the decision is pure illusion. In the movement of the multitude, it is the bodies that transvaluate values and innovate being, i.e. that decide. What greater autonomy than that of bodies?

5.5 It is the poor who participate in the decision most, not those who command.

6.1 The common name of 'the decision' is thus placed on the same terrain as that of transvaluation. The decision is another way of saying transvaluation, i.e. of saying ontological innovation on the edge of time; and the decision is in the political in the same way as transvaluation is in production (and that *kairòs* is in knowledge).

6.2 From the standpoint of political *praxis*: the decision is thus the product of the intersection of bodies and the multitude; it is the dynamic *trigger* of every innovative production of the multitude; and it is the ontological result of the fall of atoms along the line that divides plenitude from the void. In other words, in biopolitics the decision expresses its activity by turning towards the common edge of being.

6.3 The political decision is always solely the decision of the multitude.

6.4 When one speaks of the decision of the prince, one is either saying nothing at all (because when this is an individual decision it is necessarily ineffectual), or one is speaking of the entire process of the activity of the multitude that is concentrated on a point of being – like a torrent that discovers a dam that is able to determine its course. It is only in this case that one speaks correctly, because it is the edge of being that decides, and not the prince. The great political emphasis on the 'decision concerning the exception' is meaningless, because it is always the singularities that, at each instant, decide and determine the exception. What exception is there more significant than that of the innovation of being? Only this is exceptional. There is no other exception, and much less is there a political decision concerning the exception.

7.1 In the case of the theories that assume the postmodern context, we find ourselves in the presence of two opposite tendencies: the one that experiences transvaluation (and the decision) as an ascetic experience, and the other that translates transvaluation (and the decision) into a mystical experience – with reference made to the construction of political democracy. Both tendencies obliterate the power of biopolitics.

7.2 When transvaluation is understood as an ascetic experience, its capacity to act is flattened onto a genealogy of 'progress', so that the decision is diluted in a repetitive and tedious *dispositif* of normalization. In this case, the ontology of biopolitical plenitude does not risk exposure to the void, the sense of innovation knows no beyond, and consequently the transvaluation of being is only an illusion.

7.3 The concept of democracy that proclaims itself absolute is constructed in the web of asceticism. But this absolute, which arranges the multitude within a pre-constituted procedure, knows nothing of innovation. What becomes of democracy when it is not continually transformed by the desire of the common, and if it fails to recognize poverty as its motor? What can it be apart from a hypostasis, that is to say, an illusion?

7.4 When transvaluation is experienced mystically, one pretends that the determination of transvaluation (i.e. the decision) can only originate from the emptying of being, beginning from its nakedness, that is, in a residual margin. But biopolitical being is full and consistent, and its border is not residual but creative.

7.5 The democracy described by this experience is a product of ignorance of the power of the multitude, of the obsession with the negative and of the weakness of resistance. It is easy to recognize here the umpteenth metamorphosis of the decision, one that expresses not a sovereign cynicism but the return to a surreptitious eschatological perspective.

7.6 If in the case of ascetic transvaluation the decision is de-potentialized and the *to-come* is reduced to the feeble progression of the tautology of the common; in the case of the mystical transvaluation it flirts with negative theology and the *to-come* becomes a foolhardy leap that is opposed to the teleology of the common (and is an insult to the eternal).

8.1 What renders the multitude capable of transvaluation and of decision is the encounter with bodies that are placed in a relation of co-operative tension on the edge of being. But this represents merely the formal character of the transvaluation of being. For what brings it about – materially – that this encounter produces ontological meaning and is not simply the projection or repetition of the experience of a meaningless existence in the world?

8.2 We have already seen that this meeting of bodies is linguistic. Which is to say that in postmodernity language has become an encounter between bodies. The meeting of bodies creates a biopolitical context for language. We have also shown that language takes on meaning when it participates in the teleology of the common, i.e. when the common innovates.

8.3 Nevertheless, it is only when the teleology of the common is invested by love that the meaning of the common is torn away from the postmodern tautology. The biopolitical context then becomes a constitutive power that innovates the eternal. The multitude here becomes capable of innovation.

8.4 Love is not *pietas* (i.e. a power that refers to transcendence), nor is it simply *amor* (i.e. an ascetic power that operates in an atomistic context and that traverses it indefinitely). Love is biopolitical 'living labour'.

Labour comes to life by exposing itself to the immeasurable, and it is love that sustains it in the common enterprise of the construction of being (in the void).

8.5 'But noble in soul is he / Who burns to lift his eyes / Against the common doom, / And with free tongue, not docking any truth, / Admits the weak, low state, / The evil lot assigned to us by fate; He who in suffering, / Shows himself great and strong / And will not add fraternal wrath and hatred – / The worst of ills – to all / His other miseries / By blaming Man for his unhappiness, / But lays the fault on her who is indeed / The guilty one, the Power who is our mother / In that she brought us forth, step-mother in will. / He calls her enemy, and thus, believing – / As is indeed the truth – / The human race was from the first conjoined / And ranked against the foe, / He takes all men as his confederates, / Embraces all men with general love / Which is sincere; he offers, / And looks for prompt and valiant aid from them / Amid the anguish and recurring dangers / Of this their common war.' ('The Broom', lines 111–35, from *Poems of Giacomo Leopardi* [1989], pp. 61–2).

9.1 The liberation of 'living labour' (that is, of freeing itself from dead labour) has represented the utopia of every movement of the poor. 'Living labour' means, purely and simply, the power to create being where there is only the void. Living labour escapes utopia when, through the development of the teleology of the common, it also definitively escapes from the transcendental dominion of dead labour, when it reappropriates the tool and as a result is able to expose itself freely to the immeasurable on the edge of being. The liberation of living labour thus becomes dystopia.

9.2 Today, living labour has related all production back to itself. Production is language in the same way as production is living labour, because labour is immediately intellectual and affective. This labour produces the world and, at the same time, innovates it.

9.3 In the political economy of the man-man era, the production and reproduction of the world have always been separate. Man produced and woman reproduced. The sector of the economy that concerned production was the prerogative of men; the one that concerned reproduction was the prerogative of women. It is only in postmodernity, when work becomes intellectual and affective, that production and reproduction cease to be divided and come to constitute a circular whole. Living labour belongs to everyone. It is in order to signal this metamorphosis that becomes manifest in the becoming-common of living labour, that one laconically says: living labour has become-woman.

9.4 But can those who are excluded from work still be considered a part of living labour? Of course, since even the excluded are part of the common. And the poor person, who is more excluded than anyone, i.e. the singularity at greatest risk on the edge of being – at the point where Power closes off the teleological striving towards the *to-come* – the poor, therefore, are also the most common. For if it is only the common that produces production, those who are excluded but participate in the common are also the expression of living labour.

9.5 It will be said, therefore, that transvaluation and the political decision are figures of the living labour of the multitude and so participate in the common (more precisely: in the ontological constitution of the common). But we must ask ourselves, what is that extremely close kinship of living labour and love that seemed to us to constitute the opening and the meaning of the technology of love in postmodernity? Could we say that 'militancy of the common' is the 'exercise of living labour', and that transvaluation and the decision are modalities of living labour?

10.1 The *telos* of the common, driven on by love, is the living labour of a multiplicity of singularities in ever changing relations with one another.

10.2 We have seen that in production the relations of singular bodies that express living labour are ever changing. Indeed, each singular body is tested on the edge of being (if the bodies did not find themselves located on the edge of being they would not be able to place themselves in relation to one another, but would be forever immobile). But we have also seen how the living labour of bodies is manifested through a common production when work itself becomes linguistic, so that the multitude is recomposed in innovation. We experience then a double movement that goes from the multitude to the singularities in relation to one another, and from the constellation of singularities to the linguistic community. How are the extremities of this process, the singular body and the linguistic community, linked together?

10.3 We call the interweaving of singular body and linguistic community the 'linguistic body'. This interweaving is formed when the linguistic co-operation of singular bodies exposes itself to innovation. It is the ontological product of the common *telos* that integrates in a new body the tension between singularity and community, and that between the co-operation of bodies and the innovation of being. The linguistic body is increasingly new, that is, it is ever more singular.

10.4 In so far as co-operation always creates a surplus-value in living labour, the passage from linguistic community to linguistic body is a passage that creates new value. It is thus a transvaluation. This transition does not negate the singularity but posits it again as the expression of a more powerful commonality. The most singular body is also the most common.

11.1 In the teleology of the common these transitions are necessary. Indeed, they follow the arrow of time and integrate it creatively.

11.2 These transitions are called 'metamorphoses'. Metamorphosis is always singular, in as much as it constitutes itself through the creation of new being beyond the edge of time, there where one finds the seal of singularity. But this passage becomes multitude, because when the singular passes beyond the edge of being it creates new common being valid for the multitude of singularities. In this way, the teleology of the common produces metamorphoses of being.

11.3 One has a metamophosis when the singularities arrange themselves as a 'machine', or rather, when they are 'fabricated', i.e. when they compose themselves within the web of the common by producing innovation (and so establish the relation between microcosm and macrocosm). In this way the teleology of living labour contributes to the metamorphoses of the common.

11.4 The idea of 'eternal return' is false because it presupposes a movement of being across the void (and back) without producing innovation, therefore without creation. But there is no return from the void, because it is nothing. There are no strolls to be had across the ontological void. The ideology of the eternal return is thus reactionary because it does not graft innovation onto the eternal, and therefore it theorizes the impotence of the multitude.

12.1 By 'general intellect' I understand the linguistic body become biopolitical machine.

12.2 In the tradition of critical Marxism, the *General Intellect* is defined as the metamorphosis of constant social capital when, in mass and quality, it no longer needs to be activated if not by immaterial, intellectual and scientific labour, that is, by inventive-(labour)-power. The paradox of the *General Intellect* consists in the fact that when constant capital has occupied the whole of society, the intellect, that is the brain, that is the singular body, is the only productive force. This paradox is real and corresponds to the current level of development of the teleology of the common. It forms the content of the present mutation.

12.3 But if we wish to determine the current conditions of the teleology of the common, it is not so much necessary to understand the resignation of capital from the role of productive force, but above all to understand the intellect's accession to the status of sole producer of value. This dynamic of the intellect was explained above, when the brain was acknowledged as the sole tool of postmodern production.

12.4 If the intellect manifests itself as the brain, i.e. as linguistic body, then the production of the 'general intellect' is the production of brains, that is, of linguistic bodies. And the biopolitical context relates to the 'general intellect' in the form of common machine, common brain, in the same way as the brain, i.e. the linguistic body, relates to the productive tool.

12.5 From the ontological point of view, the common machine of the general intellect is the biopolitical context of life.

12.6 We find here the production of the passage from the modern age, defined as that of the man-man, to the postmodern age of the man-machine. In this last epoch, not only has the linguistic body become the tool (and so creates the productive machine), but the common machine (deploying itself in a biopolitical context) also produces subjectivity, i.e. the linguistic body.

13.1 The passage of the common from the linguistic body to the general intellect, in so far as the general intellect is biopolitical, also travels that path which goes from the machine to the body. In effect the biopolitical machine produces subjectivity.

13.2 This movement is entirely evident if one bears in mind that the production and reproduction of the world of life operate in the machine of the general intellect. In the same way as the body is author of production, the body is also the subject of reproduction, and these two powers are brought together. As far as the biopolitical body is concerned, there is no difference between production and reproduction, between man and woman, since there is no living labour that is not in some way love, and vice versa. This statement concerns – first of all – the body in its singular existence.

13.3 Living labour and love, intellectual production and expression of affect, all go to make up the body in its singularity and in its relation to other bodies, but also considered in terms of the linguistic community that metamorphoses it. In other words, the linguistic body is a body that, in so far as it is composed of intellectuality and affect, is able to expose itself to the *dispositif* of the 'beyond' that signals the singular metamorphosis of the world (through bodies).

13.4 The poorer the body – that is, the more it is exposed and open to the immeasurable – the more it concentrates the power of living labour and of love within itself. The more the general intellect is common (i.e. innovative), the more amorous it is. *Eros* and *General Intellect* celebrate their unity in the common. The body participates in this creative paradox: setting forth from poverty, it impresses the power of metamorphosis on the movement.

13.5 The passage from the epoch of the man-man to that of the man-machine, from modernity to postmodernity, posits the body as the power that forms the basis of the machine, but which is, at the same time, developed by the machine. The body is the microcosm that corresponds to the macrocosm, and the macrocosm is called the general intellect.

14.1 Through the constituent activity of the multitude on the edge of time, the innovative transvaluation configures itself as a machine that continuously metamorphoses being. The occupation of the void by living labour is, in the epoch of the man-machine, the power of metamorphic generation.

14.2 'Metamorphic generation' means (in the materialist sense of the word) teleological generation, and is thus – if you like – a generation without end. No transcendental precedes, keeps vigil or informs the effect of generation; nor is there any dialectical connection here. In our teleology, the cause is always external, because it exposes itself on the edge of time, in the place where the new rises up; and from a certain point of view, the product of innovative generation is always a 'monster'. The materialist tradition has always had an inkling of this.

14.3 The thinking that signalled the beginning of the postmodern era posed itself the question of the machine that transformed bodies. There has always been a current of thought that, through the analysis of the relation between Man and tool, conceived metamorphosis as construction, augmentation and perfection of functional and/or organic prostheses. A second current conceived of metamorphosis as a process of ontologization of virtual worlds produced by techno-linguistic co-operation. A third and final current has insisted on the effects of metamorphosis produced by the processes of hybridization on the margins of existent or future worlds. Each of these hypotheses reveals crucial aspects of the transformations of the biopolitical context, or of the real metamorphoses within the biopolitical. But none of these have so far produced anything other than hypotheses.

14.4 Perhaps these difficulties that hinder the hypotheses from verifying themselves relate to the persistence of various finalisms, that is, to their incapacity of facing up to the monster in a biopolitical way. On the contrary, in confronting the theme of metamorphosis, we insist on the fact that all ontological *dispositifs* of the transvaluation machine are free, in the same way as living labour is free; and that each of these *dispositifs* is immeasurable, in the same way that love is immeasurable.

14.5 It was around 1968 that the experiences of militant feminism knocked down the wall of transcendental ends, because they attacked it from the theoretical standpoint (i.e. from the standpoint of the irreducible creative character of generation) and undermined its ethical consequences across the whole of the biopolitical context. With feminism, singularity begins to be responsible for the eternal.

The decision

1.1 What we are trying to grasp in the constellation of bodies is that point where the common decides upon the common. 'The decision' is born of the intensity of the common singularization of bodies.

1.2 In order to advance this investigation, and so as to grasp the ethical sense of action (which cannot but root itself in the common and singularize itself within it), we must place ourselves at the heart of the corporeal constellations and observe them in the exact moment in which what we have called transvaluation is produced. Our enquiry will seek confirmation of the ethical consistency of the processes of 'transvaluation' and of the manner in which those processes come to be intensified.

1.3 If the consistency of the common exposes itself on the edge of time, ethics is this exposure to the immeasurable. Generally, it can thus be said that: in the scene of the innovation of being, we observe transvaluation singularize itself, and we call this passage ethical. If we look at this scene from below, from the singular itself, the ethical is born of a decision: it is the singularity that decides its common opening to the immeasurable.

1.4 In general, the decision (seen from below, from the singular teleological process of the common) is installed in the progression of transvaluation that passes from the body to love, from living labour to co-operation, from language to the machine. In this passage, the decision does not deny but exalts the body (and with it the constellation of bodies and the ontological machines) as constituent power. The decision is thus 'incarnated' in the common process, and materially saturated in the teleology of bodies, of languages and of machines.

1.5 All the spiritualistic definitions of the decision, that is, all those that are 'pure' or unilateral, are false. The decision is always multilateral, 'impure' and monstrous, because the singular is always an immeasurable determination of bodies, of languages and of machines. In other words, since the singularity is planted (and constitutes itself and is generated) in the biopolitical, and the decision is thus formed in 'plenitude', the act by which it leans out over the void of being will also be full.

1.6 So what is this 'event of the decision'? In order to answer this question we must avoid losing the singularity of the decision in the trans-valuation that constitutes its ontological skeleton, that is, of losing the insistence of the decision in the consistency of transvaluation. We must continue to view the production of the decision from below. Only in this way will it be possible to seize the event of the decision as such. So, what do we mean by the 'event of the decision'?

2.1 Of what event are we speaking of then? Evidently of an event that involves the common, that decides upon the common. But every decision that the singularity takes involves the common in some way. The problem is no longer that of demonstrating the ontological consistency of the deci-sion, but rather that of grasping the precise point at which the decision innovates being (not so much by insisting on the singularity, so much as on the experience of the decision, that is, in its creative expression). Only in this way will we be able to answer our question.

2.2 When we speak of the event of a common decision on the com-mon, we are saying that the singularity (the multitude of singularities) accedes to a new level of power. In other words, one can also say that the decision is the event that leads from one level of power to another; and the more powerful it is, the more open will be the field of our decision. The same can be said if we exchange poverty and love for power.

2.3 In no case can the decision be defined as a closure of possibilities, as the power of exception; on the contrary, it will have to be acknowledged as the opening of a new horizon of common power. The event of the decision is ethical when it constitutes new ontological power for the production of subjectivity.

2.4 The ethical is in no instance an example of the gladiatorial struggle of good against evil. Those who maintain this ignoble theory locate the good in the infinite, placing it in the transcendental location of judgement, and from there, in an underhand and hypocritical manner, they go on to treat the finitude of existence as 'evil'. In this way, the existent, misled, experiences astonishment in the face of its own finitude! And people's consciences are moved in the face of an aeroplane accident or an earthquake, that is, to commiserate when faced with the death of an individual. This supposed 'evil' is only the finite edge of being; and, one speaks of the finite, exactly as one does of the infinite, once it is subsumed in the eternal, and once it has been suppressed in this way, its justification becomes as banal as each sublimation is foolish. Evil cannot be confused with finitude, nor can it be attributed to it. So-called 'evil' is a condition (and a border) of existence that only the experience of passing beyond this border is able to define. Evil renders indignant and ethics shapes itself by going beyond evil.

2.5 For the man-machine, individual death is only conceivable as the common decision of overcoming death, that is, as struggle against death. It is only in taking up this choice of overcoming that the decision can be called 'ethical'. (So that from this standpoint the 'Hippocratic oath' – that demands struggle without rest against death – is more ethical than any other abstract axiology of the 'Mosaic Law' type. It is no coincidence that medicine plays a pre-eminent role in the materialist tradition, that is, when the therapy of the body and the practice of happiness are fused.)

2.6 A power that extends the common into the *to-come*, that constructs bodies in common on the edge of time, that innovates the eternal making it manifest: that is what we call the decision. But once again, what is the event of the decision? We mean, the event in its singularity!

3.1 In dialectical philosophies, the event of the decision participates in the metaphysics of dialectical supersession (*Aufhebung*), that is, of the sublimation of negation. Characterized in this way, the event of the decision does not comply with the conditions we have proposed, in as much as the *Aufhebung* is a transvaluation that conserves, i.e. which is a moment of logical continuity. The decision and transvaluation are thus drowned out in the effective necessity of the world, because rationality and reality are placed under the sign of equivalence. Singularity is extinguished; there is no more decision.

3.2 In dialectical materialism, the process of the decision is described in the same way: it organizes itself on the basis of a mechanical passage from quantity to quality that not only fails to define the Hegelian *Aufhebung*, but serves to confuse it all the more.

3.3 Despite mocking it, negative thought – although it observes the decision form itself on the edge of being, on the precipice of a desperate nakedness, understood to be the singular location where destiny is decided – is also dialectical. Alongside its sophisticated dialectical condition there is, in addition to the definition of the decision, a slide towards the negation (in any case an underestimation) of plenitude, without which the decision cannot even be conceived. There may be decision here, but one has lost the materialist event.

3.4 Dialectics, in as much as it forms transcendental thinking, denies the decision the power to generate *ex nihilo* (and to produce plenitude, fullness of being in the void, against the void).

3.5 Dialectics, in so far as it is the capitalist (bourgeois and/or socialist) form of transcendental thinking of Power, is incapable of grasping the power of the relation of poverty and love in the decision.

4.1 Even in the materialist tradition the ontological definition of the decision has frequently been missed: the irreducible and singular quality of a *clinamen* that intervenes in the eternal precipitation of atoms has not been grasped. This lack is particularly evident in that succession of attempts to solve the problem that goes from Nietzsche through to Deleuze by way of Bergson. In this tradition, which despite everything inaugurates postmodern philosophy, the *trigger* of the decision is nothing other than the limit to which the infinite acts of a 'will to power' or of an *élan vital* tend, however these are characterized. Evidently this conception approximates to the intensity of the decision in the plenitude of being, and the *clinamen* is given a subjective determination within the framework of post-Spinozism. But nothing bestows meaning on this process of decision. It revolves upon itself, unless it is a mere rejoicing in the banal duration of life – but why should it be celebrated for itself?

4.2 However, let us suppose that we can grasp the decision in the midst of an open context of microdecisions (as often occurs with these authors). In this case, the *clinamen* is the result of innumerable micro-decisions. But although materialist vitalism correctly alludes to the production of resistance and to the dynamic of a becoming-multitude (of singularities), it nevertheless risks wrapping itself in the sophisms of a bad infinity: an infinity that dilutes the intensity of the decision and that removes its singularity – an indefinite that opposes itself to the eternal. The ethics (of the materialist tradition) always lags behind the premises of postmodernity.

4.3 Ancient materialism failed to see the problem of the common decision for the very good reason that, from the standpoint of cosmogony, the name of the common did not appear as a problem. On the other hand, in modern materialism the common is subordinated to the principle of the infinite. Finally, in postmodernity, the problem is posed, but the ontologically approximated solution escapes once again.

4.4 Does the 'other history' of materialist thought offer us useful elements for the construction of the definition we are seeking?

5.1 With Machiavelli the question of the decision – both in its singular intensity and in the teleology of the common – was returned to materialism. One may consider the Machiavellian conception of the decision as generator of temporality to be incomplete; it nevertheless remains the foundation for any possible definition of the decision. In the Machiavellian conception of the decision, the constituent conception of temporality opens itself to the immeasurable: it is a decision that is, at one and the same time, singular and common.[23]

5.2 Marx's theory of class struggle as constituent of the world of life reiterates the intensity of the Machiavellian notion of the singular and common political decision, extending it into historical time. But Marx's theory is hampered by so many counteracting tendencies that only by passing 'beyond Marx' is Marxism able to confront the productive dimensions of postmodernity and decide upon the liberation of living from dead labour. Otherwise, there is always a moment in Marxism where dead labour dialectically returns to devour living labour like a ravenous Hydra.

5.3 The militant experience of the communist revolutions in the nineteenth and twentieth centuries often prefigured the biopolitical structure of the ontological decision. In the practical experience of proletarian insurrections, it was not so much a case of ideological models, so much as a transvaluation of desire, of love and of living labour by the multitude. (It is in this light that the communist revolutions, whatever convulsions they underwent, or whatever heterogenesis and/or heteronomy of ends they were subjected to, can never be assimilated to totalitarian experiences, and all comparison or analogy between communism and fascism is insubstantial and infamous.)

5.4 Foucault attempted to trace the processes constitutive of the biopolitical world, pressing forward in the formulation of the *telos* of the common conceived not as a dialectical result but as genealogical production. The Foucauldian insistence on the plenitude of difference in biopolitics, and on the singular expression of productive determination, constitutes the premonitory symptom of a postmodern theory of the decision that is at once singular and common, that is to say ethical. But who is able to explain the breakdown of Foucault's research programme?

6.1 What is the singular event of the decision upon the common? It is the triumph of love that surges up from the multitude of the poor, embodying itself in the singularity. An event that could not be any more material, any more full than it is already. It is an event of generation. And if Spinoza naturalized love, we can now see it act in biopolitical terms, that is, at once generating singularly and in common.

6.2 If this event of love is radical, it is so because it is given as power to generate on the temporal edge of being and that renders the existent immeasurable, moving beyond itself.

6.3 If to generate is to make the existent immeasurable, it is also to recompose singularity in the multitude. For it is within the multitude that the biopolitical subject of generation is constructed through language and co-operation. Here the event of the decision posits the subject in the multitude as the immeasurable of the recomposed singularities. (It is evident that if the subject is immeasurable, nothing can substantiate it.) It is in this way that temporality generates.

6.4 In the biopolitical, 'generation' means both love and living labour indistinguishably, because both the one and the other are creations of being. Generation, that is, the act of deciding to generate, is one and the same thing when it resists and when it produces, when it gives itself as (singular and eternal) intensive insistence and when it unfolds as (subjective and innovative) constituent power. It decides within the temporality of the establishment of the common.

6.5 If exploitation (or exclusion) forms a blockage in generation, resistance to biopolitical exploitation is transvaluated when it challenges the order that the organization of exploitation determines. Is thus the revolt of the multitude an act of generation? Yes, in as much as it reveals (as is implicit in its ontological name) the decision of the material *telos* of the common.

6.6 The liberty and equality of the subjects, that modernity conceives of only in terms of a vulgar formalism, are here rediscovered in the common tension of generation. It is this tension (as resistance and constituent power) that prohibits all forms of nationalism and racism, and that denies all material and/or ideological limits to biopolitical liberty.

7.1 The power of love does not only determine resistance and revolt, it is also extended (in the form of an event/decision) across the complex whole of the biopolitical field. Within this field, the event/decision must be considered alongside at least two ontological *dispositifs* that are expressed in the biopolitical field. The first is that of the metamorphosis of bodies and the second is that of the revolution of the constitution of the common.

7.2 By the 'metamorphosis of bodies' I mean the ensemble of sensorial, perceptive and mental mutations that the bodies themselves produce through the direct experience of the innovation of the world of life – within the new machines and new machinic *Umwelts*, within production and reproduction, in the metropolises and in the cosmos – produced by a permanent process of deterritorialization. Metamorphosis is biopolitical generation.

7.3 By 'new constitution of the common' I mean the ensemble of transformations of the biopolitical common within which the bodies and singularities present themselves as subjects. These constitutions are experienced as new meanings of biopolitical language (productive and ethico-political).

7.4 The subjective event of the common decision participates creatively in these *dispositifs*. The decision on the metamorphosis of bodies is encouraged by the common process of the technologies of love, which seek new productive and reproductive material configurations for the self and for the constellation of bodies. The same can be said of the decisions on the new subjective constitution of the common: they are sustained by constitutive technologies as well. Marx was well advanced in the genealogical description of the transformations of the common determined by the political and productive technologies. The Marxists who followed him were far more timid (with exception made for the thinking of post-1968 *Operaismo*, which formulated with great clarity the thematics of the new subjectivity through the analysis of struggles). It fell to Foucault to take up this thread once again, unwinding it in the construction of the 'technologies of the self'.

7.5 Love (i.e. living labour), in the relationship that links it to the power of poverty and in the exposure of the one and the other on the edge of time so as to create new being, is thus machine and motor of the subjective dispositions of the biopolitical. The common context is open: it is the technologies of love that go to work in the passage from the multitude to subjectivity. The event is finally visible: here, in these dimensions, the ethical question is posed once again. But principally we discover the question of the decision or, more precisely, that of the ethical question in the form of the decision, which is what we were seeking when we asked what the event-decision was.

8.1 To the question: what is the common event-decision in the biopolitical, we will thus give a second answer: it is the subjective transvaluation of the bodies of the multitude. The event is determined through the constellation of singularities, realizing the *telos* of the common in active form from below, in the place where the technologies of love act. The event becomes subject.

8.2 The metamorphosis of bodies and the constitution of subjects interlink in the event: the decision here is generation, that is, at one and the same time, metamorphosis and constitution of the subject. The artificial character of the biopolitical processes (but it changes nothing if we speak of their natural character), in exposing themselves on the edge of being and in going beyond, constitute a new 'nature' (that is a new 'artefact') – a second, third, enumerable natures (artefacts); but they always, and at once, constitute a new 'subject' – second, third, enumerable subjects. (For this reason it is said in postmodernity that the subject becomes *cyborg* or technological artefact. Through every previous metamorphosis, in the protracted development of the technologies of love, the body – in one way or another – has indeed become such an artefact; but this present transformation, that of the age of the man-machine, is in the real sense of the word, that of the *cyborg*; and the nature that surrounds the subject is also *cyborg*, in the same way as the subject that, with its prosthesis-tools, participates in the innovations of nature.)

8.3 In biopolitical postmodernity, the decision of the event is the event of a decision by/on the man-machine that makes of it a new subject and expresses it as a new temporality.

8.4 In biopolitical postmodernity, love is general intellect. The event/

decision thus invests the machine of the general intellect. It is put to work across its entire extension and in all its efficiency. It is this amorous explosion of the general intellect that turns resistance into power, and that makes of it the machine of metamorphic events of the common subject. It is the common *telos* that produces the subject.

8.5 The integration of metamorphosis and production of subjectivity becomes entirely evident when seen from the standpoint of the general intellect. For here fixed capital is incorporated in bodies and, consequently, the multitude is presented as a toolbox and workshop of the general intellect. Material production and production of subjectivity can no longer be separated. *General Intellect* means at once production of a new nature and of new subjectivity.

8.6 After the epoch of the centaur and the man-man, that of the man-machine will thus be defined by the metamorphoses of the human into a common amorous machine. The singular constellations present themselves as the machine of a common subjectivity. The subjective decision is the expression of this machine, and the event is its production.

8.7 Is it possible to think of a political party as a subject, that is, as the biopolitical machine of the multitude, between love and poverty? At times, in the 'other' history, the revolutionary movement of the poor has been just that. The Paris Commune was.

8.8 There is a time, there is a common *kairòs* in which one says: all together, let us decide.

9.1 Power is always domination within the common, that is, within the biopolitical common. Abstracting Power from the biopolitical context is pure delirium – as is detaching the decision from transvaluation. (Series 9 constitutes an *intermezzo* in which we will take up again some of the features of the name 'Power' that are essential to the rest of the argument.)

9.2 What differentiates the different forms of government and organization of dominion (both synchronically and diachronically) are not only the different degrees of inherence of Power within the common, but above all the different levels of intensity of the exclusion within (and never from) the common.

9.3 In the period of the man-machine, command becomes biopolitical control. What is meant by 'biopolitical control'? It is measure (that is, organization and limit) of the time of life. Control flows into time; in control, law is procedural; control is inserted into the temporal ontology of the common, i.e. of life.

9.4 In stretching out within temporality, Power wants to invest the *to-come* as well. Biopolitical domination is thus presented as a future investment whose aim is that of establishing control over present production. It is monetary, technological, terrorist (the weapons of extermination) investment, projected into the future in order to guarantee measure, beyond the limit of time as well. In this way Power submits to the lure of the common *telos* and distorts it. Once again we observe to what extent the *to-come* of the common stands opposed to the future of Power.

9.5 In postmodernity the State organizes the exploitation of living social labour through the form of control. This means that in the common the State arranges the exclusion of the poor person who is the producer of that same common. The violence of this exclusion, in as much as it is realized in the common, is extreme: it develops in the temporal continuity of life and becomes a coercive force of calculation, a block on generation and a tautological investment of linguistic production.

9.6 What Marx described – still in terms of a tendency – as the 'real subsumption' of society by capital, that is within capital, is accomplished in postmodernity. This nevertheless produces a paradox: the subsumption is so intense that it could appear to be the 'extinction' of capital in society. But it is not so. This ambiguous configuration maintains, within the postmodern society of control, a level of violence that remains absolutely unchanged: that of command, in the same way as the presumption of measure remains unchanged. What is parasitical in this configuration is the State of 'real subsumption'.

9.7 Can we define Power as the parasitical organization that seeks to bestow measure on the immeasurable? It is at once a partial and general suggestion, but nonetheless it could constitute an adequate 'ideal type'.

10.1 The decision is the subjective event of the multitude. (This is the third and definitive definition of 'the decision', after we have defined it progressively as 'technology of love' [Series 6 and 7] and as 'subjective transvaluation' [8].)

10.2 The definition of the event/decision already proposed within the biopolitical is – in the present – given within the political in the strict sense as the decision of the multitude over itself. And if rebellion is the moment of rupture and constitution, then the event/decision is within this perspective the self-governing of the multitude; that is, the dominion – or real power – of the multitude over/for itself.

10.3 The forms of rebellion are multiple: those that poverty expresses as power, that love deploys beyond the edge of time, and that the common gathers up as *telos* of multiple singularities. It is thus love (living labour) that determines the conditions of the decision as the self-government of the multitude within the common.

10.4 In postmodernity, the eminent form of rebellion is the exodus from obedience, that is to say, from participation in measure, i.e. as the opening to the immeasurable.

10.5 One can summarize in the following manner the imperatives of the immeasurable for the singularities that constitute the multitude: do not obey, that is be free; do not kill, that is to generate; do not exploit, that is to constitute the common. In other words, you will be able to decide within the common.

10.6 But rebellion simultaneously produces processes of reappropriation of the general intellect by the multitude. Exodus is a creative event. In this sense 'appropriation' reveals itself to be an abused name, and one that is perhaps now inappropriate in as much as we must now understand the 'event of reappropriation' as always (and already) a transvaluation of resistance into constituent power; moreover, the decision of rebellion is a subjective determination of the general intellect within the common.

10.7 This event of the general intellect is a process that goes from the multitude of singularities to the common machine. The self-government of the multitude is the common machine of the general intellect, and as such is revolutionary subjectivity.

11.1 But how does the decision of the multitude become subjective and political, or thoroughly subjective and thoroughly political? In order to answer this question it is necessary to take a pause and recall some of the elements of the analysis we have carried out so far. And in particular, the following definitions should be borne in mind:

11.2 We call 'political subject' that multitude of singularities which engages itself in the construction of the common *telos*.

11.3 The passage from the multitude of singularities to the construction of the political subject occurs through the 'militancy of the common' of the singularities, or rather, through the exercise of living labour that destroys every measure of dead labour.

11.4 In the epoch of the man-machine the militancy of the common is produced by a specific 'technology of love'. It is first formed and applied in the biopolitical and consists in the co-production of singularities and of the common, of co-operation and innovation, of languages and of decision. Those who are produced by the power of poverty and who generate the *telos* of the common through an amorous *praxis* are ontologically open to this co-production.

11.5 But how does this belonging to the common *telos* reveal itself? And how does the constitutive power of a political subject constructed by militancy affirm itself? What, finally, is the sense of innovation that the political subject imposes on the edge of being, in the opening to the immeasurable?

11.6 But why should we continue to interrogate ourselves when we know that the decision, in so far as it is the event of the subject, is the 'this here' – that is, is 'at the same time' the decision of the name and of the event – which is to say, the presentation of the body to the common?

12.1 Therefore, in the biopolitical postmodern, 'doing politics' means first of all to resist and rebel. But it is at the same time to express a biopolitical subject extended between poverty and love, and which decides upon the common *telos*. For that reason, 'doing politics' means to take leave of domination, to take leave of the Power of the State and every transcendental illusion in order to produce new common co-operative temporalities and spaces on the edge of being, and to realize the amorous innovation that bestows meaning on common being.

12.2 That which cannot take leave is the modern political party: that configuration which constructed itself on the basis of representation (or presented itself as the vanguard of the masses) and realized its institutional form. The political party is always constrained within that space of Power that excludes the biopolitical determination, while on the contrary, we are speaking of a subject that is at once the product of the biopolitical and that generates in the biopolitical. It is not political representation that can construct the common *telos* within the multitude, on the contrary, it can only be constructed by taking leave of representation and all the representative institutions in order to install itself in the new common temporalities. This common occupation (*Beruf*) considers the 'professional politician' as a contemptible infamous figure.

12.3 So how can one take leave then?

12.4 It is not enough to say simply that only resistance and rebellion can take leave. If resistance and rebellion were not movements of ontological constitution, they would not even be possible as common names. To take leave implies in fact a transvaluation of being. In postmodernity, when the multitude does politics and decides in relation to the common, it means that it has chosen to take leave while constituting.

12.5 If to take leave means to create new temporality in order to determine new power, it is not only a case of taking leave of Power. For if Power is the measure of exclusion, to take leave while constituting (constituting new power) is to take leave with the excluded, with the poor. The multitude that takes leave is poor.

12.6 To take leave while constituting means, in second place, to act under conditions of the most extreme deterritorialization: in postmodernity, this deterritorialization is that experienced by the bodies of the multitude. It is a case then of hybridizing in a cosmopolitan fashion the world of life, that is, appropriating global mobility through the generation of new bodies. 'Proletarians of all countries, unite' is an injunction that today means: mix up races and cultures, constitute the multicoloured Orpheus who generates the common from the human. Break down all the transcendental barriers that prevent the singular from becoming common and that block the innovation of the eternal: that is what it means to take leave while constituting.

12.7 Finally, to take leave while constituting means to construct, through the extreme reterritorialization that the bodies of the multitude experience in postmodernity, common machines through which men and women stretch out beyond the edge of time. Or rather, construct machinically and in the immeasurable, turning the technological monster into the angel of the *to-come*.

13.1 When, through a biopolitics of exodus, the singularities decide to turn the multitude into a revolutionary subject, teleological production, without prefiguring the common, exposes it to the *to-come*. The *vita activa* of the multitude is thus an open and total dystopia, and the decision to revolutionize the eternal is irreversible.

13.2 With the events of 1968, the City of Man, in an irreversible decision, loosed the arrow of the revolutionary temporality of the common. In the face of this *kairòs* of poverty and of love, the City of God is now only a bad stench.

13.3 *Alma Venus*: the daily paean to the revolution of the eternal.

Notes

Translator's Introduction

1 By 'productive aporia' I mean the blockage of the investigation brought about by the insolubility of certain problems within a particular conceptual assemblage but that thanks to that very blockage leads to the opening of new paths of investigation and a displacement of the conceptual assemblage itself. In Negri's words, 'The tension of the blockage is broken and reveals the force the blockage held back.'

2 *Operaismo* is a specifically Italian variation of Marxism, which posits the working class as the dynamic but autonomous core of capitalism. As Mario Tronti argued, in his seminal *Operai e Capitale* (Turin, Einandi Editore, 1966), the working class is in a privileged critical position from which to directly (materially and theoretically) critique capitalism, as it operates immediately both within and against capitalism. The centrality of the workers' struggles in leading development means that crisis matures through the advance of contemporary struggles and worker organization. Deeply involved in this movement, Negri rejected one later development – the 'autonomy of the political' – arguing that, contrary to the political becoming separate and autonomous from the concrete struggles on the terrain of production, 'the political tends to entirely absorb the economic and to define it as separate only insofar as it fixes the rules of domination' (A. Negri, 'Twenty Theses on Marx', trans. M. Hardt, in S. Makdisi, C. Casarino and R. E. Karl (eds), *Marxism Beyond Marxism* (New York, Routledge, 1996), p. 153). On Negri's relation to *Operaismo* see Harry Cleaver's *Reading Capital Politically* (Brighton, The Harvester Press, 1979), pp. 51–66; Yann Moulier's Introduction to A. Negri's *The Politics of Subversion*, trans. J. Newell (Oxford, Polity Press, 1989), pp. 1–44. Steve

Wright's informative – if somewhat hostile to Negri – account: *Storming Heaven: Class Composition and Struggle in Italian Autonomist Marxism* (London, Pluto Press, 2002) and Michael Hardt's 1990 thesis, 'The Art of Organisation: Foundations of a Political Ontology in Gilles Deleuze and Antonio Negri' (http://www.duke.edu/~hardt/).

3 It is only thanks to the efforts of publishers such as *Manifestolibri* and *Derive-Approdi* that many of these books are now in the hands of a new radicalized young audience in Italy, who have found in these texts of the preceding generation important contributions for thinking through the strategies of exploitation and the possibilities for collective action in Empire.

4 For Raniero Panzieri see 'The Capitalist Use of Machinery: Marx Versus the "Objectivists"', trans. Q. Hoare, in P. Slater (ed.), *Outlines of a Critique of Technology* (London. Ink Links, 1980), pp. 44–68, and 'Surplus Value and Planning: Notes on the Reading of *Capital*', trans. J. Bees, in CSE (eds), *The Labour Process and Class Strategies* (London, Stage 1, 1976), pp. 4–25. For Mario Tronti see 'Social Capital', *Telos*, 17 (autumn 1973), pp. 98–121 and 'The strategy of the Refusal', in Red Notes (eds) *Working Class Autonomy and the Crisis: Italian Marxist Texts of the Theory and Practice of Class Movement: 1964–79* (London, Red Notes and CSE Books, 1979), pp. 7–21.

5 See, for example, Robert Lumley's *States of Emergency. Cultures of Revolt in Italy from 1968 to 1978* (London, Verso, 1994); P. Virno and M. Hardt (eds), *Radical Thought in Italy* (Minneapolis, University of Minnesota Press, 1996); Wright, *Storming Heaven*. The numerous books of Antonio Negri's that have appeared in the 1990s and since should also be situated within this context.

6 For an account of the reasons for Negri's return to Italy and prison in 1997, see A. Negri, *Exil*, (Paris, Editions Mille et une Nuits, 1998). 'I am returning to signal the end of the "years of lead", and the necessity of freeing all the comrades still in prison and in exile' (p. 67 – my translation from the French).

7 M. Hardt, 'Un leviatano descritto fuor di metafora', *Il Manifesto*, 28 September 2000 and M. Hardt and A. Negri, *Empire* (Cambridge MA, Harvard University Press, 2000), p. xii.

8 The dialectic between inside and outside and the collapse of the distinction in Empire are discussed in Hardt and Negri, *Empire*, pp. 183–90. See also the interview between Michael Hardt and Thomas Dunn, 'Sovereignty, Multitudes, Absolute Democracy', *Theory and Event*, 4:3 (2000).

9 Negri makes a crucial distinction between *potere* and *potenza* in his *The Savage Anomaly* trans. M. Hardt (Minneapolis, University of Minnesota Press, 1991), which he derives from Spinoza's distinction between *potestas* and *potentia* and which is missed in the English translations of Spinoza's works. I have followed Michael Hardt's rendering of these two terms in his translation of Antonio Negri's *The Savage Anomaly* (Minneapolis, University of Minnesota Press, 1991) as 'Power' and 'power' respectively. The distinction is both a

political and an ontological one, in that *potere* (Power) stands for a centralized transcendent force of command, while *potenza* (power) denotes rather immanent and local constitutive forces. For a concise account of this distinction see the Introduction to *The Savage Anomaly*. This terminological distinction is not maintained in *Empire*, although the conceptual distinction remains.

10 Negri and Hardt take up Foucault's analysis of the changing forms of Power, although setting it in the world of real subsumption or postmodernity. They argue that Power undergoes a complete shift to become a *biopower* that takes life itself as its object and operates at the level of life itself. The question of 'real subsumption' will be considered more extensively in the discussion of *The Constitution of Time* in Part II below. In *Empire* they summarize real subsumption as follows: 'social relations completely invest the relations of production, making impossible any exteriority between social production and economic production' (p. 209).

11 One can find a transcript (in Italian) of this short paper ('Impero, moltitudini, esodo') at http://www.sherwood.it.

12 As will be argued in Part II of this Introduction. Both Negri and Hardt warn against any nostalgia for the age of the sovereign nation state. 'The state itself [. . .] is at its base an apparatus of domination' (Hardt, 'Sovereignty, Multitudes, Absolute Democracy'); while Negri is even more damning when he says that the 'furnaces of Auschwitz' were the necessary conclusion of the ideology of the nation state (see his paper given at the university *La Sapienza* in Rome transcribed at http://www.sherwood.it).

13 On the highly influential notion of the 'apparatus of capture', see G. Deleuze and F. Guattari, *A Thousand Plateaus*, trans. B. Massumi (London, Athlone Press, 1988), pp. 424–73.

14 Michael Hardt gave this paper at the *Radical Philosophy* conference, 'Look, No Hands! Political Forms of Global Modernity', London, Birkbeck College, 27 October 2001. I am grateful to him for letting me have a copy of this paper.

15 The theory of multiplicities developed by Gilles Deleuze and Felix Guattari is of fundamental importance for the investigation into the immanent organization of the multitude. Whereas philosophy – and politics – have tended to understand the many either as chaotic or as ordered through the subjection of the many to unity ('Every nation must make the multitude into a people', Hardt and Negri 2000, p. 103), the theory of multiplicities aims to subvert this duality by understanding a form of organization as immanent to the many.

16 See the following works by Antonio Negri: 'Archaeology and Project: The Mass Worker and the Social Worker' (1982), in *Revolution Retrieved: Selected Writings on Marx, Keynes, Capitalist Crisis and New Social Subjects 1967–1983* (London, Red Notes, 1988), pp. 199–228; 'Twenty Theses on Marx', especially pp. 154–6; 'From Mass Worker to Socialised Worker', in *The Politics of*

Subversion, trans. J. Newell (Oxford, Polity Press, 1989) pp. 75–88. I will return to this notion in Part II below.

17 The notion of 'class composition' is central to the analyses of *Operaismo*. The core of this notion is that the form production takes and the form of struggle are closely intertwined and can only be articulated in relation to one another. That is to say, class composition is the central determinant of the qualitative aspects of the working class. Class composition is made up of a technical element and a political one. The former is determined by conditions of exploitation imposed by capital: the manner in which workers are brought together in the process of production and the form of reproduction of the class (e.g. wage systems, family structures, etc). The political class composition, on the other hand, is determined by how the 'objective' conditions of exploitation are appropriated 'subjectively' by the class and directed against those very conditions. For a recent exploration of the history of the notion of class composition within *Operaismo* see Wright's *Storming Heaven*.

18 This is, of course, a gross oversimplification. There were a number of contributory causes, such as: the divisions within the extra-parliamentary Left; the Italian Communist Party's (PCI) decision to back the centre-left government against *Il Movimento* and the policing of struggles within the workplace by the official trade unions (both designed to lock the working class back into national wealth production); and the restructuring – on which more below – of capitalism away from the Fordist-Keynesian model of capitalist accumulation. For two accounts of this period (1968–81 and 1977–94/5) written by some of the principal participants in the history of the extra-parliamentary Left of the 1960s and 1970s, see 'Appendix: A Future History', in Virno and Hardt, *Radical Thought in Italy*, pp. 224–59.

19 In contrast to 'formal subsumption', which denotes an early stage in the development of capitalism where capital exploits labour and production as it finds it in its pre-capitalist (and relatively independent) form, real subsumption refers to the transformation of the production process itself by capital. That is, the form of co-operation in which the process of production is carried out is directly governed by capital through, for example, subjecting production to the logic of the machine: the 'nature *of the labour process and its actual conditions*' (K. Marx, *Capital Vol. 1*, trans. B. Fowkes (London, Penguin, 1990), pp. 1034–5) are subjected to and organized by the exigencies of capitalist accumulation. The *General Intellect*, on the other hand, is best understood as the embodiment in fixed capital (or the machine) of the form of productive co-operation or, more precisely, of the whole gamut of sciences, skills, techniques and knowledges of a particular level of social and productive development. Shortage of space disallows a treatment of the complex articulations and intersections between real subsumption and the general intellect here. For a recent discussion of this question in relation to *Operaismo* and Negri, see

N. Thoburn's 'Autonomous Production? On Negri's "New Synthesis"', *Theory, Culture and Society*, 18:5 (2001), pp. 75–96. For further reading on 'real subsumption' see K. Marx, 'Results of the Immediate Process of Production', which appears as the Appendix to *Capital Vol.1*; on the 'General Intellect' see the 'Fragment on Machines', in K. Marx's *Grundrisse*, trans. M. Nicolaus (London, Pelican, 1973), pp. 690–712. The Appendix to Negri's *The Politics of Subversion* contains a useful selection from both of these works. For a brief but incisive account of the history of the various readings of the 'Fragment', see Paolo Virno's 'Notes on the "General Intellect"', in S. Makdisi *et al.*, *Marxism Beyond Marxism*, pp. 265–72.

20 See Negri's 'Keynes and the Capitalist Theory of the State', in M. Hardt and A. Negri, *The Labor of Dionysus* (Mineapolis, University of Minnesota Press, 1994), pp. 24–51.

21 Maurizio Lazzarato's 'Immaterial Labor', in Virno and Hardt, *Radical Thought in Italy*, pp. 133–47 is an important contribution to the analysis of the labouring subject of post-Fordism.

22 The dominance of the service sector over manufacturing in many of the most advanced capitalist economies is evidence of how the difference in the cycles of production and reproduction increasingly fall away, or their priority is inverted, so that the 'so-called reproductive sectors now take a central role' (A. Negri, *Macchina tempo* (Milan, Feltrinelli, 1982), p. 211 – my translation). The claim is not that manufacturing disappears in postmodern, post-Fordist production practices: 'Quantitative indicators cannot grasp either the *qualitative* transformation in the progression from one paradigm to another or the *hierarchy* among the economic sectors in the context of each paradigm.' What is meant is simply that: 'Today all economic activity tends to come under the dominance of informational economy and to be qualitatively transformed by it' (Hardt and Negri, *Empire*, pp. 281, pp. 287–8).

23 'In the developments we discern in contemporary society, productive labor tends to propose completely immanent social dimensions of meaning, independent of any coercion to cooperate that could be posed outside labor itself. The increasingly immaterial dimensions of labor pose the terms and the networks of labouring cooperation at the heart of social production. Capital, displaced from its traditional role as orchestrator of productive cooperation, thus tends to take the form of an apparatus of capture' (Hardt and Negri, *The Labor of Dionysus*, p. 309).

24 See K. Marx, 'The Working Day', in *Capital Vol. 1*, Chapter 10, pp. 340–416. '[A]s co-operating workers increase, so does their resistance to the domination of capital, and, necessarily, the pressure put on capital to overcome this resistance' (ibid., p. 449); 'hence the history of capitalist production, the establishment of a norm of the working day that presents itself as a *struggle* over the limits of the working day, a struggle between collective capital, i.e.

the capitalist class, and collective labour, i.e. the working class' (ibid., p. 344); the 'establishment of a normal working day is therefore the product of a protracted and more or less concealed civil war between the capitalist class and the working class' (ibid., pp. 412–13).

25 That is, labour understood in terms of its 'abstract quality of being human labour' (ibid., p. 150), determined by the *'social configuration* in which the individual worker exists' ('Results of the Immediate Process of Production', in ibid., p. 1052).

26 On the impossibility of an independent determination of use-value in real subsumption see Negri's 'Value and Affect', *Boundary 2*, 26:2 (summer 1999).

27 What Negri also calls the 'global phenomenological fabric'.

28 The quotation comes from the paper referred to above given at the university *La Sapienza* in Rome. For more on the incommensurability of 'the people' and 'the multitude' see Hardt and Negri, *Empire*, pp. 102–3.

29 However, this position is not unproblematic, as Giovanni Arrighi argues in 'Lineages of Empire', *Historical Materialism*, 10:3 (Autumn 2002, pp. 1–14). In perhaps the most compelling critique of the notion of the multitude to date, he argues that the presupposition for the emergence of the multitude is the collapse of the distinction between first and third worlds produced by the mass migrations of capital and labour that we find in globalization. In other words, that 'capital under Empire tends towards a double equalization of the conditions of existence of the multitude: equalization through capital mobility from North to South and equalization through labor mobility from South to North' (ibid.). Arrighi insists that the extent to which the movement of capital has truly qualitatively transformed and homogenized the productive practices (and hence the technical composition) of the working class across the globe is at best empirically open to question. He goes on to argue that the flows of labour and capital were proportionately larger in the nineteenth century than today and moreover, that the distance between first world and third worlds measured in gross national product (GNP) per capita are almost completely unchanged since the 1960s. If this is so, this puts in question one of the principal conditions for the multitude and pushes us back into the arms of the social worker. It is perhaps too early to tell whether Hardt and Negri have leapt ahead of themselves or of the present historical conditions, discerning perhaps tendencies within the real that have yet to be consolidated. *Empire* remains, however, self-consciously part of a work in progress. As Negri says of the notion of the multitude, 'from the scientific point of view it remains still at an early stage, [it is a concept] that we have thrown up to see if it works' (from the paper given at the university *La Sapienza* in Rome). Hardt suggests that the multitude should – from the political perspective – be understood as a project. However, this is not to downplay the importance of the empirical element, for '[s]uch a political project must clearly be grounded in

an empirical analysis that demonstrates the common conditions of those who become the multitude. Common conditions does not mean sameness but it does require that no differences of nature or kind divide the multitude. Such differences would render the political project of commonality vain and useless' (Hardt, 'The Politics of the Multitude'). On the political demands of the multitude, see Hardt and Negri, *Empire*, pp. 396–407.

30 My translation of *Kairòs, Alma Venus, Multitudo* has benefited enormously from my being able to consult the excellent French translation of this text by Judith Revel.

31 Here, Negri's understanding of 'phenomenology' reveals its extreme asymmetry from traditional conceptualizations. Rather than a transcendent and solipsistic subjectivity, we have subjectivity as collective practice.

32 For Negri's groundbreaking readings of Spinoza, see *The Savage Anomaly, Spinoza sovversivo* (Rome, Antonio Pellicani Editore, 1992) and '*Reliqua Desiderantur*: A Conjecture for a Definition of the Concept of Democracy in the Final Spinoza', trans. T. Stolze, in W. Montag and T. Stolze (eds), *The New Spinoza* (Minneapolis, University of Minnesota Press, 1997), pp. 219–47. Jason Read's excellent 'The Antagonistic Ground of Constitutive Power: An essay on the Thought of Antonio Negri', *Rethinking Marxism*, 11:2 (summer 1999) is an important first attempt to grasp the complex relations between antagonism and constitution in Negri's readings of Marx and Spinoza.

33 'It is as if the world is unmade and reconstructed on the basis of a set of thoughts, actions, and intuitions established on the individual and collective singularity that organize it through its desire and its power' (Hardt and Negri, *The Labor of Dionysus*, p. 287).

34 In Foucault, 'biopower and 'biopolitics' originally signal the moment when the life of a population itself becomes the object of operations of control, operating alongside disciplinary regimes. The health and hygiene of a national population is then maintained and augmented through strategies that operate at the level of life itself. Negri extends Foucault's account of biopolitics, providing it with increasingly ontological, productive and collective qualities. As Hardt argues in his interview with Thomas Dunn, he and Negri contend that Foucault's 'notion of biopower is conceived only from above', while they 'attempt to formulate instead a notion of biopower from below, that is, a power by which the multitude itself rules over life. [. . .] What we are interested in finally is a new biopolitics that reveals struggles over forms of life' ('Sovereignty, Multitudes, Absolute Democracy'). For a valuable collection of articles on biopolitics post-Foucault, see 'Biopolitique et Biopouvoir', in the journal *Multitudes*, 1 (March 2000).

35 See also Hardt and Negri, *The Labor of Dionysus*, pp. 308–13.

The constitution of time

1 [Translator's note: By '*medietà*' Negri means the quantitative result of an arithmetical operation of reduction, that is, of time-as-measure.]

2 Pierre Garbero has recently and very effectively brought this into strong relief around the crucial theme of productive labour in his *Lavoro Produttivo e Lavoro Improduttivo* (Torino, Loescher, 1980).

3 [Translator's note: This section was originally planned as Part Seven of Volume 1 of *Capital*, but was not published until 1933, simultaneously in Russian and in German. It appeared for the first time in English as the Appendix to the 1976 Penguin edition of *Capital Vol. 1*.]

4 [Translator's note: See 'The Elimination of Time in Classical Science', in M. Čapek (ed.) *The Concepts of Time and Space* (Dordrecht, Holland/Boston MA, D. Reidel Publishing Group, 1976), p. 264.]

5 [Translator's note: This quotation is from Gil's entry 'Tempo' in the *Enciclopedia Tematica Einaudi*. For reasons already explained, it has not been possible to trace further publication details for this book.]

6 [Translator's note: Negri is alluding here to G. W. Leibniz's concept of time as expounded, for example, in his *Letters to Clarke*, ed. H. G. Alexander (Manchester, Manchester University Press, 1956). For a recent exploration of the influence of Ruggero Giuseppe Boscovich's post-Leibnizian notion of 'time atomism' on Friedrich Nietzsche, see Keith Ansell Pearson's 'Nietzsche's Brave New World of Force', *Pli: The Warwick Journal of Philosophy*, 9 (2000), pp. 6–35.]

7 [Translator's note: The reference is to the theories of communication found in Luhmann, Habermas, Negt, et al.]

8 However, one should be careful not to give the fairly obvious deliberations on scientific paradigms a relativistic meaning, as is frequently the case with the contemporary theorist of the paradigm, Thomas Kuhn, who is prepared to render the paradigm logically, that is formally, homologous.

9 [Translator's note: On the centrality of *mobility* for the definition of the class composition of the 'social worker', see Negri's 'Archaeology and Project: The Mass Worker and the Social Worker', in *Revolution Retrieved* (London, Red Notes, 1998), pp. 199–228. Negri's investigations into the social worker continued well into the 1980s: see his 'Twenty Theses on Marx', trans. M. Hardt, in S. Makdisi, C. Casarino and R. E. Karl (eds), *Marxism Beyond Marxism* (New York, Routledge, 1996), especially Thesis 4; and 'From Mass Worker to the Socialized Worker – and Beyond', in idem, *The Politics of Subversion*, trans. J. Newell (Oxford, Polity Press, 1989), pp. 75–88.].

10 Jean-Paul de Gaudemar has provided an effective description of this passage in 'De la fabrique au site: Naissance de l'usine mobile, in idem, *Usine ouvriers. Figure du nouvel ordre productif* (Paris, Maspero, 1980), pp. 13–40.

11 [Translator's note: In his writings of the early 1980s, Negri used the term 'hysteresis' (*isteresi*) to indicate that which is produced in the process of separation effected by the displacement, which exists not in a continuity (not even a formal continuity) with it, but as a rupture and difference: the emergence of the new. The notion of hysteresis also has a relation to time, meaning 'to come late', but also 'differently'. The work of René Thom and Ilya Prigogine were crucial for Negri in arriving at this conception.]

12 See my *Alle origini del formalismo giuridico* (Padua, Cedam, 1962).

13 Many have recently and opportunely reminded us of Ernst Cassirer's role as theoretical hinge in the development of all currents of bourgeois ideology that have attempted to reformulate horizons of meaning within subsumed being on the basis of the formal and symbolic auto-productivity of reason.

14 [Translator's note: See the 'Introduction' to Heidegger's *Being and Time*, trans. J. Macquarrie and E. Robinson (London, Basil Blackwell, 1962), pp. 21–64.]

15 [Translator's note: 'In subsuming the *time* of existence, in *subsuming it socially, capital reduces it to zero, but it restores it to us as collective essence*' (A. Negri, *Macchina tempo* (Milan, Feltrinelli, 1982) p. 23 – my translation). 'Now, with the rhythm of this new passage from quantity to quality, the field tends to reacquire the tonality of antagonism. *The figures take the form of the opposition and of subjectivity:* worker and capitalist, collective worker and collective capitalist. Once capital attains the totality of the process of valorization and of reproduction, its process is in reality once again a process of the *reproduction of the antagonisms*. Reproduction does not negate difference, does not annul antagonism; on the contrary, it exacerbates both' (idem, *Marx Beyond Marx*, trans. H. Cleaver, M. Ryan and M. Viano (New York, Autonomedia, 1991), p. 77.]

16 [Translator's note: 'In the Keynesian system, state budgeting was the means of recuperating and neutralising the class struggle in the factory, and monetary policy was the means of subordinating the wage relation' (Negri, 'Archaeology and Project', p. 207).]

17 [Translator's note: '[W]hen the whole of life becomes production, capitalist time measures only that which it directly commands. And socialised labour-power tends to unloose itself from command, insofar as it proposes a life-alternative – and thus projects a different time for its own existence, both in the present and in the future. When all life-time becomes production-time, who measures whom? *The two conceptions of time and life* come into direct conflict in a separation which becomes increasingly deep and rigidly structured' (Negri, 'Archaeology and Project', p. 220).]

18 The analogy with the physical-relativistic conception of time and of space is remarkable and suggestive: many erroneous expositions of the theory are given concerning the size of the relativistic totality – of subsumption? – as Einstein notes in particular with respect to the so-called 'spatialization of

time'. Einstein affirms that 'time and space are fused in one and the same *continuum*, but this continuum is not isotropic. The element of spatial distance and the element of duration remain distinct in nature, distinct even in the formula giving the square of the world interval of two infinitely near events' (cited in Čapek, *The Concepts of Time and Space*, p. 367).

19 [Translator's note: This quotation is from Aristotle's *Physics*, Book 4, Chapter 11, 219b, line 1, which can be found in *The Complete Works of Aristotle*, ed. J. Barnes (Princeton NJ, Princeton University Press, 1984).]

20 [Translator's note: This is the expression Marx uses for 'overhead costs of production'. Or, as in the *Theories of Surplus Value Part 1*, 'mere expenses, unproductive expenditure either of living labour or materialised labour' (London, Lawrence & Wishart, 1969), p. 167 note.]

21 [Translator's note: For as Negri had argued in his *Dominio e sabotaggio* (Milan, Feltrinelli, 1978), to say that the law of value is in crisis is not to deny that it continues to be effective, rather the crisis modifies its form, 'transforming it from a law of political economy into a form of the command of the State' (ibid., p. 13 – my translation). For more on this shift of the law of value from law of political economy to operation of command see Negri, 'Twenty Theses on Marx', Thesis 3.]

22 [Translator's note: The reference is to Walter Benjamin, and in particular to his 'Theses on the Philosophy of History', in *Illuminations*, trans. H. Zohn (London, Fontana, 1973), pp. 255–66.]

23 As Carlo Formenti underlines with reference to Prigogine, the relation reversibility-irreversibility, when it is brought into the game of an ideology of the equilibrium of micro-conflicts, of the recomposition of differences in an absolute *set*, is simply a reactionary operation.

24 [Translator's note: The reference is to Massimo Cacciari's *Krisis. Saggio sulla crisi del pensiero negativo da Nietzsche a Wittgenstein* (Milan, Feltrinelli, 1976). I would like to thank Alberto Toscano for clarifying the terms of the debate between Negri and Cacciari around this notion. This is his admirably lucid summary: 'Negri's polemic with Cacciari – with whom he had collaborated in the early days of Potere Operaio and in the journal Contropiano – is founded on a split within *Operaismo* which saw Cacciari turn, together with Tronti and others, to the PCI, in the belief that the only effective form of organization of the workers' struggle was one mediated by the party and the official workers' movement. Negri, confident that the link between autonomy and organization had to be subordinated to the subjective materiality of antagonism, and not to the directives of the party, saw the philosophy of *Krisis* – as well as Tronti's parrallel defence of the *autonomy of the political* – as the apology of a regression in the class struggle. For Cacciari, the nihilistic collapse of a foundationalist rationality, which also signals the end of any dialectics of progress and resolution, could only be assumed by a lucid thinking of the necessity of

formalism and institutional "realism", that is, by a defence of the necessity of political convention. Negri viewed this position as a denial of the constitutive and materially determining nature of living labour, as well as of the class antagonsim which is at the heart of the temporality of capitalism, a denial which subjected the workers' movement to the dubious *Realpolitik* of the PCI (i.e. the *compromesso storico*). See Negri's review of Cacciari, "Simplex Sigillum Veri" (1976) in *Macchina tempo*, Feltrinelli, 1982, pp. 39–54. For a defence of Cacciari's position, see Giuseppe Cantarano, *Immagini del nulla. La filosofia italiana contemporanea*, Mondadori, 1998, pp. 37–48.']

25 Much less outdated, if I am allowed to refer to other philosophical moments within the horizon of Italian ideology, were the attempts developed in the 1960s to pose the problem of the collective essence of praxis. Giulio Preti attempted the path of an ethical coventionalism that is strongly rooted, strongly radical and strongly social. His democratic conformism was motivated by an ethical character – constructed within and beyond the Anglo-Saxon diatribes on the 'phrastic' and 'neustic' – that, even if it prevented him from grasping the material schism of the paradigms, enabled him nonetheless to consider irresolvable – even if only in terms of a formalization of crisis – the relation between the mysticism of the collective and the ascesis of the individual. He posed the problem, which in philosophy is fundamental. [Translator's note: on the 'phrastic' and the 'neustic' see R. M. Hare's *The Language of Morals* (Oxford, Oxford University Press, 1952), especially pp. 17–28 and p. 188f.]

26 It is extremely instructive – and it is enough merely to point this out in passing because we will return to it repeatedly – to ascertain the heteronomy of ends into which neo-liberal political economy runs if one attempts, perhaps unpardonably, to take it seriously and denounce the pure and simple immediate force of its mystification. The predication of individual economic freedom, of the cuts in taxes and in social spending linked to this, unfolds *immediately* in the projection of planned support for investment (Heilbronner), in military centralization of production (Thurow) and therefore in essentially nothing less than a reformulation of programmes for capitalist reproduction and in a hierarchic proposal of objectives adequate to it (Cleaver and O'Connor). Given the level of existent antagonisms it is easy to foresee that liberalism will only be able to survive at a higher level of state planning. [Translator's note: This analysis would be confirmed in Hardt and Negri's diagnosis of the purported collapse of the Welfare State in the 1980s: 'The Welfare State was seriously eroded in the 1980s, then, in the sense that labor was progressively excluded from the constitution and the State's efforts toward full employment came to an end. If we take another perspective, however, and view the Welfare State in terms of State spending and State intervention in economic and social mechanisms, it did not wither during this

period but actually grew. The neoliberal project involved a substantial increase of the State in terms both of size and powers of intervention. The development of the neoliberal State did not lead toward a "thin" form of rule in the sense of the progressive dissipation or disappearance of the State as social actor. On the contrary, the State did not become a weak but rather an increasingly strong subject" (*The Labor of Dionysus* (Minneapolis, University of Minnesota Press, 1994), p. 242).]

27 I think J. F. Lyotard's conclusion in *The Postmodern Condition* is only apparently more restrained and optimistic: 'Still, the postmodern condition is as much a stranger to disenchantment as it is to the blind positivity of delegitimation. Where, after the metanarratives, can legitimacy reside? The operativity criterion is technological; it has no relevance for judging what is true or what is just. Is legitimacy to be found in consensus obtained through discussion, as Jürgen Habermas thinks? Such consensus does violence to the heterogeneity of language games. And invention is always born of dissension. Postmodern knowledge is not simply a tool of the authorities; it refines our sensitivity to differences and reinforces our ability to tolerate the incommensurable. Its principle is not the expert's homology, but the inventor's paralogy": *The Postmodern Condition* (Manchester, Manchester University Press, 1986), pp. xxiv–xxv. In truth, Lyotard's conclusion is merely ironic.

28 [Translator's note: See Antonio Negri's *Descartes Politico o della ragionevole ideologia* (Milan, Feltrinelli, 1970) and idem, *The Savage Anomaly*, trans. M. Hardt (Minneapolis, University of Minnesota Press, 1991). Negri continued to work on Spinoza throughout the 1980s and 1990s. See *Spinoza sovversivo* (Rome, Antonio Pellicani Editore, 1992), 'Democrazia ed Eternità in Spinoza' (1995), which appeared in his *Spinoza* (Rome, Derive Approdi, 1998), pp. 380–9 and 'Reliqua Desiderantur': A Conjecture for a Definition of the Concept of Democracy in the Final Spinoza', trans. T. Stolze, in W. Montag and T. Stolze (eds), *The New Spinoza* (Minneapolis University on Minnesota Press, 1997), pp. 219–47.]

29 The enormous importance of the work of René Thom for the social sciences consists in having inserted the concept of irreversibility, of *hysteresis*, of catastrophe into the schemas of descriptive geometric space. Following on from this, the project of the transcendental schematism and the 'necessity' of the capitalist analytic, in so far as they are geometric representations of social space, can be submitted to a system of broken figures. [Translator's note: for more on René Thom see A. Negri's 'Per un nuovo schematismo della ragione. Risposta a Petitot', in idem, *Fabbriche del soggetto*, pp. 181–7.]

30 There is another objection that we should take a look at, one that leads to the thinking of *Krisis*, as is the current mode of expression for negative thought. Here the negation of the horizon of displacement is given through the *negative hypostasis of the process of displacement itself*. Of course, it is an endogenous

process, and as such it may count as a critique of the naturalistic and post-modernist positions; but it fails precisely as a hypostatic operation. *Krisis is the analytic thing.* Here, the analytic ecstasy becomes disenchanted without the possibility of truly (that is politically) developing the negative intuition of 'thing-ness'. Scholem shows us analogous experiences in the history of mysticism: the sacrosanct idea of the critique of history and progress ends up by negating any constructive negativity – so that the mystic entrusts constructiveness to mechanical Golems within a horizon of joy.

31 [Translator's note: See Marx, *Capital Vol. 1*, pp. 128ff.]

32 [Translator's note: Negri himself takes up this thread again a decade later in *Insurgencies, Constituent Power and the Modern State*, trans. M. Bosacaglia (Minneapolis, University of Minnesota Press, 1999).]

33 [Translator's note: Negri sums this up in *Marx Beyond Marx* as the shift from money as general equivalent to money as capital. 'The circulation of money was a *"perpetuum mobile"*. Such a characteristic belongs also to the circulation of capital; but capital structures its mobility in a substantial way, that is, it is a creative mobility. [. . .] Capital circulates in time and space determining flows which are ever more coalesced, ever quicker temporally and ever more integrated spatially. [. . .] Therefore *circulation* is, above all, *the expansion of the potency of capital*; and for the same reason it entails the *appropriation* of all social conditions and their placement in *valorization*. [. . .] The socialization of capital is a process which determines, through circulation, an irresistible compulsion towards expansion, appropriation and homogenization – under the sign of the social totality' (ibid., pp. 112, 113).]

34 For example Carl Schmitt can state with some irony that: 'a new and essentially pacifist vocabulary has been created. War is condemned but executions, sanctions, punitive expeditions, pacifications, protection of treaties, international police, and measures to assure peace remain', in idem, *The Concept of the Political* (Chicago, University of Chicago Press, 1996), p. 79.

35 It is interesting to observe this move in the economists. From Keynes and from his eclectic synthesis of a classical theory of value and of a neoclassical theory of equilibrium, a school of micro-cyclical planning – productive occupation of all the pores of production and of reproduction, political cycle of capital, miniaturization of control – and a school of systemic definition, of nomenclature, take their cue. Pushed by the exigencies that are born of the crisis of each of these developments, it seems to me that both currents are trying to reach a new synthesis. If Keynes set off from the first warning signals of real subsumption, introducing time – his fundamental innovation – into the science of economics, here with the post-Keynesians, nomenclature and disciplining form the responses to a more advanced stage of the problematic of time – that is where an understanding of the operations of the link between time and command is required. In this regard, Augusto Graziani's redefinition

of the functions of inflation as a directly economic, capitalist instrument for the redistribution (*recalculation*) of revenues – as a function of accumulation, led me to some useful reflections. The concentration of profits, due to the pre-eminence of the financial sectors over the productive ones, has immediately productive aims and effects – and that is, to put into motion a 'a single mechanism which effects the desired modifications in the international division of labour through the apparently neutral mechanism of the market' (A. Graziani, *Crisi delle politiche e politiche nella crisi* (Naples, Einandi Editore, 1981), p. 62). Even in the economists, time aims to be real only through command. *Measure has become command.*

36 [Translator's note: C. Schmitt, *Political Theology. Four Chapters on the Concept of Sovereignty* (Cambridge MA, MIT Press, 1985), Carl Schmitt, p. 5.]

37 [Translator's note: 'Time and space, after first constituting the fabric of capital's expansion in circulation, appear now as barriers, as obstacles. As obstacles to be eliminated, destroyed – *by reducing space to time*' (Negri, *Marx Beyond Marx*, p. 115).]

38 The eternal dream of the analytic would like to realize itself, and the project would like to fit nature. Gertrude Stein and her neo-Platonism of Jewish origin correctly reconceive capitalist utopia in the nexus of geographical, spatial and historical relations of the USA: *mens* as unity and measure, as a nature that is a space of production. *Mens sana in corpore sano*, where the body is the railways and mass production. The last positive capitalist utopia was the frontier, the limitless nature and space to which the limitless thirst for profit adapts itself, as Marx 'On Carey' reminds us [Translator's note: See 'Bastiat and Carey', in Marx's *Grundrisse*, pp. 883–93.]

39 Rosdolsky probably displays a lot of good sense when he concludes that: 'it is not so much a case of knowing if qualified labour is a pure multiple of simple labour, so much as knowing *how* this multiple should be measured.' Now this last problem is undoubtedly one that must be tackled, but one must do so in the face of the difficulties involved in using traditional criteria of measurement.

40 [Translator's note: See Negri, 'Archaeology and Project', especially pp. 216–28.]

41 [Translator's note: In line with other translations – notably that of *Marx Beyond Marx* – I have opted for 'self-valorization', despite the risk of individualizing the process in a unitary subject. The Italian word 'autovalorizzazione' involves no such hypostasis. This should be borne in mind in the present context as well.]

42 [Translator's note: See also A. Negri's 'Sul metodo della critica storica', *Aut Aut*, 167–8 (September–November 1978), pp. 197–212, and republished in idem, *Macchina tempo*, pp. 70–84.]

43 [Translator's note: Negri provides a more substantial treatment of the

changing forms of class composition in his 'Twenty Theses on Marx' (see Thesis 4 in particular).]

44 That does not mean that a list of characteristics specific to *d* cannot be given with respect to 1, 2, 3, 4: it means that the inventory does not exhaust the concept *d*, as was the case with *a*, *b*, *c*. The terms of homologation are missing; there is an *ontological difference*.

45 [Translator's note: Although Negri here uses the term *medio*, he is nevertheless gesturing towards the notion of *medietà* spoken of above. That is, towards that which results from an arithmetical operation.]

46 [Translator's note: See Negri, 'Archaeology and Project', pp. 222–8.]

47 That the concept of *hegemony* of Gramscian origin had been considered potentially democratic, constitutes a paradox of political science. Leaving aside the obvious fact that to be hegemonic one must act among the masses, no one has wanted to question whether this is sufficient to characterize the concept of hegemony. Since this is not sufficient, one must decide whether hegemony comes *before* or *after* legitimation. It is here that the sophism is revealed. The capitalist response and that of the theory of the autonomy of the political and of the revolution from above have no doubt that hegemony is exerted *first, over legitimation*. But hegemony, if it isn't put in question, constitutes the icy condition of *dictatorship*.

48 Recently Robert L. Heilbroner has underlined the irreversibility of *State capitalism* in precisely the situations – such as Reagan's America – in which the legitimating liberal principles are proclaimed most vigorously. And the talk is precisely of 'State capitalism': nationalization and planning, macro and micro.

49 [Translator's note: A number of chapters from *La forma stato* (Millan, Feltrinelli, 1977) have been published in Hardt and Negri's *The Labor of Dionysus*. With regard to the operation of the constitutional process, see specifically 'Labor in the constitution', pp. 54–136.]

50 I derived great pleasure from reading P. A. Schiera's analysis in *La Prussia fra politica e 'lumi': alle origini del Modell Deutschland* (Bologma, Il Mulino, n.d.), where he makes of the constitutional 'enlightenment' the content of a 'police-like' constitutional ordering of time. In fact the paradox is here stretched to an extreme and is thus theoretically exemplary.

51 This old neo-Kantian awareness is slowly decantered and presented as though it were democratic and progressive by the neo-contractualists à la Rawls.

52 [Translator's note: For more on Hans Kelsen see Negri, *Insurgencies*, pp. 5–6 and Hardt and Negri, *The Labor of Dionysus*, pp. 109–12. See also Negri, *Fabbriche del soggetto*, pp. 86–91: '[T]he genius of Kelsen consists precisely in following the route that, from the old Kantian formalism, led well beyond its limits or its furthest reaches: he anticipated that formalization of the real that

we today consider proper to subsumption and the postmodern' (p. 86 – my translation).]

53 [[Translator's note: Cited in R. F. Harrod's *The Life of John Maynard Keynes* (London, Macmillan, 1951).]

54 [Translator's note: 'By *negative labour* I mean the intellectually and materially determined content of the refusal of the current social organization, and first of all of wage labour' (Negri, *Macchina tempo*, p. 208 – my translation).]

55 [Translator's note: '[F]or capital, restructuring is a political, economic and technological mechanism aimed at the enforced reduction of the working class to labour-power' (Negri, 'Archaeology and Project', p. 212).]

56 [Translator's note: The *'social worker* emerges as a new force, and as a *subjective qualification of social labour power*. The social worker completed and concluded the dynamic which existed within the mass worker as a tendency, and *transformed the independent variable into independence tout court*. This antagonism develops at a pace dictated by the rhythms of the real subsumption which capital puts into operation in relation to social labour. As real subsumption advances, so the social worker is brought into existence, as irresolvable antagonism. Antagonism as regards conceptions of life, the liberation of time, and thus in bringing about spatial-temporal conditions which are wholly alternative' (ibid., pp. 220–21).]

57 [Translator's note: 'Negative labour means that these same qualities of labour (over which capital moulds its capacity of command) are irreducible and antagonistic to command, to this command. Why? Because when mobility, abstraction, sociality become needs across the integrated field of production and reproduction, that is of life in all it abundance, the capitalist organization of production is refused in as much as it is antagonistic to the potential abundance and the desire for life that the needs of mobility (that is of freedom), of abstraction (that is of culture), of sociality (that is of community) produce. [. . .] Therefore, by proletarian institutionality I mean the coming to light of something which is identical with itself, that is individual mass substance, the enemy of exploitation, with an autonomous code of development' (Negri, *Macchina tempo*, pp. 212, pp. 212–13 – my translation).]

58 [Translator's note: See A. Negri's *Saggio sullo storicismo tedesco: Dilthey e Meinecke* (Milan, Feltrinelli, 1959).]

59 [Translator's note: The concept of 'charisma' is Max Weber's. It is succinctly explained in a note to Weber's *The Protestant Ethic and the Spirit of Capitalism*, trans. T. Parsons (London, Routledge, 1992) as 'the quality of leadership which appeals to non-rational motives' (p. 281, n. 105). But for Weber's detailed account of the notion of 'charisma' see his *Economy and Society Vols 1 and 2*, ed. G. Roth and C. Wittich (Berkely, University of California Press, 1978). See also Negri, *Insurgencies*, pp. 7–8.]

60 [Translator's note: The *Grundnorm* or 'basic norm' is the element that stands

at the basis of Hans Kelsen's juridical formalism, in which a norm is derivable from a (logically) prior and superior norm. But there is no infinite regress here. Ultimately there is a norm from which all the others derive but that itself does not proceed from a superior norm. The entire edifice is constructed upon this basis, a basis for the generation of norms. The problem is, however, that Kelsen's suggestion of versions of Kant's Categorical Imperative as examples of the *Grundnorm* do not show how one can generate the whole formal system on this basis.]

61 [Translator's note: On the 'nuclear state', see 'Some notes concerning the concept of the *nuclear state*' in Negri's *The Politics of Subversion* trans. J. Newell (Oxford, Polity Press, 1989), pp. 191–9.]

62 [Translator's note: As mentioned in the Introduction, given the conditions in which the text was written, as well as the destruction of a number of the notebooks in which Negri would jot down working notes and quotations, it should be borne in mind that he was often reliant on memory alone in the final drafting of this text. Although some of the differences in the passages cited may be due to translation, it is possible that Negri transcribed some passages incorrectly and that they found their way into the published text.]

63 [Translator's note: See Negri's profoundly innovative reading of Lenin in *La fabbricadella strategia. 33 lezzioni su Lenin* (1976).]

64 [Translator's note: These terms drawn from Louis Althusser's *Reading Capital*, trans. B. Brewster (London, Verso, 1979) (see Part II, chapter 4 in particular) describe the manner in which the linear continuity of diachronic time come to be disrupted by discontinuities, non-correspondences and varying articulations of *dislocated*, 'relatively' autonomous times.]

65 [Translator's note: Negri is here alluding to his *The Savage Anomaly*, and in particular what he terms Spinoza's shift from the 'first foundation' to the 'second foundation'. (For an informative treatment of this subject see Read's 'The Antagonistic Ground of Constitutive Power', especially pp. 2–8.)]

66 [Translator's note: This afterword was initially published as the introduction to the 1997 *Manifestolibri* publication of *The Constitution of Time* (which had originally appeared as the final chapter of Negri's *Macchina tempo* in 1982). Negri suggested, however, that it should be placed at the end of the book as it functions as a useful link with *Kairòs, Alma Venus, Multitudo*, by indicating some aporias in the text that had not been resolved here. I leave it to the reader to decide to what extent these aporias are resolved in the later text.]

67 [Translator's note: The 'Censis Reports' are socio-economic reports carried out by a private company that are extremely influential in Italian government circles.]

68 [Translator's note: The notion of the 'common name' is explored in the opening section of *Kairòs, Alma Venus, Mulititudo*.]

69 [Translator's note: This book appeared in English with additional essays as *The Politics of Subversion* (1989).]

70 [Translator's note: This book appeared in English as *Insurgencies*, Constituent Power and the Modern State.]

71 [Translator's note: *Palmiro Togliatti* was the leader of the Italian Communist Party (PCI) during the years of fascism while Gramsci was in prison, remaining at the head of the party through to his death in 1964. He lived in the Soviet Union for a number of years, only returning to Italy after the liberation of southern Italy by the allies. He established the path of the national road to socialism for the PCI and successfully transformed it into the largest Communist Party in the West. Although he never formally broke with the Soviet Union, at his death he left a document (the 'Yalta Memorandum') powerfully denouncing it and its policy of excommunicating the Chinese communists. *Massimo D'Alema* was leader of the Partito Democratico della Sinistra (Democratic Party of the Left – ex-PCI) for a brief period after 1994 and then became Prime Minister after the crisis of the Prodi government. *Fausto Bertinotti* became the leader of Rifondazione Communista (the Refounded Communist Party), following the dissolution of the PCI in 1991.

Kairòs, Alma Venus, Multitudo

1 [Translator's note: Lucretius, *On the Nature of the Universe*, trans. R. E. Latham (London, Penguin, 1994), p. 10.]

2 [Translator's note: Negri takes the notion of '*virtus*' from Niccolò Machiavelli. '*Virtus*' is one of the two apparatuses (the other is 'fortune') by means of which time is grasped and becomes constitutive of subjectivity and of politics, such that the 'political is configured as a grammar of time' (A. Negri, *Insurgencies, Constituent Power and the Modern State*, trans, M. Boscaglia (Minneapolis, University of Minnesota Press, 1999) p. 42). Negri provides an account of these concepts in his discussion of 'the decision' and of 'the multitude' in the final lesson of '*Multitudo*'.]

3 [Translator's note: Spinoza, *Ethics*, trans. E. Curley (ed.) (Princeton NJ, Princeton University Press, 1994), Part IV, P42.]

4 [Translator's note: Negri distinguishes between 'future' and '*being-to-come*'. The former is a formal category that is everywhere equal, homogenous: it is an empty space to be filled with the present without alteration, a neutral placeholder. The latter, on the other hand, is of the order of the event, steeped in being, operating on the edge of being. There is a clear link here between Negri's ontology of time and that developed by Gilles Deleuze and Felix Guattari, where the latter differentiate the time of *chronos* from that of *aeon*.

'*Aeon*: the indefinite time of the event. *Chronos*: is the time of measure [. . .]'
(G. Deleuze and F. Guattari, *A Thousand Plateaus*, trans. B. Massumi (London,
Athlone Press, 1988) p. 262; see also Deleuze's 'Twenty-third series of the
Aion', in *The Logic of Sense*, trans. M. Lester and C. Stivale (London, Athlone
Press, 1990), pp. 162–8). Negri has already engaged in a critique of time-as-
measure in *The Constitution of Time* ('First Displacement: the time of subsumed
being'). In view of the centrality of the distinction between 'futuro' and
'avvenire' I have adopted the sometime cumbersome construction '*to-come*'
(italicized). This may not always read very well, but it is important that the
distinction be held to strictly, so I have opted for this unhappy compromise;
marking off the time of the event of the '*to-come*' from that of the 'future' as
formal and empty repetition.]

5 [Translator's note: See 'The Constitution of Time', in this volume.]

6 [Translator's note: Negri takes these notions from Foucault and Deleuze. See
Deleuze's short but trenchant essay 'Postscript on Control Societies' and the
interview between Negri and Deleuze, 'Control and Becoming'. Both pieces
can be found in G. Deleuze, *Negotiations*, trans. M. Joughin (New York,
Columbia University Press, 1995), pp. 169–82. For a discussion of the relation
between disciplinary and control societies see M. Hardt and A. Negri, *Empire*
(Cambridge MA, Harvard University Press, 2000), pp. 329–32.]

7 [Translator's note: The word '*sorvolo*' is the Italian translation for Gilles
Deleuze and Felix Guattari's '*survol*', which in the English translation by
Graham Burchell and Hugh Tomlinson of *What is Philosophy?* (London, Verso,
1994) is rendered as 'survey' (see pp. ix–x of the Tranlators's Introduction).
On occasion, however, the English translation has 'state of survey'. This translation is problematic, for it renders the activity and dynamic proper to 'survey', static. In order to be consistent with other Deleuze translations, I have
opted for 'survey' or, as in Mark Lester's translation of Deleuze's *The Logic of
Sense* (London, Athlone, 1990), 'surveying'. However, one should bear in
mind that 'overflight' or 'fly over' would be the more literal translation of
'*survol*' or '*sorvelo*'.]

8 [Translator's note: One should bear in mind that the word '*vero*' includes both
the notion of the 'true' and that of the 'real'. Both meanings coexist in Negri's
account. I have selected to use one or the other according to the context,
although the one meaning should not be thought to exclude the other (when
it is particularly important that one should not lose sight of this underlying
unity of meaning I have inserted the Italian [*vero*] into the passage). One
could, appropriating Spinoza's expression, say 'true *sive* real' where, as in
Spinoza, the 'or' (*sive*) brings the two terms together rather than separating
them.]

9 [Translator's note: On the constitutive nature of the imagination see A.
Negri's *The Savage Anomaly*, trans. M. Hardt (Minneapolis, University of

Minnesota Press, 1991) and idem, *Lenta ginestra* (Milan, Mimesis Eterotopia, 2001).]

10 [Translator's note: Antonio Negri explained to me in conversation that the title *La Grandeur de Marx*, designating a mythical text about which so many stories have been told, should mark rather a period of collective discussion and reflection on Marx, and not be seen as an allusion to an actual text, whether finished or unfinished, destroyed or never even begun.]

11 [Translator's note: It is worth noting that with the notion of the 'praxis of the true' (a reformulation of the 'true in practice' drawn from Marx's *1857 Introduction* to the *Grundrisse*, trans. M. Nicolaus (London, Pelican, 1973), p. 105), we have all three elements of the methodology that Negri extracts from Marx and which guides his reading of the *Grundrisse* in *Marx Beyond Marx*, trans, H. Cleaver, M. Ryan and M. Viano (New York, Autonomedia, 1991). The other two elements are those of 'determinate abstraction' and of 'the tendency', which Negri has already discussed in his prolegomena to 'The Common name' (par. 8.6). '*The "true in practice" is thus the moment of development of the category where the abstraction finds a point of focalization and attains the plenitude of its relation to historical reality*' (Negri, *Marx Beyond Marx*, p. 49).]

12 [Translator's note: The notion of 'consisting' here contains both that of 'insisting' (as a modality of inhabiting) and – at the same time – that of 'consistency' (understood as the positivity and plenitude of the ontology being developed). So that eternity and *kairòs* exist in a productive relay, with the latter 'insisting' within the eternal whose 'consistency' it produces by always creating new being.]

13 [Translator's note: This is an ironic allusion to the famous opening to Descartes' *Discourse on Method*: 'Good sense is the best distributed thing in the world: for everybody thinks himself so well endowed with it that even those who are the hardest to please in everything else do not usually desire more of it than they possess. In this it is unlikely that everyone is mistaken. It indicates rather that the power of judging well and of distinguishing the true from the false – which is what we properly call "good sense" or "reason" – is naturally equal in all men' (*The Philosophical Writings of Descartes Vol 1*, trans. J. Cottingham, R. Stoothoff and D. Murdoch (Cambridge, Cambridge University Press, 1985), p. 111). See also A. Negri, *Descartes politico o della ragionevole ideologia*, (Milan, Feltrinelli, 1970).]

14 [Translator's note: The standard English translation makes no reference to 'power', although 'no one has yet determined what the body can do' (as it is translated by Curley) involves an implicit reference to the 'power' of the body to act.]

15 [Translator's note: The concept of *arché* appears to have entered philosophical discourse with Plato and Aristotle. In the Greek it means at once foundation, principle and commencement. But 'Aristotle is the one who explicitly joins

the more ancient sense of *inception* with that of *domination*.' (R. Schürmann, *Heidegger on Being and Acting: from Principles to Anarchy* (Indiana, Indiana University Press, 1990), p. 97).]

16 [Translator's note: Negri develops the problematic of the 'second nature' in his book on Giacomo Leopardi, *Lenta ginestra*. There, following Georg Lukács' reading of Hegel, Negri argues that the world of the 'second nature' is the set of illusions that nevertheless represent something substantive: a real illusion. 'The "second nature" is a mystification – but a destructive mystification (it destroyed the first nature, and we can no longer find it), an effective mystification (we live in it and reproduce it, living through "second nature")' (ibid., p. 57, n. 9 – my translation). See also Negri, *The Savage Anomaly*.]

17 [Translator's note: *Ethics*, Part III, P2, Scholium, in Spinoza, *The Ethics and Other Works*. See also note 14 above.]

18 [Translator's note: See the 'Fragment on Machines', in Marx's *Grundrisse*, pp. 690–712. See also P. Virio 'Notes on the "General Intellect"' (1996).]

19 [Translator's note: K. Marx, *Capital Vol. 3* (London, Lawrence & Wishart, 1984), Part V and chapter XXVII in particular.]

20 [Translator's note: For a more detailed account of the constitutive force as well as the failures of Leninism see Negri, *Insurgencies*, chapter 6. See also idem, *La fabbrica della strategia. 33 lezioni su Lenin* (Padua, CLEUP and Libri Rossi, 1976).]

21 [Translator's note: The reference is obviously to Foucault, Deleuze and Guattari. See Deleuze's 'What is a *dispositif*?', in idem, *Michel Foucault Philosopher*, trans. T. J. Armstrong (London, Routledge, 1992), pp. 159–68, as well as his brilliant *Foucault*, trans. S. Hand (Minneapolis, University of Minnesota Press, 1988). For the extraordinarily rich theory of assemblages see Deleuze and Guattari, *A Thousand Plateaus*.]

22 [Translator's note: For a brief discussion of the relation between ontology and politics see Part III of the introduction and the references contained there.]

23 [Translator's note: Negri carries out a detailed investigation of Machiavelli's thinking in relation to the notion of the decision (or *virtus*) and temporality in his *Insurgencies*, chapter 2. See also his considerations of Machiavelli and Althusser in 'Notes on the Evolution of the thought of the Later Althusser', trans. O. Vasile, in *Postmodern Materialism and the Future of Marxist Theory*, ed. A. Callari and D. F. Ruccio (New England, Wesleyan University Press, 1966), pp. 51–68.]

Bibliography

Text by Antonio Negri

(1959), *Saggi sullo storicismo tedesco: Dilthey e Meinecke*, Milan, Feltrinelli.

(1962), *Alle Origini del Formalismo Giuridico*, Padua, Cedam.

(1970), *Descartes politico o della ragionevole ideologia*, Milan, Feltrinelli.

(1976), *La fabbrica della strategia. 33 lezioni su Lenin*, Padua, C.L.E.U.P and Libri Rossi.

(1977), *La forma stato. Per la critica dell'economia politica della Costituzione*, Milan, Feltrinelli.

(1978), *Dominio e sabotaggio*, Milan, Feltrinelli.

(1980), *Il comunismo e la guerra*, Milan, Feltrinelli.

(1982), *Macchina tempo*, Milan, Feltrinelli.

(1987), *Fabbriche del soggetto*, 21st Century, no. 1, September–October, Livorno.

(1988), *Revolution Retrieved: Selected Writings on Marx, Keynes, Capitalist Crisis and New Social Subjects*, London, Red Notes.

(1989a) 'From Mass Worker to Socialised Worker', in *The Politics of Subversion*, trans. J. Newell, Oxford, Polity Press, pp. 75–88.

(1989b), *The Politics of Subversion*, trans. J. Newell, Oxford, Polity Press.

(1991a), *The Savage Anomaly*, trans. M. Hardt, Minneapolis, University of Minnesota Press.

(1991b), *Marx Beyond Marx*, trans. H. Cleaver, M. Ryan and M. Viano, New York, Autonomedia.

(1992), *Spinoza sovversivo*, Rome, Antonio Pellicani Editore.

(1996a), 'Twenty Theses on Marx', trans. M. Hardt, in S. Makdisi, C. Casarino, R. E. Karl (eds), *Marxism Beyond Marxism*, New York, Routledge, pp. 149–80.

(1996b), 'Notes on the Evolution of the Thought of the Later Althusser', trans. O. Vasile, in A. Callari and D. F. Ruccio (eds), *Postmodern Materialism and the*

Future of Marxist Theory: Essays in the Althusserian Tradition, Hanover NH, Wesleyan University Press, pp. 51–68.

(1997a), *La costituzione del tempo. Prolegomeni*, Rome, Manifestolibri.

(1997b), '*Reliqua Desiderantur*: A Conjecture for a Definition of the Concept of Democracy in the Final Spinoza', trans. T. Stolze, in W. Montag and T. Stolze (eds), *The New Spinoza*, Minneapolis, University of Minnesota Press, pp. 219–47.

(1998a), *Exil*, trans. F. Rosso and A. Querrien, Paris, Éditions Mille et une Nuits.

(1998b), *Spinoza*, Rome, DeriveApprodi.

(1999a), 'Value and Affect', *Boundary 2*, 26:2, summer.

(1999b), *Insurgencies, Constituent Power and the Modern State*, trans. M. Boscaglia, Minneapolis, University of Minnesota Press.

(2000a), *Kairòs, Alma Venus, Multitudo*, Rome, Manifestolibri.

(2000b), *Kairòs, Alma Venus, Multitudo*, trans. J. Revel, Paris, Calmann-Lévy.

(2001), *Lenta ginestra*, Millepiani, Milan, Mimesis Eterotopia.

(n.d.), 'Impero, moltitudini, esodo', presented in a discussion at the faculty of literature at the University *La Sapienza* in Rome (http://www.sherwood.it).

Agamben, G. (1995), *Homo Sacer*, Turin, Einaudi Editore.

Althusser, L. (1969), *For Marx*, trans. B. Brewster, London, Verso.

Althusser, L. and Balibar, É. (1979), *Reading Capital*, trans. B. Brewster, London, Verso.

Ansell Pearson, K. (2000), 'Nietzsche's Brave New World of Force', *Pli: The Warwick Journal of Philosophy*, 9, pp. 6–35.

Appel, Karl Otto (1973), *Transformation der Philosophie*, Frankfurt.

Aristotle (1984), *The Complete Works of Aristotle*, ed. J. Barnes, Princeton NJ, Princeton University Press.

Arrighi, G. (2002), 'Lineages of Empire', *Historical Materialism*, 10:3, autumn, Brill, Netherlands, pp. 1–14.

Augustine, St (1972), *City of God*, trans. H. Bettenson, London, Pelican.

Augustine, St (1986), *Confessions*, trans. R. S. Pine-Coffin, London, Penguin.

Baczko, B. (1974), *Rousseau, solitude et communauté*, Mondadori.

Benjamin, W. (1973), 'Theses on the Philosophy of History', in *Illuminations*, trans. H. Zohn, London, Fontana.

Bloch, E. (1986), *The Principle of Hope*, trans. N. Plaice, S. Plaice and P. Knight, Oxford, Basil Blackwell.

Bloch, E. (2000), *The Spirit of Utopia*, trans. A. A. Nassar, Palo Alto CA, Stanford University Press.

Cacciari, M. (1976), *Krisis. Saggio sulla crisi del pensiero negativo da Nietzsche a Wittgenstein*, Milan, Feltrinelli.

Cacciari, M. (1978), *Dialettica e critica della politica. Saggio su Hegel*, Milan, Feltrinelli.

Campana, D. (1991), *Orphic Songs and Other Poems*, trans. L. Bonaffini, New York, Peter Lang.

Cantarano, G. (1998), *Immagini del nulla. La filosofia Italiana contemporanea*, Mondadori.

Čapek, M. (ed.) (1976), *The Concepts of Time and Space*, Dordrecht, Holland/Boston MA, D. Reidel Publishing Group.

Cassirer, E. (1953–57), *The Philosophy of Symbolic Forms*, 3 Volumes, trans. R. Mannheim, New Haven, Yale University Press.

Cleaver, H. (1979), *Reading Capital Politically*, Brighton, The Harvester Press.

Cleaver, H. (1981), *Supply Side Economics: The New Phase of Capitalist Strategies in the Crisis*, published online, 1 June, Austin TX.

Deleuze, G. (1988), *Foucault*, trans. S. Hand, Minneapolis, University of Minnesota Press.

Deleuze, G. (1990), *The Logic of Sense*, trans. M. Lester and C. Stivale, London, Athlone Press.

Deleuze, G. (1992), 'What is a *dispositif* ?', in *Michel Foucault Philosopher*, trans. T. J. Armstrong, London, Routledge, pp. 159–68.

Deleuze, G. (1995), *Negotiations*, trans. M. Joughin, New York, Colombia University Press.

Deleuze, G. and Guattari, F. (1988), *A Thousand Plateaus*, trans. B. Massumi, London, Athlone Press.

Deleuze, G. and Guattari, F. (1994), *What is Philosophy?*, trans. G. Burchell and H. Tomlinson, London, Verso.

Derrida, J. (1982), *The Margins of Philosophy*, trans. A. Bass, Hemel Hempstead, The Harvester Press.

Descartes, R. (1985), *The Philosophical Works of Descartes Vols 1* and *2*, trans. J. Cottingham, R. Stoothoff and D. Murdoch, Cambridge, Cambridge University Press.

Foucault, M. (1997), *Il faut défendre la société*, France, Seuil-Gallimard.

Foucault, M. (2000) 'Theatrum Philosophicum', in *Aesthetics. Essential Works of Foucault 1954–84, Volume 2*, ed. J. D. Faubion, London, Penguin, pp. 343–68.

Furet, F. (1981), Interpreting the French Revolution, trans. E. Forster, Cambridge, Cambridge University Press.

Garbero, P. (1980), *Lavoro produttivo e lavoro improduttivo*, Turin, Loescher.

Gaudemar, J.-P. de (n.d.), *La crise de disciplines industrielles: un essai de definition et de génealogie*, Aix-en-Provence, CERS.

Gaudemar, J.-P. de (1979), *La mobilisation générale*, Grenoble-Paris, Éditions du Champ Urbain.

Gaudemar, J.-P. de (ed.) (1980), 'De la fabrique au site: naissance de l'usine mobile', in *Usine et ouvriers. Figurs du nouvel ordre productif*, Paris, Maspero, pp. 13–40.

Gil, F. (n. d.), 'Tempo', in *Enciclopedia Tematica Einaudi*, Einaudi Editore.

Gras, A. (1979a), *Sociologie des ruptures, les pièges des temps en science sociales*, Paris, Presses Universitaires de France.

Gras, A. (1979b), *Diogène*, 8.

Graziani, A. (1981), *Crisis delle politiche e politiche nella crisi*, Naples, Einaudi Editore.

Habermas, J. (1962), *Strukturwandel der Öffentlichkeit*, Berlin, Luchterhand.

Habermas, J. (1975), *Legitimation Crisis*, trans. T. McCarthy, Boston MA, Beacon Press.

Habermas, J. (1979), *Communication and the Evolution of Society*, trans. T. McCarthy, Oxford, Heinemann Educational Books.

Habermas, J. (1984, 1987), *The Theory of Communicative Action* Volumes 1 and 2, trans. T. McCarthy, Cambridge, Polity Press.

Habermas, J. and Luhmann, N. (1971), *Theorie der Gessellschaft order Sozialtechnologie*, Frankfurt, Suhrkamp Verlag.

Hardt, M. (1990), 'The Art of Organisation: Foundations of a Political Ontology in Gilles Deleuze and Antonio Negri', unpublished PhD thesis, University of Washington (http://www.duke.edu/~hardt/).

Hardt, M. (2000a), 'Sovereignty, Multitudes, Absolute Democracy', interview with Thomas Dunn in *Theory and Event*, 4:3.

Hardt, M. (2000b), 'Un leviatano descritto fuor di metafora', *Il Manifesto*, 28 September.

Hardt, M. (2001), 'The Politics of the Multitude', unpublished paper presented at the *Radical Philosophy* conference, 'Look, No Hands! Political Forms of Global Modernity', London, Birkbeck College, 27 October.

Hardt, M. and Negri, A. (1994), *The Labor of Dionysus*, Minneapolis, University of Minnesota Press.

Hardt, M. and Negri, A. (2000), *Empire*, Cambridge MA, Harvard University Press.

Hare, R. M. (1952), *The Language of Morals*, Oxford, Oxford University Press.

Harrod, R. F. (1951), *The Life of John Maynard Keynes*, London, Macmillan.

Hegel, G. W. F. (1977), *The Phenomenology of Spirit*, trans. A. V. Miller, Oxford, Oxford University Press.

Heidegger, M. (1962), *Being and Time*, trans. J. Macquarrie and E. Robinson, London, Basil Blackwell.

Heller, A. (1974), *The Theory of Need in Marx*, London, Allison & Busby.

Hobbes, T. (1996), *Leviathan*, Cambridge, Cambridge University Press.

Jacob, P. (1980), *L'empirisme logique, ses antécédents, ses critiques*, Paris, Les Éditions des Minuit.

Kant, I. (1987), *The Critique of Judgement*, trans. W. S. Pluhar, Indianapolis IN, Hackett Publishing Company.

Kant, I. (1990), *The Critique of Pure Reason*, trans. N. Kemp Smith, London, Macmillan.

267

Kelsen, H. (1931), *Allgemeine Rechtslehre im Lichte materialistischer geschichtsauf-fasung*, Archiv für Sozialwissenschaft und Sozialpolitik.

Kelsen, H. (1945), *General Theory of Law and State*, translated by A. Wedberg, Cambridge MA, Harvard University Press.

Kelsen, H. (1991), *General Theory of Norms*, translated by M. Hartney, Oxford, Clarendon Press.

Kelsen, H. (1992), *Introduction to the Problems of Legal Theory: A translation of the First Edition of the* Reine Rechtslehre *or* Pure Theory of Law, trans. P. L. Paulson and S. L. Paulson, Oxford, Clarendon Press.

Keynes, J. M. (1964), *The General Theory of Employment, Interest and Money*, San Diego, Harcourt Brace.

King, J. E. (1980), *Readings in Labour Economics*, Oxford, Oxford University Press.

Koselleck, R. (1979), *Kritik und Krise: Eine Studie zur Pathogenese der bürgerlichen Welt*, Frankfurt, Suhrkamp Verlag.

Koselleck, R. (1998), *Critique and Crisis: Enlightenment and the Pathogenesis of Modern Society*, trans. M. Santos, Cambridge MA, MIT Press.

Krahl, H.-J. *Konstitution und Klassenkampf*, Frankfurt, Verlag Neue Kritik.

Kuhn, T. (1962), *The Structure of Scientific Revolutions*, Chicago IL, University of Chicago Press.

Lazzarato, M. (1996), 'Immaterial Labor', in P. Virno and M. Hardt (eds), *Radical Thought in Italy*, Minneapolis, University of Minnesota Press, pp. 133–47.

Leibniz, G. W. (1956), *Letters to Clarke*, ed. H. G. Alexander, Manchester, Manchester University Press.

Leibniz, G. W. (1989), *Philosophical Essays*, trans. R. Ariew, Indianapolis, Hackett Publishing Company.

Lenin, V. I. (1977), *Selected Works in Three Volumes*, Moscow, Progress Publishers.

Leopardi, G. (1946), *Poems of Giacomo Leopardi*, trans. J. Heath-Stubbs, London, John Lehman.

Lucretius (1994), *On the Nature of the Universe*, trans. R. E. Latham, London, Penguin.

Luhmann, N. (1979), *Trust and Power*, trans. H. Davis, J. Raffan and K. Rooney, ed. T. Burns and G. Poggi, Chichester, John Wiley.

Lumley, R. (1994), *States of Emergency. Cultures of Revolt in Italy from 1968 to 1978*, London, Verso.

Lyotard, J.-F. (1986), *The Postmodern Condition*, trans. G. Bennington and B. Massumi, Manchester, Manchester University Press.

Machiavelli, N. (1983), *Discorsi*, Turin, Einaudi Editore.

Makdisi, S., Casarino, C. and Karl, R. E. (eds) (1996), *Marxism Beyond Marxism*, New York, Routledge.

Mannheim, K. (1991), *Ideology and Utopia*, trans. L. Wirth and E. Shils, London, Routledge.

Mao, Tse-Tung (1967), *Selected Works Volume 1*, Peking, Foreign Languages Press.

Marx, K. (1969), *Theories of Surplus Value Part 1*, London, Lawrence & Wishart.

Marx, K. (1973), *Grundrisse*, trans. M. Nicolaus, London, Pelican.

Marx, K. (1984), *Capital Vol.3*, London, Lawrence & Wishart.

Marx, K. (1990), *Capital Vol.1*, trans. B. Fowkes, London, Penguin Books.

Marx, K. (1992), 'Contribution to the Critique of Hegel's Philosophy of Right. Introduction', in *Early Writings*, London, Penguin.

Marzi, M. (1983), *La macchina e l'ingranaggio. Studio su Thomas Hobbes*, Padua, Francisci Editore.

Meyerson, E. (1976), 'The Elimination of Time in Classical Science'', in M. Čapek (ed.), *The Concepts of Time and Space*, Dordrecht, Holland/Boston MA, D. Reidel Publishing Group, pp. 255–65.

Moulier, Y. (1989), 'Introduction', trans. P. Hurd, in A. Negri, The Politics of Subversion, trans. J. Newell, Oxford, Polity Press, pp. 1–44.

Multitudes (2000) 'Biopolitique et Biopouvoir', *Multitudes*, 1, March.

Naville, P. (1980), *Les temps, la technique, l'autogestion*, Paris, Éditions Syros.

Naville, P. (1981), *Sociologie d'aujord'hui. Nouveaux temps, nouveaux problèmes*, Paris, Éditions Anthropos.

Negt, O. (1968), *Soziologische Phantasie und exemplarisches Lernen*, Frankfurt, Europäische Verlagsanstalt.

Negt, O. and Kluge, A. (1972), *Öffentlichkeit und Erfahrung*, Frankfurt, Suhrkamp Verlag.

Negt, O. and Kluge, A. (1993), *Public Sphere and Experience. Toward an Analysis of the Bourgeois and Proletarian Public Sphere*, trans. P. Labanyi, J. Owen Daniel and A. Oksiloff, Minneapolis, University of Minnesota Press.

O'Conner, J. (1973), *The Fiscal Crisis of the State*, New York, St Martin's Press.

Olin Wright, E. (1978), *Class, Crisis and the State*, London, New Left Books.

Opocher, E. (1977), *Analisi dell'idea della giustizia*, Milan, Giuffrè.

Panzieri, R. (1976a), *Lotte Operaie Nello Sviluppo Capitalistico*, Turin, Einaudi Editore.

Panzieri, R. (1976b), 'Surplus Value and Planning: Notes on the Reading of *Capital*', trans. J. Bees, in CSE (eds), *The Labour Process and Class Strategies*, CSE Pamphlet no. 1, London, Stage 1, pp. 4–25.

Panzieri, R. (1980), 'The Capitalist Use of Machinery: Marx Versus the "Objectivists"', trans. by Q. Hoare, in P. Slater (ed.), *Outlines of a Critique of Technology*, London, Ink Links, pp. 44–68.

Pascal, B. (1966), *Pensees*, trans. A. J. Krailsheimer, London, Penguin.

Plato (1961), *Timaeus*, trans. B. Jowett, in *Collected Dialogues*, ed. E. Hamilton and H. Cairns, Princeton NJ, Princeton University Press.

Polanyi, K. (1957), *The Great Transformation*, Boston MA, Beacon Press.

Polybius (1979), *The Rise of the Roman Empire*, trans. I. Scott-Kilvert, Harmondsworth, Penguin.

Prigogine, I. and Stengers, I. (1984), *Order out of Chaos*, New York, Bantam Books.

Read, J. (1999), 'The Antagonistic Ground of Constitutive Power: An essay on the Thought of Antonio Negri', *Rethinking Marxism*, 11:2, summer.

Rosdolsky, R. (1977), *The Making of Marx's Capital Vols 1 and 2*, London, Pluto Press.

Roth, K. H. (1974), *Die 'andere' Arbeiterbewegung und die Entiwicklung der kapitalistischen von 1880 bis zur Gegenwart*, Munich, Trikont Verlag.

Sartre, J.-P. (1976), *The Critique of Dialectical Reason*, London, New Left Books.

Schiera, P. A. (n.d.), *La Prussia fra politica e 'lumi': alle origini del Modell Deutschland*, Bologna, Il Mulino.

Schmitt, K. (1985), *Political Theology, Four Chapters on the Concept of Sovereignty*, Cambridge MA, MIT Press.

Schmitt, K. (1996), *The Concept of the Political*, Chicago IL, University of Chicago Press.

Schürmann, R. (1990), *Heidegger on Being and Acting: from Principles to Anarchy*, Bloomington IN, Indiana University Press.

Serres, M. (2000), *The Birth of Physics*, Manchester, Clinamen Press.

Sohn-Rethel, A. (1978), *Intellectual and Manual Labour*, trans. M. Sohn-Rethel, London, Macmillan.

Spinoza, B. de (1951), *A Theologico-Political Treatise and A Political Treatise*, trans. R. H. M. Elwes, New York, Dover Publications.

Spinoza, B. de (1994), *The Ethics and Other Works*, trans. E. Curley, Princeton NJ, Princeton University Press.

Sraffa, P. (1960), *Production of Commodities by Means of Commodities*, Cambridge, Cambridge University Press.

Starobinski, J. (1988), *Jean-Jacques Rousseau. Transparency and Obstruction*, trans. A Goldhammer, Chicago IL, University of Chicago Press.

Thoburn, N. (n.d.) 'Autonomous Production? On Negri's "New Synthesis"', *Theory, Culture and Society*, 18:5.

Thom, R. (1975), *Structural Stability and Morphogenesis*, trans. D. H. Fowler, Reading MA, Benjamin-Cummins Publishing.

Thomspon, E. P. (1979), *The Poverty of Theory and other essays*, London, Merlin Press.

Thompson, E. P. (1991), *The Making of the English Working Class*, London, Penguin.

Tronti, M. (1966), *Operai e Capitale*, Turin, Einaudi Editore.

Tronti, M. (1973), 'Social Capital', *Telos*, 17, autumn, pp. 98–121.

Tronti, M (1979), 'The strategy of the Refusal', in Red Notes (eds), *Working Class Autonomy and the Crisis: Italian Marxist Texts of the Theory and Practice of Class Movement: 1964–79*. London, Red Notes and CSE Books, pp. 7–21.

Virilio, P. (1986), *Speed and Politics*, trans. M. Polizotti, New York, SemioText(e).

Virno, P. (1996), 'Notes on the "General Intellect"', in S. Makdisi, C. Casarino, R.E. Karl (eds), *Marxism Beyond Marxism*, New York, Routledge, pp. 265–72.

Virno, P. and Hardt, M. (eds) (1996), *Radical Thought in Italy*, Minneapolis, University of Minnesota Press.

Weber, M. (1978), *Economy and Society Vols 1 and 2*, ed. G. Roth and C. Wittich, Berkeley, University of California Press.

Weber, M. (1992), *The Protestant Ethic and the Spirit of Capitalism*, trans. T. Parsons, London, Routledge.

Weber, M. (1994), *Political Writings*, ed. P. Lassman and R. Spiers, Cambridge, Cambridge University Press.

Wittgenstein, L. (1958), *Philosophical Investigations*, Oxford, Basil Blackwell.

Wittgenstein, L. (1974), *Tractatus Logico-Philosophicus*, London, Routledge.

Wright, S. (2002), *Storming Heaven. Class Composition and Struggle in Italian Autonomist Marxism*, London, Pluto Press.

Question what you thought before

Continuum Impacts - books that change the way we think

AESTHETIC THEORY - Theodor Adorno 0826476910
I AND THOU - Martin Buber 0826476937
ANTI-OEDIPUS - Gilles Deleuze & Félix Guattari 0826476953
A THOUSAND PLATEAUS - Gilles Deleuze & Félix Guattari 0826476945
DISSEMINATION - Jacques Derrida 0826476961
BERLIN ALEXANDERPLATZ - Alfred Döblin 0826477895
PEDAGOGY OF HOPE - Paolo Freire 0826477909
MARX'S CONCEPT OF MAN - Erich Fromm 0826477917
TRUTH AND METHOD - Hans-Georg Gadamer 082647697X
THE ESSENCE OF TRUTH - Martin Heidegger 0826477046
JAZZ WRITINGS - Philip Larkin 0826476996
LIBIDINAL ECONOMY - Jean-François Lyotard 0826477003
DECONSTRUCTION AND CRITICISM - Harold Bloom et al 0826476929
DIFFERENCE AND REPETITION - Gilles Deleuze 0826477151
THE LOGIC OF SENSE - Gilles Deleuze 082647716X
GOD IS NEW EACH MOMENT - Edward Schillebeeckx 0826477011
THE DOCTRINE OF RECONCILIATION - Karl Barth 0826477925
CRITICISM AND TRUTH - Roland Barthes 0826477070
ON NIETZSCHE - George Bataille 0826477089
THE CONFLICT OF INTERPRETATIONS - Paul Ricoeur 0826477097
POSITIONS - Jacques Derrida 0826477119
ECLIPSE OF REASON - Max Horkheimer 0826477933
AN ETHICS OF SEXUAL DIFFERENCE - Luce Irigaray 0826477127
LITERATURE, POLITICS AND CULTURE IN POSTWAR BRITAIN - Alan Sinfield 082647702X
CINEMA 1 - Gilles Deleuze 0826477054
CINEMA 2 - Gilles Deleuze 0826477062
AN INTRODUCTION TO PHILOSOPHY - Jacques Maritain 0826477178
MORAL MAN AND IMMORAL SOCIETY - Reinhld Niebuhr 0826477143
EDUCATION FOR CRITICAL CONSCIOUSNESS - Paolo Freire 082647795X
**DISCOURSE ON FREE WILL -
Desiderius Erasmus & Martin Luther** 0826477941
VIOLENCE AND THE SACRED - René Girard 0826477186
NIETZSCHE AND THE VICIOUS CIRCLE - Pierre Klossowski 0826477194

www.continuumbooks.com